THE MORVILLE HOURS

THE MORVILLE HOURS

Katherine Swift

BLOOMSBURY

Bloomsbury Publishing, London, New York and Berlin

A CIP catalogue record for this book is available from the British Library

ISBN 978 0 7475 9258 7

10 9 8 7 6 5 4 3

Typeset by Hewer Text UK Ltd, Edinburgh
Printed in Great Britain by Clays Ltd, St Ives plc

The paper this book is printed on is certified by the © 1996 Forest Stewardship
Council A.C. (FSC). It is ancient-forest friendly. The printer holds
FSC chain of custody SGS-COC-2061

FSC
Mixed Sources
Product group from well-managed
forests and other controlled sources
Cert no. SGS-COC-2061
www.fsc.org
© 1996 Forest Stewardship Council

Contents

A Note about Books of Hours

The Hours of the Divine Office are very ancient. They were already ancient in the sixth century when St Benedict codified them in his Rule, a practical guide for the monastic life. They consisted of seven Day Hours together with Vigils, the Night Office (also known as Matins). Each Hour was made up of a selection of prayers, psalms, hymns and readings that changed with the seasons and together spanned the whole twenty-four hours. The exact timing of each of the Hours varied according to whether it was winter or summer and, when Benedict's Rule was adopted by other communities of monks, also from one religious house to another. Vigils was originally said at midnight, but in the Rule of St Benedict was prescribed for 'the eighth hour of the night' – 2 a.m. – because 'by sleeping until a little past the middle of the night, the brothers can arise with their food fully digested.' Lauds might then follow Vigils immediately or be said separately, three hours later, with a period of study in between. Then came Prime, after which work began, followed three hours later by Terce. Three hours later again came Sext and the main meal of the day. Then came None (pronounced to rhyme with 'stone'), at about 3 p.m., followed by Vespers, often celebrated with great solemnity, at about sunset, and finally Compline, celebrated at

9 p.m., after which the community retired to bed. The Hours still provide the basic structure of monastic life today.

   The text of the Office (from the Latin *officium*, meaning 'duty' or 'service') was contained in a compendium known as the Breviary. Books of Hours were smaller portable versions of the Office for use by laypeople. They contained a simplified scheme of the eight Hours, known as the Little Office of the Blessed Virgin, together with other prayers and devotions, including the Litany of the Saints, the Seven Penitential Psalms and the Office of the Dead. Books of Hours are the most numerous class of books to survive from the late Middle Ages. They are at once the most visible and the most intimate of medieval books, very widely disseminated yet used in an intensely private manner by individuals, often women, in the privacy of their own chambers. Mass-produced by workshops in France and the Low Countries, they were exported to this country in their thousands – the 'best-sellers' of their day. The middle classes bought them ready-made; the wealthy commissioned them splendidly embellished in gold and colours, with special prayers to their patron saints and miniature paintings by the greatest artists of the day into which their own portraits might be incorporated as bystanders – looking on at the Nativity, as it were – or their favourite castle adopted as the backdrop to some scene of rural life.

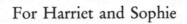

For Harriet and Sophie

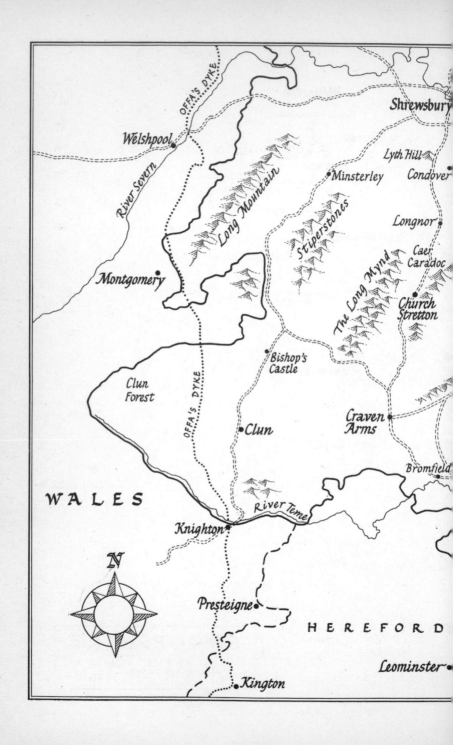

Newport

Wellington

Wroxeter
The Wrekin
Buildwas
Telford
Shifnal

Coalbrookdale
Ironbridge
Albrighton

Broseley

Much Wenlock

Aldenham

Ape Dale

Wenlock Edge

MORVILLE
Bridgnorth
Quatford

Corve Dale

Dudmaston

Brown Clee

Clee Hills
Highley

Titterstone Clee

Cleobury
Mortimer

Ludlow
Bewdley
Kidderminster

Tenbury
Wells
R. Teme

WORCESTERSHIRE

...SHIRE

S T A F F O R D S H I R E

River Severn

SHROPSHIRE

0 1 2 3 4 5 miles
0   5   10 km

The
Dower House Garden
Morville

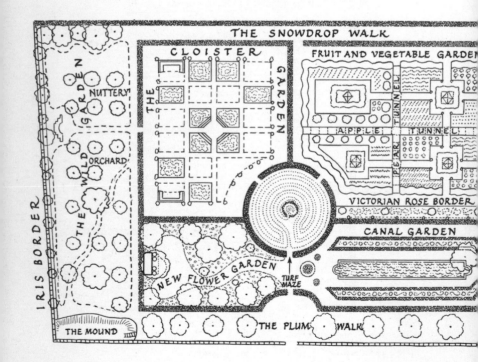

THE SNOWDROP WALK

CLOISTER GARDEN

THE GARDEN

NUTTERY

N GARDEN

THE WILD GARDEN

ORCHARD

IRIS BORDER

FRUIT AND VEGETABLE GARDEN

PEAR TUNNEL

APPLE TUNNEL

VICTORIAN ROSE BORDER

CANAL GARDEN

NEW FLOWER GARDEN

TURF MAZE

THE MOUND

THE PLUM WALK

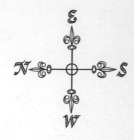

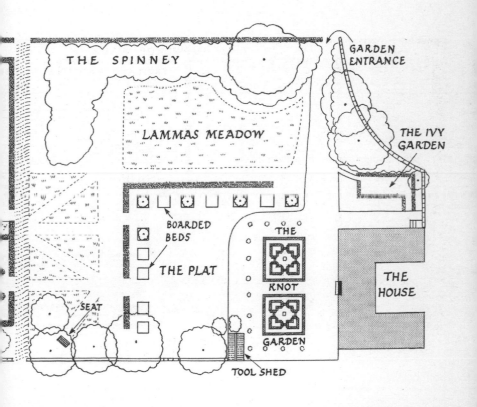

THE SPINNEY

LAMMAS MEADOW

GARDEN
ENTRANCE

THE IVY
GARDEN

BOARDED
BEDS

THE PLAT

SEAT

THE

KNOT

GARDEN

THE
HOUSE

TOOL SHED

I Come to Morville

S ome people watch birds. I watch clouds. Sometimes it's the same thing, as when the buzzards soar on a rising thermal above the garden, or the swifts and house martins chase high-flying gnats on a summer's day. But mostly it's just clouds I watch: the hard edge of a retreating cumulonimbus, the thin veil of cirrostratus as a warm front comes in, the halo of rainbow-coloured ice crystals around the moon in a mackerel sky. In winter the clouds run down from the north and the east, from the open land beyond the garden; in spring they come bowling up the valley from the south-west, their shadows scudding across the hillside, the fields darkening and brightening with their passage.

I came here to make a garden. In the red earth I find fragments of blue-and-white willow-pattern china, white marble floor-tiles, rusted iron nails. A litter of broken clay pipes in the flower-beds, their air holes stopped with soil. Opaque slivers of medieval glass, blue as snowmelt. Flat wedges of earthenware dishes with notched rims and looping patterns of cream and brown. Who drank from that cup, who smoked that pipe, who looked through that window? Did they stand as I stand now, watching the clouds on the hillside?

Angles and Romans, Cornovii and Normans, monks and soldiers, herdsmen and farmers; millwrights, iron-founders, carpet-makers and railwaymen, they came this way too – following the valley, up from the river, looking for land, iron, work, a home, the hillside brightening and darkening with their ebb and flow. Only the land remains, and the land remembers – in crop mark and hollow way, ridge and furrow, bell pit and Roman road, turnpike and stew pond.

I first came to Morville in the dark; felt, rather than saw, that same high horizon and that round bowl of land. Driving down from the Holyhead ferry in a winter dusk, I made a detour off the old A5 south of Shrewsbury. Night had fallen before I reached Morville. The hairpin bend at the turn to Ludlow was as sharp as it appeared on the map, and there, by the light of the headlamps, were the gate piers to the Hall. I left the car at the end of the drive and walked down the avenue to the house, my feet feeling for the road in the blackness. Emerging from the trees I was conscious of open space curving away from me, and of the dark bulk of the Hall beyond. I kept my distance, half-embarrassed, half-unwilling to be seduced by this new place. I stood, instead, looking across the lawn at the illuminated windows on the first floor, at the light streaming from the narrow embrasures of the turret stair. I could see two pavilions, one on either side, joined to the main house by high curving walls. In the light from the windows, the outline of cupolas was just visible, with a glint of filigree ironwork from the weathervanes above. To the right, the untenanted Dower House; dark, its windows yielding nothing. To the left, a high wooded horizon, black against the first stars. Water rushed somewhere below. And then, high up, behind me, a clock struck the three-quarters – two bells combined in a musical phrase of two notes, one high and one low, repeated three times – their softly muffled sound drifting out into the darkened valley. A church! I had not expected that.

I was at that time working in Dublin as Keeper of Early Printed Books in the library of Trinity College, and commuting back and forth from Oxford. My husband had a bookshop in Oxford, and he was still living there. Morville was his plan to lure me home. He used to meet me from the plane at Heathrow every Friday night with a wallet of photographs of all the houses he had been to see in the previous week – diminutive Georgian manor houses we couldn't afford; gaunt brick ruins with walled gardens filled with nettles; sagging timber-framed palaces. They haunt me still, the ones that got away; like parallel universes, the alternative lives I might have led. In Lincolnshire, Cumbria, North Devon, Wales, Yorkshire – anywhere where land and houses were (at that time) relatively cheap.

And then he found Morville. Shropshire had always shimmered on the periphery of my vision: Housman's *A Shropshire Lad* was an anthem of my childhood, a copy always in the house (though it was not until later that I understood why). Ludlow and Clee were familiar names, though as yet unvisited; Wrekin and Wenlock Edge were tinged with longing and regrets, though not mine. My father bought me books every Christmas and birthday. When I was twelve he gave me the poems of Mary Webb. I learned them by heart.

> We were in the hills of heaven
> But yesterday!
> All was so changeless, quiet, fair,
> All swam so deep in golden air;
> White-tapered chestnuts, seven by seven,
> Went down the shady valleys there . . .

'I think this is the one,' said my husband.

We agreed to take the Dower House on a twenty-year lease, but I had yet to see it, except in photographs. I was reluctant to leave

Dublin and my job and friends there, and I was unsettled by the impermanence of a lease. But as I stood in the darkness that night and listened to the bells dying away and the sound of the stream welling up into the silence, everything suddenly seemed possible. We moved to Morville August 1988, with two removal vans of books, three cats and two carloads of plants.

The sound of the church clock became the regular accompaniment to my daily labours in the garden. It provided a sort of basso continuo to life at Morville, so quiet that the fog across the Church Meadow could stifle it, or the north wind blow its notes away into the trees. In the warm wet violet-smelling air of April, a gusting south-westerly would bring the notes in breaths and snatches. One heard it best in summer dawns before the drone of road or field; or on winter evenings when Orion burned coldly above and the congregation made its way over the potholed road towards the lights of the church; or in the watches of the night, when the clock numbered the long sleepless hours till dawn. For much of the year, I could see the clock from the garden, glinting gold on the north face of the church tower. I would watch the interplay of light and shadow, perpendicular and horizontal, plane and angle – tower, nave, chancel, aisle – as the sun made its daily revolution around the church. In high summer the tower was hidden in the green leafiness of the trees, and that was when the clock would chime clearest of all, the sound vaulting over the empty air in the valley bottom where the sleek brown mill-race ran, springing up into the bright wooded air beyond, and echoing back from the high horizon.

One day I climbed the tower with the clockwinder to look at it, clambering hand over hand up a zigzag of wooden ladders inside the dim void of the tower to a platform halfway up where a confection of shining brass cogs gleamed in a cupboard in the dust-smelling darkness. Vast counterweights on chains disappeared into the gloom below. Hawsers ran up the rough surface of the stone walls above and disappeared into the floors overhead, linking the clock's mechanism to the dial and to the bells on which it struck the hours – a Victorian mechanism attached to eighteenth-century bells in a Norman church – the counterweights rising back up the tower like buckets from a well, like water brought up slopping from the past. The church was built in the early twelfth century by the monks of the Benedictine Abbey of Shrewsbury, twenty miles away. Then in 1138 the Abbot of Shrewsbury received permission from the Bishop of Hereford to appropriate the church into a new daughter house, a priory he wished to build at Morville, to be headed by a Prior drawn from the senior monks of the Abbey.

The names of the priors of Morville survive – four Johns, two Williams, two Richards and a Walter – scattered here and there in miscellaneous documents over the succeeding four centuries. There are many gaps. Where a name is recorded, it is more often than not because of some misdeed or inadequacy. The Priory seems to have begun in a grand enough way: in about 1168 additions were made to the church which included an extended chancel capable of accommodating two dozen or more. But in later years the size of the community seems to have shrunk to just two or three. It cannot ever have been a rich living. In 1253 Prior John Wallensis (John 'the Welshman') was charged with receiving part of a deer poached from the royal forest. In 1290, when the Bishop of Hereford visited Morville with his retinue, the Prior managed to provide fodder for the thirty-five horses, but the Bishop had to provide the greatest part of the food for his men himself.

For four hundred years the monks worked the land around the village: the flat land near the church, the heavy land down by the stream, the sloping side of the hill, the stony ground where my neighbours and I garden. Then came the Reformation. The Priory was dissolved, the monks ejected and the land bought by the local merchant who built the big house here. Of the Priory buildings now there is no trace. Even the site itself is now in doubt: perhaps it lay beside the church, to the north, where the remains of buildings still show themselves as parch marks during drought; perhaps to the west, underneath what is now Morville Hall; perhaps at the crossroads, on the high ground where the road to Ludlow meets the road from Shrewsbury, sliced through now by modern roadworks. Only the church still stands, with its eighteenth-century bells and its Victorian clock striking the hours.

The word 'clock' comes from the Middle English *clok*, the bell that called monks to prayer. And as I stood in the garden in those early years listening to the church clock striking the hours, it recalled for me the Hours of the Divine Office, that ancient system of worship followed by the monks who once worked this ground under the Rule of St Benedict, with its discipline of physical labour in all weathers, tempered with the injunction to study. It recalled the rhythm of a day which began with Vigils and Lauds, then Prime, Terce, Sext and None, Vespers and Compline, the bells raising the monks before dawn, guiding them through the day in measured steps of work, study and prayer, and delivering them safely back into the night once more. It also recalled for me a half-forgotten time in my childhood when I too had been part of that world. My mother had converted to Roman Catholicism in the mid-1950s and, increasingly drawn by the monastic life, she had become what is known as a secular tertiary, a member of the Third Order of St Dominic. (The first order consisted of monks, the second of nuns, and the third of lay-people, one of several such institutions founded in the thirteenth century in response to a surge in popular religious feeling.) A tertiary commits him- or herself to the Rule of the Order, as far as that is compatible with life in the world, and to the recitation of the Hours of the Little Office of the Blessed Virgin, the shorter version of the Divine Office devised for the use of laypeople, at the appointed times each day. My mother used to take me on retreats to Dominican abbeys, and while she was at her prayers, I – a child of eight or nine – would roam about the grounds or help the lay brother in charge of the gardens as he weeded the paths or dug the vegetable patch.

Among the books I brought with me to Morville was my mother's Dominican prayer book, containing a modern text of the Hours. Slim, black-leather-bound and discrete, almost devoid of illustration or decoration, it was a far cry from the gorgeousness of the medieval Books of Hours. I went to the Bodleian Library in Oxford to look at some of them. Tiny, of a size made to be held in the hand or carried in a pocket, they opened like small dark jewel boxes to reveal a kaleidoscope of colour – lapis lazuli and turnsole violet, verdigris and vermilion, orpiment and cinnabar. Whole processions of saints filed by as I turned the pages, each with his or her identifying object – St Peter and his church, St Catherine and her wheel, St Cecilia playing the organ – the richness of their robes set off by the plump gold-leaf cushions of their haloes. There were complete cycles of images of the Passion of Christ or the life of the Blessed Virgin, each gilded page more splendid than the one before, bordered with curling tendrils of foliage or a scattering of *trompe l'oeil* flowers rising from the page as if newly picked. Books of Hours like these are among the treasures of Western art.

As I followed the familiar words in the unfamiliar script, each letter as narrow and pointed as a Gothic arch, I was decoding the sources of my mother's spirituality, rediscovering something which for me as a child had been a daily reality. Books of Hours now are studied in minute detail, the chain of their ownership traced, the location of the workshops tracked down, the artists identified, their handiwork exhibited in art galleries and printed catalogues. But I was less interested in the iconography of the saints, in the delicacy or psychological realism of the paintings, than in the words themselves, and in the half-remembered music they conjured up: the haunting cadences of the Gregorian chant, at least as old as the Hours themselves. I found, as I read, that I could still sing the Latin text of whole prayers and hymns – learned fifty years ago and buried in the back of my memory – *Glorias* and *Credos* and *Salve Reginas; Kyries, Sanctuses* and the *Dies irae.*

And there was something else too, something which in those days when I was first beginning the garden, and would stand, spade in hand, listening to the church clock striking the hours, had for me even greater resonance: the calendars that prefaced the Books of Hours, with their illustrations of the horticultural and agricultural tasks appropriate for each month; their tables of saints' days and holy days, Simple and Double, Semi-Double and Greater Double, Doubles of the Second Class and Doubles of the First Class – the 'red-letter days' of joyful celebration – picked out in red ink; their columns of Dominical Letters and Golden Numbers for calculating Sundays and the date of Easter; their days marked 'D' for the *dies Aegyptiaci* or *dies mali* – the bad-luck days (from which our word 'dismal' comes), when anything begun would come to naught and seed would shrivel in the furrow; their dual system of dates – Arabic figures and Roman numerals, the one counting by tens, the other by ides, nones and kalends (the source of the word 'calendar'); and their ancient Babylonian signs of the zodiac tracing the sun in its annual progress across the sky, each governing not only a segment of the heavens but a part of the human body, dictating what medical treatment might or might not be appropriate that month. The calendars made up a cycle of multiple resonances, spiritual and secular, terrestrial and sidereal, liturgical and agricultural, pagan and Christian, breathtaking in its richness and antiquity and in the geographical spread of its references, but also grounded in the here and now, in the everyday.

In the world of the Books of Hours, tiny emblematic figures dig, prune, sow, chop wood, mow grass, reap grain, tread grapes, each in their allotted month. There are animals being fed, tended, led to market, slaughtered, consumed. There is an interlude in April and May for picking flowers, courting, making music. Another at Christmas for feasting. In a world of electric light and central heating, where one month is much like another and vegetables are flown in daily from Kenya and Spain, this all seems like an echo from a vanished world. Nowadays, adrift in an affectless no-man's-land, we are cut off not only from the hopes and fears, the triumphs and despairs of the agricultural year, but from the shared emotions of the great story which plays itself out month by month in the liturgical year. The twenty-first century is fighting a losing battle to keep its calendar. Gardeners of course have never lost it.

So it was that the Hours came to mirror my life in the garden – not only the calendar illustrations with their regular round of tasks, but also the feasts and the fasts, the highs and the lows, the red-letter days and the *dies mali*: from the crunch of grass underfoot at midnight on a frosty New Year's Eve, to the drip of trees in a melancholy March dawn; from a perfumed May Day morning when the whole world seems sixteen again, to the enervating heat of a midsummer noon; from the bloom of blue-black damsons picked on a golden September afternoon, to the smell of holly and ivy cut in the dusk of a rainy Christmas Eve. Senses seemed keener in relation to the Hours, with their lesson of attentiveness. Theirs was a world where time was accounted for, each second precious: instead of hearing, one listened; instead of seeing, one looked; instead of tasting, one savoured; instead of touching, one felt. 'Listen,' said St Benedict, 'listen with the ear of your heart.'

Books of Hours were family treasures, expensive items in a world where books were scarce; a place where births and deaths might be recorded, at a time when such records were few; pious relics, handed down from one generation to another, with the impreca-tion, written or implicit, to pray for the soul of the departed donor. With the advent of the printing press, their numbers multiplied. They became the single most common book – often the only book – in English households. But once Henry VIII declared himself head of the Church in England, their use became increasingly problematic. References to certain saints had to be deleted (to Thomas à Becket, a saint who had famously stood up to a king), the title of Pope to be scratched out wherever it occurred, certain prayers excised. A new prayer book was com-missioned, the Book of Common Prayer, enforced by the Act of Uniformity in 1549. The reforms were repealed and the deletions reinstated under Mary Tudor, but were re-imposed under Eliza-beth. By the 1560s Books of Hours had become off limits to all but the defiant few. The calendars, however, with their calcula-tions of good- and bad-luck days and their counsels of the right time to prune, sow, reap or harvest, survived into an age of mass print as secular almanacs.

In addition to my mother's Book of Hours, I had an un-identified fragment of such an almanac, given to me by my husband: lacking the first and last leaf, it was illustrated with black-and-white woodcuts of the same familiar labours of the year, but with the addition of proverbs and wise sayings, the phases of the moon and mnemonic rhymes about the weather. It proved to be a fragment of the Shepherds' Great Calendar, which began life in 1491 and remained in print for three hundred years, with sporadic revivals thereafter. To the monthly recital of saints' days and its portrayal of the agricultural labours and their accompanying signs of the zodiac, the Shepherds' Calendar also adds another dimension: the years of a human life, six for every month – the infant, the child, the schoolboy, the adolescent, the lover, physical prime, maturity, the beginnings of decline, pros-perous old age, senility, decay, final extinction. And gradually I began to see that in the Hours – with their joyful *Te Deum* and litanies of praise, their Office of the Dead and Penitential Psalms, their despairing *De profundis* and final serene *Nunc dimittis* – was reflected the arc not only of a single day or a single year, but of a whole lifetime, with its trajectory from darkness into light and from the light into the darkness once more.

And in the background, as in the calendars' scenes of rural life where the activities of the year were played out against a painted backdrop of high-walled castles and turreted towns, was Morville itself: the hill, the house, the high-wooded horizon, and the church tower with the gilded hands of the clock turning, turning.

But then the clock stopped. There had been aberrations before, as when the clockwinder was on holiday and his deputy proved forgetful, or when hard weather froze the hands on the clock face, but this time the fault was mechanical, more serious, the stoppage of the clock prolonged. In its absence, I pined. Seen across the Church Meadow in the swooning heat of midsummer, the church tower appeared to shimmer, encircled, unreachable, drowned in a spell that would last a thousand years. I remembered Brid Ellen, who had run widdershins round the church through the shadow of the tower into an enchantment so deep that she was spirited away to faerieland. A kindly neighbour, missing the point, said, 'Don't you wear a watch?'

Unlike a watch, which marks off how much time has gone and how much remains, the sound of the bells ringing the quarters had seemed to say, 'Stop. Think. This is *here*. This is *now*.' In my previous life there had never been enough time: time was always running out. But in the garden, where I was acutely aware of the passage of time – the changing light as the hours of the day passed by, the shifting pattern of the seasons as the years passed by – there was paradoxically the feeling of having all the time in the world, of hours and days stretching and expanding into a shimmering pool of *now*.

All gardeners are aware of that sense of flow, of losing oneself. Modern timekeeping is too rigid for the likes of us – pinned like a moth to a framework with no give in it. Modern hours are set at one-twelfth of the day or night at the equinox: sixty minutes, three hundred and sixty seconds of tedium. In the garden, a single minute, a single second, can be an eternity. In classical times, the Horae were bringers of blessings, invited to weddings; now they are the presiding deities of the time-clock, the stopwatch, the facelift. There were originally three Horae – goddesses not of times of the year, but of processes: of growing, flowering and fruiting. Only later did they come to be associated with periods of time: the four seasons, the hours on a clock. Ordinary people told the time by natural events, cock-crow and noon, full market and first sleep, the lighting of the lamps. When hours were used, in the sense of formal divisions of the day and night, they were calculated as one-twelfth of the day or night at that particular time of year, and so varied according to the season. I like that. I like the feeling of time expanding with the unfolding of the leaves, contracting again with the first frosts of autumn.

As my days spent alone in the garden turned into weeks and the weeks into months, I got into the habit of leaving the front door of the house open – not just unlocked, but standing open to the garden – from spring to autumn, all day long. I would open it first thing in the morning to smell the air and close it only at midnight as I went to bed. House and garden became extensions of each other. The kitchen filled with plant pots and tools and string, the hall with boots and jackets and gloves, the bathroom with tender seedlings. Plants spent part of their year in the house and part outside in the garden; I could tell the time of year from the tide of greenery in the house. And gradually I came to know the creatures who shared the house and garden with me: the jackdaws who roosted in the roof space; the black newts in the cellar, dining on woodlice; the harvest spiders and the tortoiseshell butterflies who found a winter home in the dim recesses of the ceiling; the swallows who reconnoitred the bookshelves in the hall for nesting places in spring. Outside, there were other creatures and other worlds to discover: the citadels of bees and ants, the papier mâché galleries of the wasps, the subterranean refuges of badgers and moles. Then there were the wanderers – the animals who came and went unseen: the night owls and the foxes, the birds who left their arrowed footprints in the snow. The cats were louche go-betweens, at home in both worlds, belonging to neither.

I found companionship too in the other people who inhabited

the same landscape – the tramp, the hedge-layer, the stockman, the gravedigger; the sheep-shearer, the farm labourer, my neighbour who tended the vines, the lad who brought the logs, the butcher who delivered the meat – present-day inheritors of those figures in the calendars of the Books of Hours. Country people seem to have all the time in the world. Not really, of course. Concerns are as pressing here as elsewhere. But there seemed to be a country courtesy which required that conversations over the field gate or in the lane or down in the Church Meadow be unhurried – a mutual satisfying of curiosities, an exchange of information, a bond formed: Welsh voices, Shropshire voices, Black Country voices, telling stories of the land and the village and its people.

Other voices too, the competing voices of those who lived here in the past, jostling for my attention – the monks of the Benedictine Priory and the dynasties of Smyth, Weaver and Warren, their voices rising up from deed boxes and document cases, rustling like dry paper. They cajole and wheedle and sigh. Make us a herb garden and plant valerian and poppy and wolfsbane for Prior Richard, the last Prior of Morville. Sweet-smelling knots for me, sweet Frances Cressett, a bride when Elizabeth was on the throne. A parterre of clipped box and yew of which Arthur Weaver could approve. A rose border of pillars and swags for a Victorian patriarch. A gentle wilderness for Juliana, 'fifth and last surviving daughter'. And there were others, nameless, numberless, the self-confident and the lost, the careless and the carefree, their existences reduced to a fragment in the earth, to a single instant – the sound of a willow-pattern cup shattering on a stone floor, the blur of a hand throwing away a broken clay pipe. I came to make a garden, but found that one garden was not enough to tell all their stories.

Gardens are about people first and plants second. Like our

multi-layered language, gardening is made up of different elements, bits and pieces from far and near, now and long ago, taken and incorporated into the vocabulary of plant and tree, the grammar of path and hedge. I divided the garden up, hid each part from the others behind high yew hedges, played a game of multi-dimensional chess with myself. In my twenty-first-century garden, bits of the seventeenth century are still here – and the nineteenth and sixteenth and eighteenth – poking through the gauzy surface of the present like Marley's pigtail. And there is China and America and Africa, as well as Shropshire. And stories – many stories, of this house and the people who lived here, and of the people who live here still – handed on from person to person, told and retold, a skein of stories. Like the lavender my father took as he moved from house to house, from one job to the next, and I from him, taking cuttings of the lavender, and cuttings of the cuttings, and cuttings of the cuttings of the cuttings, rooting it each time in a new garden.

And me? What is my story? My father carving my name in the speckled green side of a vegetable marrow so that I could watch the letters stretch and grow as wide as my own four-year-old smile. Violet-blue Michaelmas daisies and basking Tortoiseshell butterflies. Fossils in wrappings of cotton wool. Books on leaning metal shelves. The smell of pipe smoke in a cold room. A typewriter. Blue hyacinths. Iron Age forts and the worn steps of church towers. A dozen clocks chiming the hour for dinner. A black-and-white marble floor. A yellow climbing rose. Clouds passing over the hillside. Each a fragment of memory, a lost moment, a shining and irreducible 'now'.

So come with me now into the garden. It is New Year's Eve. This is here. This is now.

Listen.

Vigils

Listen.

In the dark tower the cog wheels spin and whir, readying themselves. Silence, deeper than before. And then with the thud of the detent dropping, the striking-train lurches forward, heavy with the weight of accumulated minutes and seconds, and the year and the night topple over into the black abyss of another day, a new year. This is the night when Feasting Janus faces both ways. In pub and farm, manor house and cottage, the old rituals of propitiation are observed. This is the night when revellers keep the lights on late and drink to keep out the dark.

But in the hollow centre of the garden the encircling yews dream their deep winter sleep. The soil beneath the fibrous net of red roots is warm and dry. My breath steams in the darkness. No moon, only faint shreds of high cloud. A rat-tat of fireworks marks the hour, then faint, distant shouts. The two cats reappear: they have followed me on my midnight progress through the garden, felt presences rather than visible companions. Now they shadow me, left and right, as together we cross the turf maze with its circular hedge of yew and emerge into the western side of the garden. A glaze of ice is forming in the middle of the canal; the long lines of hedges and *plates-bandes* recede into the darkness.

On into the Orchard now, greeting each tree in turn, each thicket of wild rose, with a salutation for each of the silent beehives, their roofs slicked with silver by the falling frost, for each clump of hazel and willow. Tonight each rose must be named, each tree acknowledged. This is when it all begins. This is the Night Office, the Vigil before the dawn. *Te deum laudamus*, 'We praise thee, O God . . . Heaven and earth are full of the majesty of Thy glory.' *In te, domine, speravi*, 'O Lord, in Thee have I hoped: let me not be confounded forever.' I used to dread New Year's Eve: wept, hid, was slung out of pubs. Until I started to garden.

The grass crunches underfoot. On into the Cloister Garden now, the weathered oak of trellis and arbour, pale against the dark earth, enclosing a memory of summer like a lingering perfume – a bower of roses, red and white. Then down through the fruit tunnel, turning towards home, the cats ahead of me. The silvered grass of the path reaches out in front, broad and straight below the airy colonnade of the tunnel, the ribs of apple and pear cordons black overhead against the sky. On either hand, the Vegetable Garden stretches away, an interlocking pattern of black and white, dug earth and frosted grass: tonight each bed must be visited, none forgotten; each path trod, none omitted. We emerge halfway along the rose border with its pillars of larch poles and swags of rope, edged now with rime. I pause on the grass terrace at the edge of the upper garden: below, the uncurtained windows of the house gleam, throwing pathways of light across the Knot Garden; behind, the dark bulk of the Hall; and beyond, the backdrop of wood and hill, massive under the stars.

Last shouts of neighbours going home: 'Goodnight, Arthur. Night, Pat!' Cars on the road. Then silence again. Slight wind. Bark of dog fox, far out, patrolling the valley floor. Swift ack-ack of pheasant from the wood. In the silence of the church tower, the counterweights tock downwards on their chains, inch by inch. Tomorrow the clockwinder will come to wind the weights back up to the top of the tower, his heels echoing on the stone floor as he crosses to the vestry and climbs the zigzag of shaky wooden ladders to the platform where the clock stands. But until then the church is empty, silent. Except for another sound, a small sound, more regular than the mouse gnawing a forgotten prayer book, quieter than the scuffling of the velvet-eared bat brushing the roof with its leathern wings, as soft as the spider spinning its web: the sound of a pen scratching in the darkness. High up in the nave, above the pillars of the Norman arches, the four wooden Evangelists sit, chroniclers of the village for four hundred years, each with his book open before him, each with a large white goose-feather quill in his carved hand. Matthew with his angel, Mark with his lion, Luke with his ox, John with his eagle. For four hundred years they have kept watch in Morville church, observing the congregation come and go; recording christenings, weddings, burials; keeping a tally of tolls, calculating the tythes; overseeing the distribution of bread and coals to the poor, funeral hatchments for the rich, memorial tablets for the fallen – Lucknow and Cambrai, Le Cateau and the Somme. What secret glances, what lovers' trysts, what hopes and fears, faded now into dust! What spring mornings, what early frosts, what mothers' tears – writing it all down, their pens scratching away into the night.

But what of those who came before, tumbled now, dumb and blind, in the deep soil of the churchyard? Of the flint traders who walked the ancient ridge-way along the hill? Of the first farmers whose ashy remains lie scattered under the round barrows on the ridge? What of the builders of the hill forts – the people of the Wrekin and the Clee? Who tells their stories?

Only the flints and the loom weights and the rusted sickles in the soil. No monuments of wood or stone; only the mute witness of the hill forts. Yet from that distant past comes the echo of a sound – something as fragile, as insubstantial but indestructible, as that: no more than a breath. Breathed across the generations, its form changing like Chinese whispers: Morville, Marvil, Morfelde, Momerfeld, Membrefelde, Mamerfeld. From the drawl of an eighteenth-century English gentleman, back through Elizabeth's time to the Wars of the Roses, back past the coming of the Normans and the Anglo-Saxons, back to the ancient Britons – the sound changing shape in their mouths as it passed from one to another – the word that defines this place. Mamerfeld, the land by the hill. In that first syllable there may be the echo of the name the first Britons gave to the hill – a mysterious, irreducible sound. The hill has no name now. The Ordnance Survey map calls the two ends of it Meadowley Hill and Aston Hill, from the two villages that lie adjacent. We who live here just call it 'the bank' or 'the hill'. But its name may once have been something like the 'Mam', a name going back as far as the builders of the hill forts or even earlier.

It is impossible to overestimate the reverence of early peoples for hills – high, separate places, remote from everyday affairs, their separateness signalled by a drop in temperature, a thinning of the air as you climbed, a covering of snow, often veiled from view in mist and cloud – places where you went for worship, sanctuary, to bury the dead. Our hill still affects our lives today: a landmark when returning home from a journey, a shelter from storms, the gateway to the rich lands of Corve Dale beyond. On the map the road still curves around it; its steep escarpment is still accessible only on foot. It is a place where buzzards wheel, the place where the midwinter sun still sets.

That first winter at Morville I walked the empty fields, my boots growing heavy with the bare wet earth. I followed the Mor Brook and the Tiddle Brook, peering into the furrows, tracing the lines of vanished hedges. I scrambled up the steep bank of the hill, the Wrekin behind and the Clee in front rising up over the horizon like two dark planets ringed with snow, rising higher and higher the further I climbed. I scoured the light dry soil on top of the hill, with its big knobbly lumps of what the farmers up here call catsbrain. I peered at the rich pebbly loam of the broad ridge to the south-east of the village – 'rather stony, locally very stony', the Government soil survey had said – with its string of prosperous farms. I wandered the shining red clay of the land around the church and stream where the medieval village once was, and the big field where the combine harvesters in summer work all night long by the light of their headlamps. And I wondered about the soil in my garden: about the large rounded cobbles – white and red and grey (rounded by what? I wondered) – that I found below the surface. And I began to see that the whole landscape was a book, if only one could read it – a manuscript written and rewritten, over and over again, a palimpsest of texts, decipherable still . . .

Shropshire is the coldest of the shire counties, an English outpost hunched beneath Welsh mountains. Locked in by land, the county is ridged and furrowed like the frozen fingers of an outstretched hand – a left hand, with the Clee Hills as the thumb, and Wenlock Edge, Caer Caradoc, the Long Mynd and Stiperstones as the fingers. The names clang and slide like horses' hooves on frozen ground. On winter mornings the low sun glances from ridge to ridge, lighting the tops of the hills in sequence, east to west, as if with a chain of beacon fires – signalling to the Long Mountain, rippling on into Wales. But below the hills, the valleys shiver in shadow. Our valley is the gentle Corve Dale, beneath the high shoulders of the Brown Clee, where on warm April days the brook meanders down to Ludlow – but the valley holds its breath now in the icy maw of winter, while above on the Clee the hill forts flare before the sun. In broad and grassy Ape Dale too, beneath the wooded flank of Wenlock Edge, modern farms and homesteads lie silenced by the cold, united in chilly equity with abandoned priory and empty cloister. Beneath lowering Caer Caradoc – was it here Caractacus made his last stand? – where the narrow Roman road runs arrow-straight to Viroconium, the valley is still fathoms deep in frozen dark, while in the air above, the tremendous whale-like bulk of the Long Mynd breaks the surface into a glittering sea of frozen bracken. And in the far valleys beyond, high in the lee of the Stiperstones, the remains of old lead mines show black against hills where quartz and calcite mimic the frost and the villages have names like White Grit, Gravels, Snailbeach, Shelve.

Back. Further back. Back beyond the lead miners, back beyond the flint traders, back to a time when the last glacier, as high as a dozen church towers, ground to a halt here: a time when the Welsh borderlands were invaded by twin streams of ice fed from the mountains of Wales and the Irish Sea – two groaning, creaking, grinding sheets of ice, carrying with them sand and gravel and pebbles and boulders and rocks, scratching and scrap-ing and gouging, overtopping all but the highest hills; the jug-gernaut of the Welsh ice swinging south and east, deflected around the Long Mountain, the Stiperstones, the Long Mynd and Wenlock Edge, into the valleys of the Usk and Wye, tongues of ice licking round Norton Camp and up into Corve Dale, probing the soft underbelly of Ape Dale; the tidal wave of Irish sea ice parting on either side of the Wrekin, then reuniting, crashing down into Ape Dale from the north, engulfing the valley, shearing the side off Wenlock Edge, overtopping it at its lower northern end, and pushing on through the valley of the Severn, lapping the skirts of the Brown Clee, until the ice hung poised above Corve Dale, on the brink of the soft land below. And then stopped. Right here.

Morville was glaciated only once – in the last and coldest phase of the Pleistocene Ice Age. Over central England the ice was a mile thick. There are striations on the side of the Wrekin four hundred metres above the surrounding plain. Even here at the edge, the ice would have been fifty metres high – a vertical cliff-face, its upper surface rent by fissures into a maze of pinnacles like a forest of frozen termites' nests. For three hundred years the ice sheet surged and retreated and surged again, fed by snow falling in the mountains at its source, sometimes moving forward several metres in an hour, juddering onwards inch by inch, second by second, the ground vibrating with a roar like that of a continuous volcanic eruption; at other times wasting backwards, streams of soil-laden meltwater gushing from channels beneath it, the dirty white snout of the glacier and the pale blue of the sky reflected in pools of water trapped behind the mounds of debris the ice bulldozed before it; all the time accompanied by the trickling of gravels, the noise of stones falling from the hillsides; never standing still.

For a few short weeks each year, the temperature here at the edge would have soared, flooding the surface with meltwater: the brief hectic summer of the tundra, full of noise and movement and

the glitter of sun on water, the cries of waterfowl, the flash of
wings in the sun, air shimmering with dancing clouds of gnats,
when lush green grass and thick tussocks of sedge would carpet
the ground and flowers would burst into life – the vivid green-
and-yellow clumps of marsh marigolds reflected in the pools of
the valley bottom; the fragile white eight-petalled cups of mountain avens blooming on the bare rocky ledges of the hillside; dwarf
willows and birch on the drier ground, their catkins heavy with
yellow pollen, loud with the humming of bees.

The marsh marigolds are still here: *Caltha palustris* – kingcups,
the villagers call them. They thrive on the edges of the village, in
the boggy places north of the Ash Bridge and around the pools of
Morville Heath: treacherous ground, camouflaged with a litter of
fallen branches, the water gleaming dark and deep – deeper than
you think. The dwarf willows and birch retreated long ago to the
far north of Scotland. I went to look for them, hiking across the
high bare tundra of the island of Hoy to a remote valley where
they survive, an untouched fragment of ancient post-glacial flora,
huddled in a fold in the land. Their thickened furry leaves and
shoots are still adapted for sub-zero temperatures, though the
enemy now is not the intense cold of the Ice Age but the incessant
wind that sweeps the island. The mountain avens retreated with
the ice to the mountains of Snowdonia and Scotland, and to the far
west of Ireland, where I found them on the limestone pavements
of the Burren in County Clare, their tiny oak-shaped leaves
carpeting the naked rock. In England the mountain avens survive
only as pollen grains and fragments of plant material in the peat
laid down after the Ice Age; once they were so abundant that they
even gave their name, *Dryas octopetala*, to the two periods of
intense cold – the Older and Younger Dryas – that marked the
end of the Pleistocene epoch.

The Younger Dryas ended with a period of rapid warming, caused in part by a massive increase in atmospheric methane (a greenhouse gas even more potent than carbon dioxide) pumped out by newly forming peat bogs. Within fifty years it was all over. Vast plains of outwash flooded from the retreating ice sheet. Torrents of meltwater burst through the watershed at Barrow and carved out the Ironbridge Gorge. A group of woolly mammoths drowned in a kettle hole in the ice at Condover, sixteen miles away. At Morville, the dying glacier disintegrated into a wilderness of shifting meltwater channels, blocks of ice, debris, lakes and pools. It dumped its freight of gravel, the heaviest, largest pebbles first: my garden, and those of my neighbours, curving like a terrace above the valley floor, along the side of the glacier. Then the medium-sized pebbles, washed further by the tide of meltwater, adding to the piles of moraine bulldozed by the glacier in its youth: the mounds to the south and east of the village. Then the finer gravels, carried further still, down the valley to Harpsford, where the meltwater was damned by ice into a vast lake. Here the two streams of the Mor Brook and the Tiddle Brook – the 'large' brook and the 'little' brook – still join. I stand below the high stone bridge with its triangular breakwater and tangle of tree roots testifying to the ferocity of winter spates, and I imagine the lake, the sediment softly drifting down through the water, fathoms deep above my head.

North-west of the village, the big field below the gardens is plastered with boulder clay, or 'till': the finest grains of all, ground to a powder by the motion of the glacier while it was still moving forward. The word comes from the same root as 'tilth' and 'to till' (the land). Thousands of years later the big field became one of the open fields of the village, divided into strips which were distributed among the villagers so that each had a strip of the best (and the worst) land to cultivate. I think of the machines working here in summer, of the badgers rustling through the corn on Midsummer Night. This is the fertile red clay of the valley floor, which cracks open in summer like rows of bricks laid out to dry, like the crackle of glaze on a terracotta tile, like a sheet of squared paper, the stubble plotted like a graph.

I took some of the cobbles from the garden to the geologist at the Ludlow Museum. From the Lake District, he said; ground smooth by the glacier. It makes for hard digging.

I am greedy for facts. I want to know who first tilled this ground, who first dug this earth. I am curious about them, my first, nameless neighbours. It was the soil that brought them – us, all of us; the pattern of the village and the lives of its inhabitants, human and non-human, all predetermined by the patchwork of soils left by the ice. The trees came back first – pine and birch, then oak and ash and hazel – and the wandering herds of bison and mammoth, feeding on the fresh grass. Then the men, following the herds. They came first to the thin soils of the high plateau on the western edge of the village, scraped bare by the passage of the ice, a route for hunters and traders above the dense forests of the valley, carrying axes of polished stone and flint: greenstone from Cornwall, granite from Wales and the Lake District, flint carried all the way from East Anglia and the chalk uplands of southern England. They were the first British farmers. They buried their dead in megalithic chamber tombs and long barrows. But not here. Here, they seem merely to have passed through, following the ridge-way from the Radnor Hills, along the spine of the Brown Clee, down past Ouseley and out over the plain, carrying their precious load of flint to settlements on the banks of the Severn. Their track still runs today, a dotted green line across the modern Ordnance Survey map, down between the stone quarry and the motocross track. The farmers on the hill still find their flints, gleaming in the furrows like wet coins. One of the farmers told me how, when still a boy at the village school, he was caught carving his name on his desk; sent to the headmaster and asked to hand over the penknife, he opened his hand to reveal a Neolithic arrowhead – a sliver of flint, barbed and tanged, as slim and deadly as the day it was made.

No, the first farmers here were a different people. They came later, and chose the broad ridge of gravel on the south-east of the village, with its well-drained fertile soils, easily cleared of trees. I see it beyond the garden, its easy gradient picked out by the rising curve of the street lights at night. The straight road along the ridge still swerves to avoid the site of their cemetery, its groups of round barrows and massive incurving entrance banks ploughed out now to crop marks and dark patches in the soil, to shadows and less than shadows. These were people who marked the seasons with standing stones and stone circles, honouring the movement of the sun from midwinter sunset to midsummer sunrise. They made pots, shaping them by hand, and decorating them with patterns of lines and hatching: you can still see the impress of their fingertips in the wet clay. And they knew the secret of metalworking: they had tools and weapons of bronze which they cast in stone moulds. And perhaps they told stories too, their voices rising and falling around the campfires at night, stories of which the tale of Arthur's Excalibur, the sword in the stone, may be the last faint echo.

I didn't yet know what form the garden would take, but I had an atavistic desire for the extremes of midsummer sunrise and midwinter sunset. I wanted the garden to reflect the sweep of the year, the lengthening and shortening of the shadows, the turning wheel of the stars. I wanted to mark where the midsummer sun rose and set – the azimuth, where the apparent orbit of the sun bisects the horizon – describing in the course of the day a great arc from the trees north-east of the school house right round to the barn north-west of the big chestnut. I wanted to mark the position of the midwinter azimuth, when the arc of the sun contracted to a scanty 100°, hardly clearing the bowl of the hills on either side of the church tower. I was already aware that the land itself, the plot which was to become the garden, was oriented more or less precisely upon the cardinal points of the compass, since it was aligned with the house, which itself was oriented on the lines of the big house beyond, which was in turn oriented on the church, which was itself oriented to the east – the direction of the sunrise, adopted under Christianity as a symbol of the risen Christ. But due east is, loosely, a sort of average for sunrise throughout the year or, more precisely, the direction of the equinoctial sunrise, when day and night are of equal length. It is the direction of balance, reason-ableness, the golden mean; of confidence, trust and hope. But I found myself wanting the extremes, north and south, black and white, midsummer and midwinter. I wanted to feel that succession of despair and elation, to stand in the frost or snow, with the low shadows striking across the face of the garden, watching the sun turn back from its midwinter nadir and start to inch its way up the heavens, pushing the curve of the azimuth wider and wider, week by week, like a swimmer breasting the waves.

And yet the Christian liturgy too taps into the same drama of the slain god, of the darkness before the returning light. I remember the anguish of Good Fridays as a child, when my mother would fast all day, white-faced and fainting, meditating on the brutal facts of Christ's death and descent into the tomb; then the release and joy of the ceremony the following night, when a lone candle would spark into life in the darkness, and '*Lumen Christi!*' sang the priest, and again '*Lumen Christi!*', his voice rising higher, and a third time '*Lumen Christi!*', the candles kindled one from another until the whole church was filled with flickering light. 'Christ is risen!' 'He is risen indeed!'

Offa was King here once. The second half of the place-name Mamerfeld is the Anglo-Saxon word for an open tract of land: something broader and wilder than a field in our modern sense, clear of trees perhaps, but not necessarily cultivated. Much of the land around the village would already have been cleared by Bronze and Iron Age farmers. First the gravelly land on the ridge; then, as heavy ploughs were developed which were capable of turning the sod, the flat land in the valley bottom, with its wet, claggy soil and impenetrable thicket of alder carr. The Anglo-Saxons arrived here relatively late, and not as farmer-settlers, as they were in the south and east of the country, but as part of the final push westwards by the Angles of Mercia in the late seventh century, as a ruling élite. They brought us their language, consolidated the land into big agricultural estates with specialised satellite settlements, gave them the place-names we still use, defined the boundaries of the shire and sub-divided it into smaller administrative districts known as 'hundreds', each with its own court.

The origin of the Anglo-Saxon hundred is lost in the mists of time. A hundred what? Men-at-arms? Hides of land? But it's their landscape we still inhabit today. You can map it in the names they gave to the villages – all compounds of 'tun' (a settlement) or 'leah' (a woodland clearing): a land of woods and fields, hamlets and scattered farms, as it remains today. South and west of here, they filled the good farming land of Corve Dale with new settlements and arable fields – Aston and Weston, Acton and Upton, Shipton, Stanton and Hopton (later Monkhopton): East Settlement and West Settlement, Oak Settlement and the Settlement on the Hill, Sheep Settlement, Stone Settlement, the Settlement in the Little Valley. On the poorer ground to the north and east, the place-names tell a different tale, of woods and clearings – Meadowley, Broseley and Linley; Nordley, Astley and Willey: Meadow Clearing, the Clearing of the Guardian of the Fort, the Clearing in the Lime-Tree Wood; North Clearing, East Clearing, the Clearing in the Willow-Wood. This is a vocabulary of usefulness, of practicalities; of assets and production. But for the principal features of the landscape the Anglo-Saxons co-opted the old British names: the Wrekin, the Long Mynd, Wenlock Edge, the rivers Severn and Teme, the forest of Wyre. A name is a name, one as good as another – why bother to change it?

Their attitude to the British themselves was similar: practical, robust, dismissive. They called them Wealas, 'the foreigners' – which is where our words 'Wales' and 'Welsh' come from – rather than their own name for themselves: Cymry. At Morville they called the gravel banks where the round barrows once stood Walton (now Bridgwalton): 'the place where the foreigners live'. Far from being wiped out or driven into the far west, the British were permitted to remain in many of their old haunts, tolerated by their new overlords, the two communities living side by side.

But although the British were a subject people, they were also the inheritors of the Cornovii, the warrior tribe that had built the great hill forts of the Clee and the Wrekin. Allied peoples still controlled all the land beyond the Long Mountain. So forty miles west of here, in the second half of the eighth century, Offa built his dyke, separating England from Wales, Anglo-Saxons from foreigners, 'us' from 'them'. With its ditch and embankment still swelling across the landscape, the dyke was more control point than frontier or border – there were after all Anglo-Saxon settlers further west – but just in case. Just to make sure.

Shropshire still has an air of being on the frontier, the nearby towns strung out along the border like pieces in a chess game: Kington, Knighton, Presteigne, Bishop's Castle. You enter Shrewsbury by the English Bridge and leave by the Welsh one. As late as the eighteenth century the River Severn was still the boundary between English- and Welsh-speakers. And at the Shrewsbury Flower Show each August you still hear as many Welsh voices as English ones. I like it here; I like the feeling of ambiguity, of being on the edge; of being in a sense in no-man's-land, between the Welsh mountains and the West Midlands. Between. I feel comfortable with that. I feel comfortable here.

Christianity came late to Shropshire: Mercia was the last of the Anglo-Saxon kingdoms to embrace Christ. One winter's day when it was too cold to garden, I went to Lichfield Cathedral to see St Chad's Gospels, a treasure-book dating from Offa's time or slightly before. It was made in about 730 in the scriptorium of one of the Anglo-Saxon monasteries connected with the Irish saint Columba (a group that includes Iona, Lindisfarne, Durrow, Kells and Lichfield itself). Christianity had first been introduced to Britain by the Romans, but had lapsed after the withdrawal of the legions. It was brought back to Britain in the second half of the sixth century from the shores of Ireland by St Columba, who founded the community at Iona off the west coast of Scotland. At about the same time, the Pope in Rome sent St Augustine to England on a similar mission. Augustine landed on the coast of Kent and set up his see at Canterbury in 597. There were thus two sources of the re-Christianisation of Britain: one formal, centralising in tendency and hierarchical, spreading from the south; the other tribal and bardic, with an emphasis on the spirituality of place and the poetic imagination of the individual, spreading from Ireland and the north-east. The collision of the two ideologies can be illustrated by the events of 651, when Oswy, the Christian King of Northumbria who followed the Irish Rule, found himself celebrating Easter on the day that his wife, Queen Eanfled, who followed the Roman Rule, was still fasting and keeping Palm Sunday. So Oswy called for a debate, the Synod of Whitby, which was convened in 664. Ostensibly the issue was to settle the date of Easter, though in fact nothing less than the future of the Celtic Church itself was at stake. After hearing both sides, Oswy decided in favour of Rome, a decision subsequently imposed upon the whole country in 669.

The spiritual tenor of Celtic Christianity survived, however, and survives still, increasingly prized for its reverence for the natural world and the individual expression of that feeling in the medium of religious poetry. Typical of the spirit of the poems of wandering Irish monks, transcribed into the margins of manuscripts in far-flung monasteries, is this gentle hymn of praise from one monk to his cat:

> I and Pangur Ban my cat,
> 'Tis a like task we are at:
> Hunting mice is his delight,
> Hunting words I sit all night.
>
> Better far than praise of men
> 'Tis to sit with book and pen;
> Pangur bears me no ill-will,
> He too plies his simple skill.

'Tis a merry task to see
At our tasks how glad are we,
When at home we sit and find
Entertainment to our mind.

Oftentimes a mouse will stray
In the hero Pangur's way;
Oftentimes my keen thought set
Takes a meaning in its net.

'Gainst the wall he sets his eye
Full and fierce and sharp and sly;
'Gainst the wall of knowledge I
All my little wisdom try.

When a mouse darts from its den,
O how glad is Pangur then!
O what gladness do I prove
When I solve the doubts I love!

So in peace our task we ply,
Pangur Ban, my cat, and I;
In our arts we find our bliss,
I have mine and he has his.

Practice every day has made
Pangur perfect in his trade;
I get wisdom day and night
Turning darkness into light.

                    Anon., eighth century, translated
                    from the Irish by Robin Flower

St Chad was one of the spokesmen for the Irish side at Whitby. He had trained at Lindisfarne under Aidan, one of Columba's disciples, and in 669 he became the first Bishop of Mercia, setting up his see at Lichfield. It is said that he travelled round his enormous district on foot, in the Irish tradition, until commanded by his exasperated Archbishop to ride on horseback. The Gospel book associated with his name surfaces first in Wales, at the church of St Teilo at Llandeilo Fawr. The first intimation of its presence in Lichfield Cathedral is no earlier than the tenth century, but tradition has it that the Gospels were made for Chad's shrine, which in the years following his death in 672 became a place of pilgrimage. Books like the Gospels of St Chad, the Lindisfarne Gospels and the Book of Kells were powerful religious symbols, sacred objects like saints' relics, liable to be poached from one ecclesiastical institution by another which felt the need of a boost to their status – a magnet for pilgrims, the lucrative tourist industry of the day. They were also worldly treasures – their covers encrusted with gold or silver and precious stones – and thus liable to be looted by marauding armies. In time of war the books would be hurriedly buried or spirited away by their custodians to prevent them falling into the hands of pagan invaders. The St Chad Gospels were probably removed from Lichfield Cathedral when it was sacked by Vikings in the ninth century; the shrine was destroyed then, and the Gospels were probably plundered for their rich binding or hidden away for safekeeping. Perhaps both, for only a fragment of the original survives, containing the Gospels of Matthew and Mark and part of Luke. The opening of Matthew is worn and bereft of its first page as if the book had long ago had its cover ripped off.

The last time the Gospels of St Chad were hidden was during the siege of Lichfield in 1646, when the cathedral was bombarded by

Cromwell's troops and the library ransacked and dispersed. Only the Gospel Book survived. It was returned after the Restoration, in a gilded wooden case which can still be seen in the cathedral.

The cult of St Chad continues at Lichfield to this day. The well where he used to pray is dressed each September with patterns of flowers in a modern revival of ancient well-dressing rituals. And when in 2003 a carved stone panel – which may be a sole surviving fragment from his shrine – was discovered during excavation work in the nave, people flocked in their hordes to see it. Dubbed 'The Angel of Lichfield', it showed an angel with lilies, the figure framed by huge feathered wings, the drapery of its tunic delicately moulded to suggest transparency and movement. Perhaps it was part of an Annunciation scene. The discovery coincided with the completion of a British Library project to digitise the manuscript, and people queued for hours at a computer terminal to 'turn' the pages the shrine had once contained.

Absorbed in looking at the manuscript with its rounded Insular script, its painted portraits of the evangelists – Mark with his lion, Luke with his ox – its illuminated initial letters and its interlacing borders like finely wrought metalwork, its swirling 'carpet page' of red and pink and silver beasts meshed tight as a school of silver fish, overlaid with the outline of the Celtic cross, I didn't notice the light growing dim, didn't feel the temperature dropping. When the storm finally broke, the huge north door crashed back on its hinges under the impact, revealing a white whirling world of snow and darkness outside, as if the Vikings themselves were once more at the doors.

Now it was the Anglo-Saxons who found themselves on the western side of someone else's border. Now it was they who were being harried westwards across the country by a fresh group of invaders, this time from Denmark. Offa had in his time ruled almost the whole country south of the Humber; now his capital at Tamworth and his cathedral at Lichfield were overrun, his kingdom peeled back to this sliver of land between Watling Street and the Welsh mountains. The final frontier, only a dozen miles from Morville, was negotiated between Alfred and the Danish leader. But the people here lived in constant fear of incursions. In 895/6 a Danish army overwintered on the bank of the Severn not five miles from Morville. In 910 the Severn was crossed at the same place by another band of Danes, 'rejoicing in rich spoil'. In 912 Aethelflaed, sister of Alfred and Lady of the Mercians, built a *burh* to defend the western bank of the Severn, one of a string of fortified places she had constructed after Alfred's death in response to the Danish threat. The name of the *burh*: Brycge. Bridgnorth, our closest town.

We know, because they wrote it all down – the Saxon monks of Winchester, Abingdon, Peterborough, Canterbury and Worcester – from the ninth to the twelfth centuries, continuing even after the last Saxon King was dead, keeping a record of the great events of each year – battles, laws, kings and saints – writing what came collectively to be known as the Anglo-Saxon Chronicle. It is the single greatest achievement of the Anglo-Saxon people, the first continuous national history of any Western people in their own language, begun perhaps as a single manuscript in a single place – tradition has it, at the direction of Alfred himself – then copied and sent out to the monasteries with instructions to continue the record and keep it up to date. Alfred knew that it was words as well as fortresses which would hold the newly created English nation together, that books and libraries were needed as well as weapons and armour to hold the line. And the line held: there are no Danish settlements in Shropshire. Christianity was preserved.

*

It's a quiet sort of heroism, the making and keeping of books. You don't get medals for sitting in the library each day, scratching away, writing it all down. Still less for dusting the shelves. But it is what civilisation is made of: the collective memory, passed on, passed down. All my adult life had been spent in libraries of one sort or another – research libraries, national libraries, college and university libraries. Now it was the local library at Bridgnorth which began to fill in the missing pieces of the jigsaw. I learned that, before the Benedictine monks of Shrewsbury built the stone church at Morville, the Anglo-Saxons had built a minster church here, probably of wood, mother church of a huge parish which ran north-east/south-west across the Severn, covering an area of 140 square miles from Broseley and Willey in the north-west, to Tong and Albrighton in the north-east, and from Charlcot, Aston Botterell and Pickthorn in the south-west, to Quatford, Eardington and Glazeley in the south-east. The church was served by a community of eight secular canons – not monks, but priests who lived communally and who, like Chad, would have travelled their enormous district on foot.

So had I found it at last, the first garden here? The Anglo-Saxon monks of Winchester and St Albans and Ely had gardens, and so, according to Bede, did St Chad's monks at Lichfield. Seeds from long-vanished monastic crops still turn up during excavations: vegetables and fruit; medicinal plants to cure the monks' ailments or at least to dull the pain with morphine extracted from opium poppies; dye plants like madder and woad to colour textiles and the vestments for the Mass; strewing herbs to sweeten the air and drive away fleas; butcher's broom to tenderise their meat. There were flowers, too – roses and lilies, for their beauty as well as their use – and more: Aelfric's *Colloquy*, a Latin vocabulary for speakers of Anglo-Saxon written in 995, includes the Anglo-Saxon names of more than two hundred plants and herbs. There would also have been fields of wheat (the area between Bridgnorth and Much Wenlock is still known locally as The Wheatlands), from which the first ripe grains, in thanksgiving for the harvest, would have been baked into bread and consecrated on 1 August, Lammas Day. The word *Lammas* – meaning 'loaf mass' – first occurs in its Christian context in the writings of Alfred, though the date of 1 August seems to suggest that the Anglo-Saxons had adapted the older Celtic festival of Lughnasa, which itself probably marked the opening of the harvest season. The practice of baking the Lammas loaf has long since dwindled away, but the date is still observed on the water meadows of the River Lugg near Hereford, where a system of strip-farming survives from medieval times, Lammas being the date by which crops of hay must be cut from strips of land rented at Candlemas which at Lammas revert to their owners.

No one quite knows how the Anglo-Saxons arranged their gardens, but I saw that I could at least grow the herbs and vegetables, fruit and flowers that those eight Anglo-Saxon clerics would have grown here at Morville. And I could make a little hay meadow too, to be mown at Lammastide, with wild fritillaries in it, as on the water meadows of Hereford, commemorating Alfred and how he loved books and beat back the Danes. And I began to see how I might make a whole sequence of gardens stretching from Alfred's day to the twenty-first century, commemorating all the people who have lived and worked here, dug the same soil as I do now and watched the clouds scudding across the same hillside, sniffed the air and felt glad to be alive.

Food is the most basic reason for making a garden. Cast out of the Garden of Eden, where food grew itself, man was ever afterwards obliged to grow his own by the sweat of his brow. But for me, growing vegetables was never a penance. My father always grew all our food. Who needs roses when in winter you can have the smooth gleaming curves of red cabbages; hostas when you can have huge dark heads of savoys quilted like elephants' skin; lilies when you can have blue-leafed leeks with sword-like leaves which turn purple in the frost and gauzy mauve seed heads as large as footballs? Who needs hollyhocks when you can have the magnificent grey foliage and towering electric-blue thistle-heads of cardoons – immune to rust and perennial too? In spring and summer there are the black-and-white flowers of broad beans, as luscious as any *Papaver orientale* 'Perry's White' and smelling far more delicious; pale lilac flowers of the graceful climbing mange-tout 'Carouby de Maussanne'; dark purple pods and flowers of dwarf French bean 'Royalty', dramatic as any hellebore; mahogany flowers of the curious winged asparagus pea (*Tetragonolobus purpureus*); pyramids of scarlet runner beans (grown for their flowers long before anyone thought of eating them), violet 'Viola Cornetti' pole beans and 'Meraviglia di Venezia', with its bright yellow pods and yellow-flushed vines. You could make a flower garden from peas and beans alone.

In the calendars of the Books of Hours, each month is illustrated by the social or agricultural activity that most typified it, the repertoire of images remaining virtually constant throughout the whole period of their production. For January the image is always Feasting. Christmas then used to last right up until the end of January. Who now even keeps the Twelve Days of Christmas, let alone the thirty-one days of January? For all our complaints about present-day Christmases beginning earlier and earlier, with Christmas trees and Christmas decorations appearing in the streets as soon as the sun-tan lotion of summer holidays has been put away, nowadays the event itself is a poor thing. By Boxing Day it's all over, with everyone off to the sales, and the newspapers full of advertisements for next year's summer holidays. In the Middle Ages, Christmas Day was only the beginning: for four weeks people had been limited to a diet of fish and gruel (meat, cheese and eggs being restricted during Advent, as they were during Lent). So on Christmas Day they made up for it with a gargantuan feast. There then followed twelve days and twelve nights of feasting and merrymaking, culminating on 6 January – Twelfth Night, the Feast of the Epiphany, kept with almost as much magnificence as Christmas itself.

We always keep Twelfth Night here: winter feasts are important to keep out the cold. The table groans with food – on one memorable occasion, six ribs of beef, a foot high; a boned, stuffed cockerel; a roast shoulder of pork, stuffed; a boned leg of lamb, rolled; two pieces of pickled beef; a steak-and-kidney pudding; roast parsnips, roast potatoes, a whole gleaming red cabbage, braised in the oven; mustard sauce, redcurrant sauce, creamed horseradish, braised apples; Stilton, Cheshire, Cheddar; pineapple, grapes, mangoes, mandarins, pippins, plum pudding and cream. After the Twelfth Night feast, all the winter greenery brought in from the garden on Christmas Eve is ceremonially burned on the fire: garlands of shining holly and black-fruited ivy, branches of pine, juniper and yew, banked up in the grate until the whole room is filled with the pungent smell of resin, the sparks shooting into the dark night sky like a gigantic Roman candle, the golden globe of mistletoe, cut from one of the apple trees in the Orchard, burned last, its white berries hissing in the fragrant ashes.

In the Bodleian Library's most precious Book of Hours – known as the Breviary of Henry VII or the Hours of the Fastolf Master, sumptuously illuminated in France in about 1440–50 for a wealthy English patron who may or may not have been Henry VII – it is Janus himself, the Roman god of gates and beginnings (who gives his name to the first month of the year), who presides over the feast, one face knawing a chicken leg, the other drinking from a goblet; one face bearded, looking back towards the Old Year, the other young, facing towards the New. Servants ply both faces with more food and drink. There are rushes strewn on the floor; behind him the leaded windows are dark. Under his feet is a plump red cushion to keep the draughts away.

In the more modest prayer book commissioned in about 1488 by George Talbot, 4th Earl of Shrewsbury, a nobleman sits at table in his manor house. We see it in section, the front cut away like a child's dollhouse, with columns, heavy red curtains draping the elaborate interior, and snow outside on the steeply pitched roof. The nobleman is waited upon by a serving woman, while another man warms himself at a blazing fire. The one figure missing is Lazarus at Dives' door: the tramp. Tramps seem to be invisible now too: the urban homeless, air-brushed out of the view; beggars you avoid eye contact with; crazies you cross to the other side of the road to avoid. But I remember the rural tramps of my childhood as familiar faces, each with their regular round of house calls and seasonal migrations. Their coming was as natural as the turning of the leaves, their due a screw of tea, a piece of cheese, a bundle of old clothes in the days before Oxfam.

I have a complicated reaction to homelessness. On one level, a mortal terror of being homeless – a phobia, like falling through floors (I have that one too). I have a nightmare vision of myself rootless, wandering, my possessions in white plastic supermarket bags; perhaps that is why I took to gardening – to feel safe, to feel rooted, to have a place to belong to. On the other hand, as a student I used to hitch-hike the fledgling motorways of Britain, leaving on a whim, often in the small hours of the morning, going wherever the cars or lorries might be going, sleeping rough in barns or in an abandoned car, waking cold and cramped in a Lakeland dawn or to the roar of early morning traffic. The soundtrack was Dylan – the self-conscious melancholy of 'one too many mornings and a thousand miles behind'. I had read Kerouac, of course. I too wanted to be *On the Road*. Going somewhere, nowhere, anywhere, so long as I was going. My hero was Bashō, the poet-wanderer of seventeenth-century Japan. I too dreamed of following 'The Narrow Road to the Deep North', of recording my travels in limpid haiku. My father had told me tales from the *Odyssey* in place of bedtime stories, and almost before I could walk I was as familiar with Odysseus's heroic wanderings as I was with the geography of my own street. It was only later that I learned that the *Odyssey* was one of the *nostoi* – tales not of journeys but of homecomings. However far his wanderings, Odysseus had a home to return to. As did the hero of Kerouac's novel. And Bashō too.

Sidney didn't. One bitter winter afternoon, soon after I began the garden, the doorbell rang. 'I'm a pilgrim,' he said, standing at the door with the snow whirling at his back. 'Have you got any old clothes? Can I chop some wood for you? I always work for anything I get.' I had abandoned any idea of gardening that day and was sowing seeds at the kitchen table in the warm. He looked too frail to wield an axe, and you wouldn't have left a dog outside on a day like that. 'Come in,' I said. I fed him soup and bread and cheese, and all afternoon he sat at the kitchen table, drinking cup after cup of coffee and smoking endless thin roll-ups which kept going out, all the while prattling on about this and that, while I went on sowing my seeds; and all afternoon my eyes were drawn to his hands which he rubbed compulsively – swollen and scratched and bloody, like lobster claws. I found him some clean clothes and socks and a better pair of boots, and he had a bath – three baths – draining the hot-water tank and flooding the yard below with soapsuds. After he had gone, I found his discarded shirt. It was encrusted with blood from the eczema that must have covered his whole body.

No, I don't have a romanticised view of being a tramp. If you are homeless, for every night when you get a hot bath there must be ten – twenty – when you go to sleep wet and cold and hungry. Goodness knows what Sidney's story was, what misfortune or tragedy underlay his wandering life. But there was a sort of heroism about it. To have and to keep nothing (for each thing I gave him, he left a corresponding thing behind); to cast oneself so utterly adrift, so completely trusting of the kindness of strangers; to give them in turn a chance to trust, to give, to care. Like a feather upon the breath of God.

As the days get longer, the cold gets stronger. So says the adage. Nowadays we can garden up to Christmas and beyond. The really cold weather saves itself for January and February. This is when the snow comes, transforming the crisp geometry of house and garden into billowing arches and domes, neighbours into bundled babushkas. I adore the snow, but am torn between the urge to see and the desire not to spoil. I creep round the outside of the garden, peering through gaps in the hedge, unwilling to set foot on the perfect expanse within. The cats hate it, preferring to spend their time indoors, curled up beside the Rayburn. Our fierce little white cat is shamefully revealed as a dirty yellow and, suppressed, keeps miserably to the margins. The meek pale tortoiseshell on the other hand, her smooth coat a decorous mixture of beige and brown and cream, is transformed into a startling redhead, her tawny coat bristling like a small plump lion. She skips and scutters about in the snow, tail in the air, whiskers resplendent. The large grey tomcat, however, entirely disdains leaving the house except to perform the necessary offices, when he springs fastidiously from one frozen human footstep to another before gaining the shelter of some frozen shrub, and then, turning his back, he languidly sprays the snow with a perfect arc of golden urine.

The garden is abandoned to other creatures: fox, weasel, stoat, badger; fieldfare and blackbird; pheasant and vole. I can see their tracks in the new snow. Whose territory is it anyway? They were here before me. They ignore the divisions of beds and paths, taking their own lines, disregarding my interventions. I see that a fox has been in the Cloister Garden, his sharp-clawed prints arrowing across it in a single line like a cat's, hindfoot lining with forefoot in perfect register, ankles delicately swinging in. I follow his track back to the point where he entered the garden under the yew hedge, see where his belly scuffled a trough through the snow, how he trotted diagonally across, halted, then doubled back, circled round. I try to imagine him – his colour, his dark muzzle, his smell, his warm breath, his motion as he trots and pauses and trots again – trying to make a narrative, to see the unseen. Like tracking the past, reconstructing the trajectories of other people's lives. I piece the story together, following it, then losing it, making patterns where perhaps none exist – like the constellations traced on the night sky four-and-a-half millennia ago, to enable priests and farmers to make sense of the turning year and travellers to find their way: unrelated stars, making a pattern only in the eye of the beholder, each a million miles from the Earth and from each other. On winter nights Taurus the bull charges across the sky, his massive head aggressively lowered, his long horns ploughing the furrow of the ecliptic. Above his back dance the Pleiades like a swarm of bees, goading him to greater fury. The Hyades which make up his face and the red star Aldebaran – his angry bloodshot eye – are light years apart: Aldebaran is sixty-five light years from us, the Hyades more than twice as far, the Pleiades two and a half times as far again. Except on the clearest of nights, the Pleiades are visible only if you don't look at them directly. You have to look away in order to see them, catch them unseen in the corner of your eye. Maybe this is a better way of understanding the past: not looking directly, but letting it emerge. Like the pattern of fields on the hillside at night, made visible by snow against the black calligraphy of hedgerow and copse; like the white spaces between letters written with invisible ink, warmed against a candle flame.

I have always liked the cold. I relish the sense of siege, that heightened sense of the boundary – the walls of the house – between our territory and the cold's. Perhaps this is because my first winter was the year of the Great Freeze, that first winter of austerity after the war, when the coal stocks ran out as the temperature plunged. The passageways dug through the frozen snow were too narrow to admit a pram, and for the whole of that winter I never left the comforting womb of the house. Occasionally my mother would put me in the front parlour with the windows thrown open, and there I would lie, swaddled like an Eskimo child, cocooned in warmth, looking out at the frozen world. Much of the time I think I was alone – my father away at the university in Manchester, my mother beginning that slide into depression which resulted in her hospitalisation the following spring – and even now I still associate cold weather with a not unpleasant sense of solitariness.

She said: 'Having you ruined my life.'

He said: 'We love you now, of course, but it would have been so much better for us if we had never had you.'

'Don't have children, dear,' they said.

I have a photograph of my parents taken the summer they first met. My mother is the centre of the picture. She draws the other figures around her, her arms through theirs. She is laughing. She is unrecognisable to me. In the next photograph she holds me. She looks like a death's-head.

Yet I knew I was loved – perhaps too intensely: there was no refuge from the searchlight of their attention, no shelter from the tempest of their lives together, no evading their competing claims for love and allegiance. Ice crystals grow in different patterns according to the temperature. From 0 to –3°C the ice forms thin hexagonal plates; a degree or two lower, and needles result; a few degrees colder still, and you get hollow prismatic columns. At –12 °C the ice is transformed into dendritic growth – the curling, swaying fronds of frost flowers on glass. This is the temperature at which snowflakes form, high in the troposphere; any colder and the air begins to be too dry for snow. Each snowflake is unique, repeatedly falling and being carried upwards in the up-draught of the great weather systems – her depressions, his rages – the conditions around each one varying from minute to minute, the final shape reflecting the snowflake's precise history. Many are damaged by collisions as they fall, blown about by surface winds; others, falling into warmer air, melt away to rain or sleet. The biggest, most perfect snowflakes fall during calm weather and when the temperature is close to zero. Isolation: it's what I do best.

Gardening, reading and writing. All solitary pleasures. One year I was snowed in alone here at Morville. The roads were blocked, the ice brought down the power lines, the milk froze in the tanks, the mail piled up undelivered, and the wind blew the snow in the lee of hedges and walls into hollow arching parabolas like Atlantic breakers, frozen in a breath. A band of wood pigeons took up winter quarters in the cherry tree overlooking the Vegetable Garden, spying out the land. When disturbed, they rose heavily into the air in a muffled whirl of feathers the same colour as the snow-laden sky. I waded thigh-deep through the snow to visit a neighbour, guessing where the field path lay, returning by the main road, skidding down the hill in the middle of the empty carriageway, the whole countryside silenced. And that first night, in the book-lined house, with the shutters closed, the heavy curtains drawn, the candles lit and an armchair pulled up to the fire, I was supremely content. The next day, as the great yews bowed their heads under the weight of snow, I read on by the fire. With computer screen blank, and telephone, TV and radio all silenced, absolved of all quotidian cares, I read *The Secret Garden*, itself a winter book, set in another gaunt old house with the wind wuthering around it in the darkness, the tapestries stirring in the draught, the carpets lifting on the bare boards of the corridors, and outside the mysterious garden, where all seems dead – or waiting.

Lauds

Wait. That's the advice given to anyone starting a new garden: wait for a year, and see what comes up in the existing garden. But I can't wait. I can't sleep at night. My head is buzzing with ideas. I wake at 3 a.m. and prowl the corridors of the house. I look down into the moon-washed garden and imagine a pair of knot gardens below the windows, their interlacing patterns picked out by the frost in stark black and white. I conjure cones of box and pyramids of yew casting long moon-shadows across the frosted grass, like a Kip and Knyff engraving; high hedges with flat frost-whitened tops; moonlight flooding through a receding perspective of massive yew arches.

It is the moonlight that has awoken me, flooding through the crack between the curtains, flaring around the edges of the shutters, throwing a hopscotch of black-and-white window-panes on the floor of the room. The air inside the house crackles with cold. I open a window and lean out. The moon is high in the west, huge and pale, draining the stars to faint pinpricks, closer to the earth now, in February, than it will be at any other time during the winter, closer than it ever will be again until the Harvest Moon of September. It fills the high narrow yard behind the house full to the brim with its light, pinning every crack and crevice to the cliff-face of the walls like moths caught in a searchlight.

It is an old house: a two-storey, three-sided range adjoining the big house next door; part dower house, part brewhouse or bakery, sometime laundry and apple store, cobbled together from disparate spaces at different times. People have lived and worked here, century after century, reshaping it according to new tastes, new needs. Doors have been patched and reversed, rehung; new door-ways cut through walls, old doorways blocked; new corridors sliced from existing rooms, old ones reduced to ghosts under the wallpaper. Rooms have expanded and contracted – appearing and disappearing – as walls were demolished, windows blocked, floor levels raised, ceilings dropped. One room was forgotten entirely, blocked in, blocked up, entombed above the hall. Beneath the layers of paint and paper are other layers of paint and paper, blue and yellow, pea-green and dark brown, a record of other people's lives, life upon life, back through the centuries to the bare stone from which the house was constructed; sandstone, quarried from the hillside above the house, its layers of green and grey and purple sediments continuing the story, back and back, year on year like the growth rings of a tree, laid down in flood or drought, recording the seasons, the centuries, the millennia, the history of this place.

The glass in the leaded lights of the casement windows is a patchwork of panes. The oldest glass is thinner, greener, flawed with the elongated scars of air bubbles. Through it the garden looks different – there's a different cast to the light, as if the weather out there were about to change; a ripple of disturbance as you pass, as if someone had just walked quickly by outside. Under the eaves, across the east front of the house, there is a row of rooms with low sash windows, broader than they are high. Here the panes are younger, larger than the leaded lights of the casements, many with the swirl of crown glass. In winter, on the inside of one of the panes – always the same one – the mist of condensation clears and then mists over again, every few seconds, over and over – always in the same place, slightly below the middle, a little towards the bottom – at about head-height: a regular pulse, starting from the centre and spreading outwards, as if an exhalation of breath had momentarily warmed the cold pane – as if someone were standing at the window, as if all that remained of them were that warm breath and that lingering gaze, looking out into the garden.

Like sheep on the hillside, we are hefted here, the ghosts and I. How could you bear to leave? Not to feel the wind on your face or crumble the soil through your fingers; not to hear the buzzard's cry or sip dew from the honeysuckles in autumn; not to smell the spring when it comes lilting over the hedges in April. Seeing the world at one remove, from the other side of a cold windowpane. That must be how it feels to be a ghost.

My garden was conceived in winter: a garden of ruler-straight lines and precise measurements, of black ink and white paper, moonlight and shadows – the plan of a city which did not exist; a map of a place yet to be discovered. My America, my New-found-land. I shaped coastlines, created continents; laid out city streets and broad thoroughfares, gave them names. Complete in itself, it needed no projection into the actual; it was almost more real than the 'real' garden is to me today. Even now, the 'real' garden is haunted with the ghost of this ideal garden. It still appears at night and in the winter. Is this what I am searching for, on my noctural perambulations?

The silhouette of the garden was pegged out in autumn mist, the lines of string receding into indistinctness. Mr Day who kept the churchyard tidy came to help and together we planted yew hedges in midwinter fog, each isolated in his own world, only the sound of distant spade on stony ground signalling the presence of one to the other. When the first beds were cut out of the turf – a pattern of dark interlocking L-shapes beneath the pale cupola of the Gatehouse – the ground froze hard into an icy chess board of black earth and frosted turf.

I still love the garden best in monochrome: in snow, in moonlight, in frost, in heavy dew, in fog – especially in freezing fog, when whole trees are drowned fathoms deep in arctic air and the boundaries between sky and ground blur, when the silvered paths of the garden seem to float over the black earth of the empty beds like slender bridges cantilevered out over a chasm, and twigs and branches are transformed by the hoar frost into fragile constructions of air and ice, each day a little longer, growing in the direction in which the air is flowing, like fingerposts to the far north.

I dress in monochrome, too: working with old books in out-of-the-way corners of dusty libraries I long ago adopted black as a simple everyday expedient. Is there a connection? The subfusc of academic uniform, the black velvet of winter parties, the black and white of text on page, this liking for winter?

It is said we have five senses: hearing, touch, smell, sight, taste. Only five? Surely others too, in that passionate engagement with the garden. The sense of time – of before and after, of not-now, of anticipation and memory – that so enriches our perception of the garden, as in the white lilac which grew outside my bedroom window when I was a child, or the gardener's posie of rosemary and rue given as a house-warming present half a lifetime ago, remembered now and planted again to make a new garden in another place, another time. The sense of space, the perception of volumes – high or low, wide or narrow, big or small – and the feelings they provoke of containment or exposure, prospect or refuge, connection or separation, end or beginning. And the sense of motion – the sense of moving through space: gardens are experienced not simply as pictures, but as series of shifting perspectives, changing volumes – as movement, as progression. Long before I began the garden I knew that there would be certain ways, certain routes through it – stopping places, vistas, views, curving paths, straight paths, right angles, detours and diagonals. I imagined how it would feel to move through it long before I knew what form 'it' would take: I knew only that it would be a garden where you took your time.

Anticipation is one of the gentler pleasures of gardening. We sow seeds and then wait for them to come up. We plant trees which we never see in maturity, except in our mind's eye. When the gardens of Studley Royal in Yorkshire were rescued from dereliction in 1966, the deputy county architect's report warned that the restoration would take a considerable number of years. But this, he felt, was acceptable, in keeping with the world of the garden's creators, the eighteenth-century Aislabie family, for whom there would always have been 'a respectable pause for anticipation between the conception of a project and its realisation'. Anticipation is the imaginative leap which enables us to picture how a garden will look in ten, twenty, a hundred years' time, and yet still relish the time in between; to enjoy not knowing, too, or half-knowing, savouring the delights of gardens which tantalise us into wondering what is through the arch, around the next corner. Playing with our sense of anticipation is one of the great devices of garden planning. As Alexander Pope put it:

Let not each beauty ev'ry where be spy'd,
Where half the skill is decently to hide.
He gains all points, who pleasingly confounds,
Surprizes, varies, and conceals the Bounds.
Epistle IV, To Richard Boyle, Earl of Burlington,
Of the Use of Riches, 1731, lines 53–6

At the heart of the garden I planned a circular enclosure through which all the other parts would connect. At first I saw it merely as a restful interlude between one part of the garden and the next, just high hedges and mown grass – no more – a relief from the colour and incident elsewhere. There were to be three exits, little openings in the hedge which would provide access to the other areas. But as the hedges grew, the views through the openings began to assume almost more importance than the openings themselves. They were odd, unintentional little views, set on the diagonal, concealing more than they revealed: intriguing glimpses rather than deliberate vistas. The space within the hedges also started to acquire its own unexpected personality. I had mowed the grass in concentric circles; now I mowed only the alternate ones, making a pattern of long and short instead of the expected smooth expanse. Eventually this became the Turf Maze. So now, although you can still choose to cross this circular space, selecting another path and deviating from the direction in which you were travelling, the Turf Maze mown in the grass at your feet gently discourages you from doing so, teasing you into exploring it first – only for you to discover that, having once set out upon it, it returns you to the place where you first started.

Although the garden is divided into separate areas by high hedges, it is less a succession of garden 'rooms', each leading into the next in an orderly sequence, than like a medieval church, with nave, transepts and aisles, choir and apse, little side-chapels and chantries, glimpsed sideways through arches and arcades in an ever-shifting perspective. There's a transparency about it – the way an overture before an opera introduces all the themes that will be elaborated later – yet it retains its secrets, its ability to surprise. Both the maze and the views from it heighten the visitor's sense of anticipation by refusing to resolve matters in the expected way.

Morville Hall and the surrounding land is owned by the National Trust. Before they would give permission for the garden they wanted to see plans. So I worked on the design all that first winter, and by spring I had my outline – a grid of hedges dividing the garden into six unequal spaces: Vegetable Garden and Cloister Garden, Canal Garden and New Flower Garden, Wild Garden and mown-grass Plat. Not that the garden was really 'designed' at all. There was a feeling of inevitability about it – not in the sense of restoring or recreating what had been lost, but in its inevitable geometry, as dictated by the buildings, the shape of the plot, the slope of the land, the line of the horizon, the positions of roads, walls, gate. That first winter, as I began to draw the plan, the process of 'designing' felt more like patiently waiting for the garden to reveal itself than any active pursuit on my part; a matter of asking the right questions. Alexander Pope said: 'Consult the Genius of the place.' The answers are all there; the trick is to find the questions.

'What if?' – the most exciting question in the world.

And when the design is finished, it should snap shut like a box.

But I wasn't ready to produce the detailed planting plans the Trust would have liked. And I wasn't able to produce three-dimensional visualisations either, for I could only draw in the most rudimentary fashion. So I wrote about the garden instead – in the present tense, as if walking around in it – pointing out the view through the hedges here, the shape of a shrub there, the scent from the wigwams of sweet peas over there. Even now I am still introduced, in the manner of Bateman cartoons, as the person who wrote the guidebook before the garden had even been begun. But for me the garden was already so real that I could walk about in it and smell the flowers. In my imagination I could feel the different spaces of the garden alternately opening and closing around me, sometimes narrowing to no more than a corridor, at other times widening into a pool of space. I could see the patterns of light and shade as I walked under the tunnels of trained apples and pears; I could feel the alternation of warmth and coolness on my skin. I could taste the fruit and hear the birdsong: I hardly needed to make the garden at all. Except for my husband Ken's sake, who said: Make it for me, so that I can see it too.

February begins with the great feast of Candlemas, celebrated on the 2nd. This is the feast of the Presentation of Jesus in the Temple, and was traditionally the day on which people brought candles to be blessed in church. The custom arose from the opening words of Simeon's canticle where he recognised the child as the Messiah: *Lumen ad revelationem gentium*, a light to lighten the darkness of the world. After the blessing of the candles some of them would be lit, and the congregation and celebrant would process round the church carrying them. Then the priest would change out of his purple vestments into white for the feast of the Purification of the Virgin Mary, which is celebrated on the same day. Candlemas was my mother's favourite feast day. In northern lands, it has always been seen as a time of renewal and rebirth, signalled outside by the yellow flowers of the winter aconites and inside by the candle flames of Candlemas, blooming together in the darkness of winter.

The Roman month of February took its name from the adjective *februus*, meaning 'purifying' (*Februa* was the feast of purification held by the Romans at the end of February). This was the month of ritual cleansing, when worshippers washed away the pollution of the previous year and prepared themselves for the year ahead. According to Hebrew law a woman also needed to be purified forty days after the birth of a child. These two things seem to have combined in the institution of the Christian feast of the Purification of the Virgin, placed in accordance with Hebrew law forty days after the Nativity – on 2 February.

But in Celtic lands Mary shares the opening of February with another figure, St Brigid or St Bride, whose feast day falls on 1 February. Brigid is sometimes called 'Mary of the Gael', and is the most important figure of the early Irish church after Patrick himself. She is said to have been Abbess of Kildare, a shadowy figure about whom little is known for certain, though she is venerated all over Ireland and her feast (and its eve) was until the nineteenth century the occasion of elaborate rituals performed by the women of the household. Behind her seems to stand a powerful Celtic goddess associated with healing, learning and poetry, a friend of animals, closely associated with nature, whose feast was anciently celebrated on the same day. That day in the Celtic world was the festival of Imbolc, signifying the end of winter and the beginning of spring, characterised in the tale of Emer and Cú Chulainn as the time when the ewes begin to lactate

again. The great festivals of the Celtic calendar, instead of celebrating the cardinal points of the sun – spring equinox, summer
solstice, autumn equinox, winter solstice – as the Roman calendar
did, marked the openings of the seasons: Imbolc at the beginning
of February, Beltane at the beginning of May, Lughnasa at the
beginning of August, Samhain at the beginning of November.

Mary and Brigid, Candlemas and Imbolc: the importance
attributed to these two feasts, and to the beginning of February
as the time when the success of the coming agricultural year might
be determined, is reflected in the number of surviving weather
rhymes which use Candlemas as a marker.

> If Candlemas Day be fair and bright,
> Winter will have another flight:
> If Candlemas Day it be shower and rain,
> Winter is gone and will not come again.

Or more succinctly:

> *Soleil de Chandeleur*
> *Annonce hiver et malheur.*

February's occupations in the Books of Hours are Keeping
Warm and Chopping Wood. In the Hours of the Fastolf Master, a
prosperous man sits at his ease in front of a roaring log fire, one
hand raised to feel the heat, one leg bared to warm his toes, a
cauldron simmering over the flames. More logs are stacked in a
neat pile outside. In other Books of Hours, peasants chop logs and
bear them into the seigneur's hall. But in the calendar illustrations
to the Earl of Shrewsbury's prayer book, three villagers are
lopping trees with curved billhooks while a woman gathers the

loppings together. Logs were for the rich. The lord of the manor would have owned the timber of the trees on his estate; the villagers – if they were lucky – would have had the right to cut the underwood and to pollard or coppice some of the trees for firewood. Otherwise they were reduced to gathering fallen sticks. The thinner the stick, the faster it burned. At the time these miniatures were painted, Europe was slipping once more into a period of profound cold. Poor summers were followed by bitterly cold winters. In 1431 all the rivers in Germany froze over; in France most of the vines were killed by frost. The woman in the calendar illustration is tying the loppings into a faggot to make them last longer on the fire.

There's an art to stacking a log pile: selecting the appropriate sizes and shapes so that the pile will be stable and self-supporting; weighing them in the hand, and placing the heavier ones at the bottom and sides, with the lighter ones at intervals between, so that each basketful will contain some of each; making the pile neat, regular, like building a wall – a wall against winter, like the shelves of pickles and preserves lining the walls of the larder. In the winter of 1946/7, as the country ran out of coal and the thermometer stayed below zero for weeks on end, Pa chopped up the kitchen shelves to keep us warm. He was a theology student, away in the university at Manchester twelve hours a day. He used to sit up with me at nights, wrapped in his overcoat to keep warm, studying his Greek grammar: both of us insomniacs even then. When we all got whooping cough, he took his final examinations with bandages strapped around his chest to disguise the coughing.

I still have his Greek primer – like all his books, covered with notes, underlinings, exclamations, their backs stuck together with Sellotape, the endpapers filled with page references and quotations. I am more than twice the age that he was then. I open his books now, looking for messages from the past. What were you thinking of, Pa? What did you mean me to be, when you sat there, rocking the cradle with one hand, your Greek primer in the other? As I pace the house at night, I think of him looking out over the snowy roofs of Accrington, over the black-and-white pattern of yards and alleyways, over the railway lines and mill sheds, the rows of back-to-back houses and the corner shops, the pubs and the post office, the churches and chapels, out to the wild un-marked sweep of the moors beyond – back to where he came from.

Lives are decided by accident: he was a fatherless child of the slums whose life was transformed by a boyhood meeting with the local Unitarian minister. All it takes is a split second, a moment when what-might-have-been hangs in the balance with what-never-was.

Our logs are brought by Nick, who has been delivering logs to us ever since he was sixteen and got his tractor licence. He's a handsome lad with broad shoulders, newly married and with a baby of his own now. It was often a Sunday morning when he brought the logs, as he worked during the week at the farm in the next village. He would come before I was up, and I would find the logs already tipped in a heap on the gravel when I opened the door. But once, in hard weather, I opened the door to find him still standing there beside the trailer, white-faced, the load un-tipped. He had borrowed the trailer, he said, and loaded it the night before, but when he came to tip it he found that the logs had frozen together, jamming the tailgate, so he jacked the trailer up higher to try to dislodge the icy load, and higher again, jiggling it up and down. He was standing beside the load, between the trailer and the pick-up, when the jacking mechanism failed and the trailer came crashing down. It missed him by a hair's breadth. Only a moment before he had been standing beneath it. 'I might have lost an arm, or might've been . . .' It didn't need saying what he might have been.

Logs are my one great extravagance (apart from books). The glowing heart of the house in winter is really the coal fire in the Rayburn: lit in the autumn, it stays in all winter – a sturdy, neat, workhorse of a fire, heating the water and warming the house. I like the thought of it, methodically going about its business in its little cast-iron range; I like knowing it's there without having to look; I like the routine of feeding it night and morning, going outside to fetch the coal, looking at the stars, sniffing the air for frost. But there's something special about the log fire. I like the smell of it. I like its companionable ways, how it flares and flickers like a conversation, animating the room. I like learning about the different woods Nick brings. In hard weather I keep the fire burning all night, banking it up before I go to bed with big dense logs of yew or wind-blown tulip wood retrieved by Nick from an old garden nearby; in the morning I'll throw dry bits of old apple wood from the Orchard on to the hot ashes, filling the room with sweet woody fragrance; later perhaps some smooth grey-skinned birch logs smelling of Russia-leather boots, leaping into mid-morning flame but gone long before midday; or green holly, flaring and sputtering like hot wax. Perhaps there will be red-fleshed alder (known as waller or wallow around here, says Nick. 'How do you spell it?' I ask. He shrugs. On account of its watery habitat? I look it up in the *OED*: it comes from the Old English *alor*, meaning 'reddish-yellow' – the wood is white when first cut, then changes to red as it oxidises. I also learn that it makes the best charcoal for gunpowder – an alarming thought), good to slow the fire down again before I go to bed. Occasionally there will be a bit of sulky chestnut from the big old tree beyond the bonfire yard which blew down in a gale, hardly worth burning at all, and one or two leftover logs of larch, pine or spruce, from the trees felled years ago down the back drive – resinous and sticky and smelling of forest, but banging and crackling and spitting out sparks on to the carpet until I have to leave off writing and go and fetch the fireguard.

But best of all I like the sound of it – the first crackle as the fire starts to take hold of the kindling, how it whispers and sighs as each log falls into ashes, how it responds to the rising wind. I don't need a weathervane to know which way the wind blows. As my neighbour Pat says, 'In winter the weather either comes up the valley from Joy's – when it's perishing cold – or down the valley from Joyce's – when it pours with rain.' Today the house vibrates with the wind: doors banging, chimneys thrumming, the corridors creaking and rustling. An east wind. The cat flap in the kitchen door lifts open, horizontal: the cats flatten their ears and narrow their eyes before breasting the tide of freezing air like Christmas Day swimmers taking the plunge. Little pots of seedlings freeze solid on the back steps. I don overcoat and gloves, and go out to fetch a box of apples from the fruit store for the blackbirds – little brick-red 'Margils' with orange stripes, huge yellow dumplings of over-ripe 'Lord Derbys', tiny leftover 'Pitmaston Pineapples', all beginning to go soft now – rolling them out over the frozen ground, allowing each bird its territory so they will not quarrel. But they do, darting forwards and backwards in fierce little rushes, clacking their alarm calls, tail feathers spread, backing and advancing like Spanish dancers: my fierce little black chickens.

I have two places in the house where I work. The downstairs room with the fire, and upstairs a monkish cell from which I can look down into the garden. In summer, with the window flung open and the jasmine in bloom, the upstairs room fills with the scent of the garden. The cats keep me company then, lounging on the sill or lunging at the house martins swooping up to their nest in the recess above the window. But in winter, when the wind is in the north and the curtains stir in the draught, they mostly desert me, preferring the Rayburn and the warmth of the kitchen. I sit with a shawl over my knees, the most loyal of the cats perhaps curled against the small of my back for warmth. The papers rustle on my desk. I try to work, but I'm distracted, restless now, thinking about the garden. And soon the thought of tea lures me too down to the kitchen.

And there, on the kitchen table, the seed catalogues, unopened in their plastic wrappers, glow. All winter I have been trying to resist them. But now, with somnolent cats at foot and elbow, the sharp dry smell of airing linen in my nostrils and my back to the door of the Rayburn standing open on the fire within, I make a start. First to list the seed saved or unused from last year. Then to list what new seed needs to be bought. And then, only then, cautiously, to open the catalogues, with their honeyed promises of shapes and tastes and smells; their coloured photographs of laden baskets and ripe pods, purple aubergines and ruby chard; yellow flower of courgette and soft sweet flesh of parsnip; leeks like thighs and lettuces like the frilled red skirts of cancan dancers; flowers like butterflies, like birds, as blue as lapis lazuli, as dark as bitter chocolate. And every year, despite my resolutions, I fall, succumbing to their thousand- and-one temptations and ordering far more than I need.

Outside, unnoticed, the snowdrops have begun to bloom, the tips of their leaves specially hardened to pierce the armour of the frozen ground. First the doubles, then the taller slimmer singles. I feel like Ebenezer emerging on Christmas morning to find that I haven't missed them after all. They grow in the shady places under the hedge between my neighbours' gardens and mine, not visible from the windows of the house. They are like forgotten patches of snow left over after the thaw, drifting downhill in twos and threes before widening into a pool in the shade of the young trees in the spinney. I follow them back along the hedge and up into the nuttery where I planted some clumps 'in the green' last year, dug from the hedge bottom as the flowers began to fade – the surest way to get them established. And there they are, beneath the hazels, flowering among the drifts of dead leaves and the bright patches of green moss. Planted dry, in autumn, they would not have flowered for another year or more.

I take the car and drive down into Corve Dale to see Old Tom the shepherd, who has been planting snowdrops for more than fifty years. He started in 1953, the year he married. The date is written in snowdrops on the front lawn of his cottage, flanked by two snowdrop pheasants (grown portly now with age, like Old Tom himself). He lives at Broncroft Parks, where in winter the Tugford Brook spills out over the flat land of the valley bottom, carrying snowdrop bulbs down from the Clee and out into the fields and woods. Old Tom rarely gets beyond his own garden now, but he used every year to take clumps of snowdrops from the banks of the brook and plant them out along the lanes, each year a little further – from Broncroft Parks to Broncroft, and on towards Broncroft Castle. And now other people have begun to do the same, carrying on where Old Tom has laid off, continuing the work of the brook, spreading the snowdrops from Broncroft to Broadstone, from Broadstone to Tugford, from Tugford to Holdgate, lining the lanes with snowdrops, a ribbon of white.

With the bitter cold days of February often come brilliantly starry nights. February is the month for star-gazing. The ancients divided the stars into 'wanderers' and 'fixed stars'. The wanderers were the five planets observable with the naked eye – Mercury, Venus, Mars, Jupiter and Saturn – which appeared to wander across the heavens against the backdrop of the fixed stars. Our word 'planet' means just that: a wanderer, from the Greek *planēs* (plural *planetes*), via Latin and Old French. After millennia of observation and recording, the movements of the planets were sufficiently known to be predictable, but were still inexplicable – now bright, now dim, now here, now there, now you see me, now you don't – until in the sixteenth century Copernicus posited a solar system with planets moving around the sun and then Kepler demonstrated the elliptical shape of their orbits.

Venus is the nearest planet to us, and is the brightest object in the sky after the sun and the moon. Her retrograde motion was a source of special puzzlement to the ancients. As I come down the garden trundling a wheelbarrow at twilight, or scrape frost from the windscreen of the car before sunrise, I gaze up, searching the constellations for her – as morning or evening star, dazzling in Sagittarius or brilliant in Pisces; sometimes crossing the path of

Jupiter, sometimes that of Saturn; hanging like a pearl from the ear of the new moon: capricious, wayward, unconfined.

It seems that the world is divided between those who go and those who stay, the wanderers and the fixed stars, the rootless and the rooted. There are those who wander from choice – nomads, travellers, gypsies-at-heart – whose home is wherever they happen to be. And there are those who stay, who live quiet lives within the distance their feet will take them – or at least no further than the compass of a Saturday morning bus ride to the local supermarket – whose home at last is the same earth they have known all their lives. But then there are those at home nowhere – the restless, the dispossessed, the homeless, refugees.

My parents had a knack for starting over, for reinventing themselves – he changing jobs, changing places; she changing her name (she left one city as Edna May and arrived in another as Anna), changing religion (from Anglicanism to Communism to Catholicism to Buddhism); both continually in a ferment of new ideas, literary, political, philosophical, theological; educated out of the working class but never arriving in the middle, uncomfortable with both. They compulsively moved house from one end of the country to the other and back again: Lancashire to Somerset to north Lincolnshire; south Lincolnshire to Leicestershire to Gloucestershire; Gloucestershire to Oxfordshire to Shropshire. He was a quick-tempered man, proud, prone to take offence where perhaps it was not always meant.

For me our moves seemed always to come at some natural break in my schooling or growing-up – or perhaps, with my books for company, I hardly noticed. But for my brother, fifteen months older, the moves disrupted an already troubled childhood and adolescence. It seemed we were always turning up at a new school with the wrong accent – a West Country burr in north

Lincolnshire, the flat vowels of Lancashire in rural Somerset – in some new place where alleys had become ten-foots and marbles had become alleys. For a time we lived in a house sandwiched between the Great North Road and the main railway line from London to Edinburgh. I used to lie in bed listening to the trains passing at night at the bottom of the garden, used to watch the students thumbing lifts from the lorries thundering by in front. When a by-pass was built, I used to cycle up to the flyover to watch the cars. It was the going I liked: destinations not arrivals. I never thought of them coming back. But wherever we were, Pa always planted a garden. Like tent pegs hammered into the ground, it anchored us.

I came to Morville and found a home. I'm digging in. I travel in time now rather than space, my expeditions only as far as the end of the garden. Distance has nothing to do with remoteness. I am obsessed by roads, but never go anywhere. I pore over maps, but am rooted to the spot. I dream of distant islands, but found one here, bounded by my own garden wall. Bridgnorth begins to seem like a metropolis.

The Romans arrived here in AD 47. There wasn't much resistance. And when the frontier rolled on, and something like normality returned – the same round of agricultural tasks, the same worries about the weather – the countryside itself seemed little changed. Except for the roads, gleaming white and straight, on the way to somewhere else. Military roads, serving the army's objectives – fast communication over long distances, fort to fort – ancient motorways, ignoring settlements or places, without meaning for the local people: for them the old routes still obtained, along the high ridge-ways. (There is a Roman road at the end of the garden:

I catch glimpses of the cars going by as I pause in my pruning –
brief flashes of colour between the garden wall and the old stone
barn. The people in the cars – where they come from, where they
are going to – are almost as impenetrable to me now as the
comings and goings on the Roman road were to the first century
inhabitants of Morville. The road was, in the Roman scheme of
things, only a minor road; hardly even a B road. The modern
B4368 diverges briefly from it in the field beyond the garden,
hurrying on, crossing the stream at the Ash Bridge before swerving left to rejoin it as together they plunge down into Corve Dale.
But the old barn follows the Roman alignment. It stands at the end
of the garden, tip-tilted off at an angle, pointing nowhere. Passing
motorists now use the odd triangle of land it leaves between itself
and the road as somewhere to take mobile-phone calls, somewhere to check the map.)

The roads; and the taxes. The British submit cheerfully enough
to taxation, said Tacitus, provided there is no abuse. But the
weather had been getting steadily worse for decades, making it
ever more difficult to make ends meet. The great Iron Age hill
forts, far from being constructed as a defence against the Roman
invaders, may have begun to be abandoned long before the
Romans came, as part of a general retreat from high land in
the face of the worsening climate: by the time the Romans arrived
the once great tribe of the Cornovii, with its fortresses of Wrekin,
Clee, Caer Caradoc and Bury Ditches, was already fragmented,
the people living in small ditched farmsteads on the flat land of the
valleys, eking out a livelihood from the sodden soil. A land of
continual rain, according to Tacitus. Rain, and the ceaseless tramp
of marching feet.

In Shropshire, at any rate, it was soon over. And in the middle
of the sodden land they built Viroconium, for thirty years the

nerve centre of the Roman advance into central and northern Wales, garrisoned with the 5,500 men of the *Legio XIV Gemina*. Every spring and summer the legion pushed forward into the territory of the Ordovices, one of the last tribes to continue to resist; and each year as the weather closed in, the legion fell back to Viroconium, taking up winter quarters there on the banks of the Severn like overwintering geese: crowded, voluble, exotic. The soldiers came from Gaul and Thrace, Syria and North Africa. How they must have shivered in the wooden watchtowers of Viroconium, stamping their feet to keep warm, looking out over the desolate land, waiting. Waiting for spring. Waiting for their discharge. Waiting for an attack that never came.

In AD 78 military command was transferred to Chester. The fortress at Viroconium was demolished and in its place a new civilian town was laid out: Viroconium Cornoviorum, a planned New Town, a school for new Romans, the fourth-largest city in Roman Britain, eventually extending over 180 acres of flat Shropshire countryside. Here the upper and middle classes of the Cornovii turned their back on the land to experience urban life for the first time. Not for them the virtuous country living extolled by Horace and Virgil: the Shropshire countryside is virtually empty of the gracious Romano-British villas and prosperous estates found in Gloucestershire. Instead there was Viroconium Cornoviorum, with its broad thoroughfares and grid of secondary roads, all intersecting at right angles; its rows of houses and dense network of alleyways, all teeming with life. It was a city of extraordinary magnificence – a magnificence still largely unexplained, given the apparent poverty of the surrounding countryside – with splendid baths and a palatial basilica-like exercise hall; forum, shops, temples; an arena for horse racing and, most luxurious of all, hypocausts – underfloor central heating by hot air. Hypocausts were originally designed for use in the *caledarium* and *tepidarium* of the Roman bathhouse, but in the chilly cities of Roman Britain they were installed in the living quarters of private houses too.

There was every amenity. Fresh vegetables and fruit were supplied by a ring of market gardens at the town's perimeter. Fresh water was brought by aqueduct from the Severn, piped not only to the baths and other municipal buildings but also to the large private houses that lined the central streets. There were pleasure gardens too: some of the larger houses surrounded by their own grounds had projecting dining rooms from which the gardens could be admired; others were set back from the road with a portico and garden in front. There would have been box hedges and topiary shapes; blossoming fruit trees and bright beds of flowers; trellises and pergolas and statues; perhaps even water gardens like those in more civilised parts of the Empire, with stone-edged rills, formal pools and fountains fed from the river which looped lazily round the city's rolling boundaries.

The ghost of Roman gardening lingers still. The Romans brought the walnuts and sweet chestnuts I planted in the nuttery; the quinces and medlars I chose for the Plat; the sour cherries and sweet apples, the artichokes and asparagus, the leeks and lettuce and cucumber, the marjoram, parsley and dill I grow in the Vegetable Garden. Latin is still the lingua franca of gardens. Their style of gardening, forgotten in Britain after the demise of Roman rule in the early fifth century, was re-exported from Italy in the fifteenth and sixteenth centuries with the fashion for interlacing knots and parterres; their grottoes and water features were cribbed by the Grand Tourists of the seventeenth and eighteenth centuries, their pergolas and colonnades by the neo-classicists of the nineteenth. I see a twitch of the toga in the medieval arbours and trellises of the Cloister Garden; an echo of the *Hypnerotomachia* in the patterns of the Knot Garden. I hear Pliny's voice beside the pools and topiary of the Canal Garden; Cicero in the Temple and formal wilderness of the New Flower Garden; Columella beneath the tunnels of trained fruit in the Edwardian Vegetable Garden. Even the little paved area beside the kitchen steps – the 'patio', a late twentieth-century borrowing from a Spain newly discovered by British package-tour holidaymakers in the 1960s as an area for outdoor dining – is ultimately derived from the Roman peristyle, a fashion brought from Rome to Spain in the second century BC.

Roman gardeners adored box – *Buxus sempervirens*, or common box, native to both Italy and Britain, and still the staple of formal gardening everywhere (despite the inroads of box disease in the late twentieth century). The Roman word for 'gardener' – he who clipped the hedges and maintained the pleasure garden – was *topiarius*, giving us the English word 'topiary'. We even use the same one-handed shears to do the work (modern electric hedge-cutters bruise the stems of the box and mangle its leaves). Over the centuries, various forms and cultivars of box have been selected – dwarf forms, variegated forms, forms with differently coloured leaves – and new species have been introduced from the Far East and the Himalayas. I grow three kinds of box: *Buxus sempervirens* itself, for large topiary shapes; *B. sempervirens* 'Suffruticosa' for the low hedges in the Canal Garden; and *B. balearica* from the Balearic Islands and nearby parts of Spain and Algeria – larger-leaved and faster-growing but less hardy – for big round topiary balls. Derby Day (the first Saturday in June) is the traditional time for clipping box – any later and the resulting surge of new growth is too soft to endure the winter, making it liable to be damaged by frost (but choose an overcast day: bright sun will brown the cut edges of the leaves). As I prepare to cut, I switch on the garden radio to listen to the big race, and I fancy I hear, mingling with the cheers of the crowd at Epsom, the distant shouts of race-goers in the arena at Viroconium.

There's not much to see at Viroconium now. Part of the wall of the basilica, the ruins of the forum, the remains of the hypocausts. On the surface. But beneath the soil of the present-day village of Wroxeter the plan of the great city is still intact. In 1788 the great engineer and road-builder Thomas Telford noted that in hot summers 'the stone foundations of ancient buildings at no great depth under the surface of the ground are manifest in long continued drought so that when the occupiers of the land need any stones for building, they mark the scorched parts and after harvest dig out what serves their purpose.' This had already been going on for more than a millennium. In fact, so successfully was the site robbed that twentieth-century archaeologists considered the city to have been a failure – a projected New Town that failed to take off, a place of uncompleted buildings and blank spaces, of high hopes not fulfilled. Then in 1995 new archaeological techniques of gradiometry and automated resistivity metering revealed the true extent of the buried city in all its teeming density, a mesh of streets, alleys and townhouses, a heaving mass of people and markets and lives.

As the plan of the garden started to take shape on the ground, another New Town was spreading across the fields near Viroconium – not, like the Roman city, all ruler-straight lines and right angles, but a town with hardly a straight line in it – all loops and curves, roundabouts, slip-roads and bypasses – a New Town for the automobile age: Telford New Town, named after the great

engineer and road-builder. Telford was county surveyor for
Shopshire from 1788 until his death in 1834, and he was one
of the first scientific investigators of the site of Viroconium. The
two towns, ancient and modern, are linked by Watling Street – the
Roman road that carried the legions into Wales and later served as
the border between the Danelaw and Alfred's England; the same
road that formed the basis for Telford's great highway linking
London and Dublin after the Act of Union in 1800; the same road
I travelled back from Dublin to Morville in 1988 – the old A5,
downgraded here to a B road, and replaced with a new dual
carriageway and a motorway buzzing irritably away across the
fields.

Roads are not shown on English county maps much before
the end of the seventeenth century, creating an impression of
an empty landscape devoid of roads. Not true. There was a
dense network of roads, paths and tracks. On moonlit nights I
fancy I see them still, those wandering old roads, crossing the
Church Meadow, swinging round the curve of the vanished
graveyard, bone-white in the light of the moon: from Much
Wenlock in a diagonal across the Church Meadow to the lych
gate; from Haughton down over the little stream and into the
back of the churchyard; from the church and mill down the
valley to The Lye – all cleared away with the huddle of houses
around the church to improve the view from the windows of
the big house.

The coming of the turnpike reduced the multiplicity of local
routes still further by concentrating traffic on a single main road.
The main road through Morville to Shrewsbury was turnpiked in
a series of Acts passed in the eighteenth century, the road down
into Corve Dale not until 1839. The aim of a turnpike – like that of
a modern motorway – was to shorten and straighten the route. It

was the quickest way from A to B. It bypassed villages. It reduced gradients by means of cuttings and embankments, and – like a modern toll-road – was paid for by those who used it, thus ensuring that its surface was maintained in good order. Before the age of tarmac, roads – except those deliberately constructed, like turnpikes and Roman roads and eighteenth- and nineteenth-century enclosure roads – were temporary, pragmatic, local: created by custom, maintained by the passage of feet. They had no made-up surface. In bad weather they quickly became rutted and worn, and as quickly, if abandoned, became over-grown. They might last fifty years or a thousand. Of their nature they are undated and undatable. Some of the oldest look the youngest – entombed beneath modern trunk roads, like Watling Street – and some of the youngest look the oldest, like Miss Bythell's road, built by John Lane, the farm manager, in 1978.

Audrey Bythell was the daughter of the last owners of Morville Hall. In 1966 she presented the house, outbuildings and 140 acres of surrounding land to the National Trust. She continued to live at the Hall as resident donor, and to farm the land. Her pride and joy was her herd of pedigree Guernsey cows, based at the farm in the neighbouring village of Aston Eyre. 'She would visit them cows of hers any time of the day or night – sometimes as late as eleven o'clock at night. But after she lost her sight her wasn't safe in that old Land Rover of hers, so I built a road for her to drive on through the fields.' She had gone blind quite literally in the course of a night the year before, and only her peripheral vision remained. 'Many's the time I had to leap in the wheat to get out of her way. Her couldna see me!' Within a year of her death in 1984, Miss Bythell's road was gone, ploughed over, reabsorbed, sunk back into the fields from whence it came. Only here and there does it survive, in part as a half-remembered footpath through the wheat, in part as a field track, as overgrown as any prehistoric trackway.

Down in Corve Dale and on the side of Wenlock Edge, the winter landscape expresses itself as a pattern of roads and hedges, raised lines on the Braille map of the fields. With the land frozen into immobility, the hedges are home to a shifting, rustling, twittering population of birds, voles, shrews and mice, larger mammals like rabbits and hedgehogs, insects, invertebrates, the occasional frog or toad or newt in the damp places at the bottom – the hedges providing shelter, nesting sites and food, tiered like a high-rise city round the edges of the vacant fields. It is a role they have filled for millennia. Longer lived than trees, more durable than stone walls, a hedge may be as much as a thousand years old – older. If regularly layed, they continually renew themselves, gaining species with every century. There is a strong correlation between the age of a hedge in centuries (whatever the soil or climate), and the number of tree or shrub species in a thirty-yard run. Thus a nineteenth-century enclosure hedge typically has only one species, usually hawthorn; a Georgian enclosure hedge might have two, a late medieval hedge between four and seven, an early medieval hedge from seven to ten, a pre-Conquest hedge ten or more. This is partly because older hedges were planted with more species to begin with and partly because all hedges acquire more species by self-seeding and by the action of birds. I see this process happening before my own eyes. Modern garden hedges are usually a monoculture: hawthorn, beech, hornbeam, holly, yew. I planted a thousand feet of yew hedge in the garden here as a matt dark-green close-textured back-drop to the medley of brilliant colours I planned for the flower-beds. Elegant, neat, discreet. But that first winter, when walking the country lanes, I was struck by the vivacity of the field hedges – primarily blackthorn and hawthorn, but enlivened in winter with the glossy leaves of holly and ivy, and in spring by the bright new leaves of the hawthorn and the white blossom of the cherry-plum and sloe. I relished the way the low sun glinted on them, in contrast to the funereal aspect of the yew. So I also planted a smaller mixed hedge of holly, yew and hawthorn to divide the upper and lower parts of the garden. And already it has been colonised by silver birches, brambles, ivy, honeysuckles and two species of wild rose. My instant Elizabethan hedge.

Hedge-laying is an ancient trade: Julius Caesar encountered 'plashed', or layed, hedges during his Flanders campaign in around 55 BC:

> [The Nervii] cut into slender trees and bent them over so that many branches came out along their length; they finished them off by inserting brambles and briars, so that these hedges formed a defence like a wall, which could not only not be penetrated but not even seen through.
>
> *De bello Gallico*, II. xvii

Many farmers nowadays cut their hedgerows with mechanised flails, producing ageing hedges which are gappy at the bottom: all the new growth comes at the top, where it is continually cut off. Laying a hedge thickens and rejuvenates it, with all the new growth coming from the bottom. A laid hedge gets better and better, a flailed one worse and worse.

It was while I was roaming the fields at Morville that I became aware of the presence of Karl the hedge-layer. Lengths of overgrown untidy hedge would suddenly assume a new guise: neat, stock-proof, workmanlike, the new cuts white against the bark. But it was months before our paths actually crossed. Nick knows his trees by their quality as firewood, Karl by their usefulness in making a hedge. Elm is good, he says – long-fibred and strong – 'and laying the trees keeps them young and out of reach of the Dutch Elm Disease'. (The trees seem not to be susceptible to the disease until they reach twenty feet or so; coppiced or maintained as what are in effect shrubs, they are capable of living long and useful lives.) Elder on the other hand is useless: 'It doesn't respond to cutting', becoming neither twiggy nor bushy; worse, it grows quicker and wider than its neighbours, shading them out. Karl cuts it down wherever he finds it, and poisons it. He cuts out ash and sycamore too, for much the same reason. But holly is good, he says, though it has a shorter fibre than elm, so is less strong. Hawthorn and hazel are best, because they respond well to trimming and spring up readily from the base. Blackthorn is both good and bad: it suckers so vigorously that unless there is stock grazing on both sides the hedge gets wider and wider; but on the other hand the blackthorn will spread along the length of the hedge, filling in any gaps. I ask him about the birch in my hedge. Neither good nor bad: 'benign', he says. He uses a pair of curved billhooks like the men in the Earl of Shrewsbury's prayer book: one is a short Staffordshire billhook, the other a long Yorkshire one, both kept lethally sharp. His other tools are two axes, which double as wedges to prise open the cuts, and a spade to find the roots. He makes the cuts with surprising delicacy, half-cutting through the trunks, laying them down, and weaving them through the upright stakes of ash or hazel he has brought with him. Finally he binds the top of the hedge with wands of hazel cut from Wenlock Edge, twisting them into a braid.

Each hedge is different, and so too is each individual tree. It's a slow, meditative process. The traffic passes in a blur, Karl seeming to inhabit a parallel dimension, moving slowly, thinking, planning, measuring by eye – which to keep, how to lay – pruning away everything he doesn't need, shaping the hedge he has before him to the hedge he sees in his mind's eye. Gradually the hedge extends along the roadside. With its rhythm of bright freshly cut vertical stakes hammered in at intervals, its long swathes of laid boughs, and its trills and top-notes of twisted hazel, it looks like a line of music, a tune only he can hear.

Karl lays hedges in winter, from September to March or April, depending on the weather. Holly hedges are cut last – they are sensitive to the cold, he says, like all evergreens. In summer he repairs stone walls. 'You sort the stone into functions,' he says. 'Facers, through-stones, fillers, top stones – a heap of each, so that your hand goes straight to what you need.' It becomes a point of honour that no stone, once picked up, is discarded; each must find its place within the wall. I'm reminded of my father's favourite text for a sermon, one of these hammered out each Saturday on the battered old typewriter in the cold book-lined room with its leaning metal shelves, his pipe clenched between his teeth: living, like hedge-laying, like building a drystone wall, is a question of using what is to hand, making the best of what you've got. But it is the creative power of the imagination – selecting, rearranging and unifying – that transforms the trees into a hedge, stones into a wall, experience into art.

In the calendar illustrations for February the occupations of chopping wood or lopping trees are sometimes replaced by pruning vines. Tacitus, writing in the first century AD, had considered the British climate unsuitable for grapes because of the excessive rain, but from late Roman times the British climate steadily improved. In AD 280 the Emperor Probus issued an edict removing the prohibition on the cultivation of vines in Britain. By late Saxon and Viking times the island was experiencing a climate more closely approximating that of the Continent, and Bede, writing in 731, could record vineyards at several localities. By the time of the Domesday survey in 1086, thirty-eight vineyards were listed. New grape varieties imported by the Norman invaders flourished in the warmer conditions.

The peak of this period of better weather lasted from the middle of the eleventh century to the early years of the fourteenth. By then all the great monastic houses boasted vineyards. But by the fifteenth century, when the Books of Hours were being produced, the climate had worsened again. There was a shortage of skilled labour due to the ravages of the Black Death, and widespread social unrest. Agriculture in general (and with it vine-growing), was in decline. Much of the European countryside was reverting to wasteland, or was turned over to less labour-intensive crops like sheep or cereals. Devoid of people, the late medieval landscape eerily resembled the countryside of the early twenty-first century, with its set-aside and its vast empty fields of agro-prairie. It seems that, even at their height, the Books of Hours were an exercise in nostalgia.

We are now in a period when the climate is warming again, and there are vineyards once more at Viroconium – ten acres of vines planted in 1991, enclosed by the still-visible bank and ditch of the Roman perimeter defences. In the Hours of the Fastolf Master, pruning vines is the illustration given for March, but in our warmer climate this is far too late. Vines should always be pruned in early or midwinter, never in spring, for in common with mulberries, walnuts, birches and maples, they weep uncontrollable tears of clear sap if pruned when the sap is rising, ceasing only at bud-break. I once came across a friend trying to staunch the flow of sap from a late-pruned vine in his garden by fitting it with a brass tap bought from the plumber.

I like the stripped-down quality of the garden in winter, the transparency of it. I like winter tasks, an opportunity to be outside the house. But pruning is not a job for the rawest weather when fingers and toes are quickly chilled, especially if, like me, you tend to stand and stare. Bud and bark and thorn – in winter there is so much more time to *look*, and to learn: how the fat white fruit buds of the pears on their short knobbly spurs are precisely spaced along the vertical and horizontal ribs of the cordons like rows of Gothic crockets, easily distinguishable now from the slim, scrolled extension buds which would carry the framework of the tree and which now need pruning back. The thorns of the roses too, overlooked in summer when I am bewitched by flower and leaf, are as various as the families of the rose, signalling lines of kith and kin unthought of in the heady scents of June. I see that the huge triangular black thorns of 'The Garland' (like sharks' fins, and almost as lethal, catching in my hair as I pull the long shoots down to prune them) are shared with *Rosa moschata*, from which it descends, and that the old gallicas in the Cloister Garden, with their small, slim, sloping thorns set sparsely among bristles, are quite distinct from the albas, with their large hooked thorns and smooth pale-green bristle-less shoots. I like this feeling of intimacy, this close looking, this sense of time extending. But meanwhile, as I stand and stare, the cold strikes through the rubber soles of my boots, and my fingers grow numb inside the stiffening leather of my pruning gloves.

A better task for this weather is dealing with the manure that has been tipped at the far end of the drive – manure fresh from the byre, hot and sweet and redolent of summer hay, with fans of yellow straw mixed in with the dung, trodden flat by the cows' hooves. It is too hot yet to use: hot enough to scorch the tender new stems of the roses; so hot that I need to take off my jacket and gloves as I work. In twelve months, when the straw is well rotted and the heat has gone out of it, that's the time to barrow it up into the garden and spread it on the rose beds. For now, I stack the manure into a tidy pile, lofting it into the air with the curving prongs of the pitchfork, making a steaming fragrant mountain, the garden all around frozen and white while I stand on top of the heap in shirtsleeves, enveloped in a cloud of sweet-smelling steam.

The manure comes from Miss Bythell's cows. In summer I watch their daily progress across the hillside as I work in the garden: 140 matched Guernseys, the taut horizontal line of their spines as straight as a washing line from poll to tail, the blades of their hips protruding through their tawny-gold hides like super-models in blond cashmere. One frozen February afternoon I walked the line of Miss Bythell's road from Hall to farm to watch them being milked. John had already started milking before I arrived, and from outside I could already hear the rapid breathy pulse of the compressed air, the soft rattle of cattle-cake pellets dropping into the metal feeding troughs, the clatter and bang of the metal barriers as six by six they came from the byre into the milking parlour, nosing the sweet molasses smell of the cattle cake. Here all was warmth and wetness: the steaming pools of piss, the soft splatter of cow-pats, the warm milk purling down inside the glass collectors. Condensation trickled down the outside of the chilled steel tank. I could see the warmth of their sweet damp breath in the air, feel the heat of their bodies as they pressed past. It's not for nothing that earlier ages of farmers shared their living quarters with their beasts in winter.

The cows were given names at birth, each starting with the same letter of the alphabet for all those born in a given year. They spent their summers on the hillside and their winters in the shippon, a long narrow stone-floored byre across the yard from the black-and-white farmhouse where John and his wife Brenda lived. Here Pipkin and Primrose, Polly and Petula dreamed away the time from October to April, their shadowy, reclining forms looking in the dim half-light with its receding perspective like figures in a Henry Moore painting of wartime Londoners sleeping in the Underground. Here all was order and patience, each beast with her favourite stall, sounds muffled by the deep straw of the bedding.

When I left the milking parlour it was quite dark, with gusts of sleet in a rising wind. Huddled in my jacket, I trudged home through the frozen stubble of the fields, thinking of the warmth and somnolence of the shippon with something close to envy.

Despite the weather the wild daffodil buds are showing their first pale glimmer of colour. Their country name is the Lenten lily, because they bloom in the liturgical season of Lent. An older name is '*Laus tibi*', from the refrain *Laus tibi, Domine, Rex aeternae gloriae* ('Praise be to thee, O Lord, King of Everlasting Glory'), said at Lauds instead of 'alleluia' from Septuagesima until Easter. Lauds is all about praise: the name comes from Psalm 148, a litany of thanksgiving said at Lauds which begins *Laudate Dominum* ('Praise the Lord') and in which every aspect of creation joins with mankind in a paean of praise: sun, moon and stars; 'fire, hail, snow, ice, stormy winds'; mountains and hills; 'beasts and cattle'; 'serpents and feathered fowls'. February has something of the feel of Lauds about it: of candle flames in the darkness, gratefulness for small comforts, little bits of beauty in a wintry landscape. In winter, Lauds begins in the dark and ends with the first glimmer of light: in the words of Psalm 62, 'O God, my God, I watch for you at dawn.' There's a feeling in both of waiting: waiting for spring, waiting for Easter, waiting for dawn.

It is almost dawn now. Listen. The birds are beginning to sing, their first tentative notes piercing the darkness. First a high clear trill from a lone wren, far away at the bottom of the garden, his song echoing in the stillness. Then again, high and fast, this time twice in quick succession. Then a chaffinch, high up in a tree on the left, his notes tumbling over themselves, louder and faster as they fall. Now a song thrush on the other side of the garden, repeating everything in triplicate, short phrases, disjointed, like a virtuoso trumpet player warming up, trying things out, practising. And then the blackbird, his long liquid notes fluting over the garden in silver loops and curls of sound. And then another and another, until birds are calling back and forth, from tree to tree, from side to side, high to low, front to back, from the thickets of wild roses in the Wild Garden to the topmost branches of the pear by the Canal, from the big hawthorn near the house to the yew trees on the other side, an acoustic geometry, a picture in sound of the still-invisible garden.

All winter the blackbirds and thrushes have been silent. Now in the darkness of a February dawn they are beginning to sing once more.

Prime

Something is different.

As soon as you open the door you know it. Everything is loosing bounds, changing shape, morphing into something else. Surfaces are wet to the touch, slicked with water. Even the ground underfoot seems unfamiliar, the gravel soft and yielding. The cats, alerted by the spill of light from the door, return early from the night's hunting, their coats peaked with moisture. You don't need to see in order to know. The thaw has come at last.

There's an hour or more between first light and sunrise. I've been up since half past five, getting some work ready for the post. From time to time I raise my head and look out of the window. Slowly the garden begins to emerge, like a photograph lifted dripping from the developing tray. First the big trees, dark against the less dark sky – flat shapes without mass: the dome of the horse chestnut beyond the bonfire yard, the ragged outline of the tall old hawthorn near the house – everything below still wrapped in darkness. Then the smaller trees, and the ramparts of the hedges, everything quickly gaining definition now. In the west the sky is still dark, a deep midnight-blue spangled with the last faint stars, but in the east the sky is paling to a luminous turquoise, hovering between blue and green, paler and paler each time I look, until, at the horizon, a rim of gold – crocus-yellow: the sun. In December the sun rose behind the church tower; by June, the sun's rising will be lost in the trees on the far side of the school; now, in early March, it rises almost halfway between, moving a little further north each day, grazing the ridges of the ploughed field at the top of the village.

By the time I've finished my parcel it's past seven and the sun is up, gilding the east face of the church tower and flooding into the room where I am working. Gradually the dawn chorus dissolves into a chatter of diurnal preoccupations and is lost in the growing noise of traffic from the road. I pull on my boots and go out into the garden. After the long confinement of winter, it's like walking on the moon – the mossy turf responds to my tread, putting a spring in my step. I bound to the top of the rise, my two arms outstretched like a kid playing aeroplanes, as if I might take off altogether. The blackbirds who have had the garden to themselves since the freeze started now erupt in a flurry of wingbeats and rattling alarm calls, scattering at my approach.

One of the first jobs of the thaw is to turn the garden stopcocks back on and check whether the pipes have been damaged during the freeze. The water for the garden comes from a spring half a mile away on the hillside above the house. It is shared with the cattle at the farm down the road, and in the early days of our tenancy it provided water for the house, and for our neighbours' houses, too. We are all on mains water now, piped from goodness knows where and paid for by the yard. But the old water is still here, keeping its head down, running beneath and beside the new plastic pipes, going about its business. Occasionally, like an old dog, it contrives to get back into the house through a maze of ancient brick culverts and old lead pipes, rising up through a grating in the cellar and spreading stealthily across the floor, its dank odour seeping up the cellar steps. But today there's no more than a gritty trickle from the taps, and my next-door neighbours Arthur and Ian must shoulder their spades and set off down the fields, looking for tell-tale muddy patches where the pipe has sprung a leak.

In summer there are regular pilgrimages up the hillside too, to check the little underground reservoir into which the spring gushes. Ian cocks his head as the water falls into the enclosed tank, listening to the echoes, estimating the gap between the source and the surface of the water, guessing its depth, its rate of flow. In good years there's enough for all, both farm and gardens, with a surplus running down into the Mor Brook. In bad years he puts us on the alert: we must ration ourselves, only water what is necessary.

Ian and Arthur dig down and splice the old pipe together again – a patchwork of ancient mends and joins – and the water is back before they are, gushing out of the taps clear and cold, the chill of the ice about it still.

It's never taken for granted, this water, with its visible-invisible almost miraculous source. It has to be placated, its rituals observed. We are its acolytes. Without it, the garden would wither and the cattle die. In prolonged frost, more plants die of drought than of cold. No wonder springs were sacred places. Much Wenlock, five miles away down the road, used to be full of them, bubbling up into the town from the limestone at the foot of Wenlock Edge. Most are now bricked up, built over, diverted, but there are three left, each with its presiding deity – Christian now (two attributed at one time or another to St Mildburg, the seventh-century Abbess of Wenlock Abbey, the third to St Owen, adviser at the French convent where Mildburg was educated) – though still venerated in the old way with tributes of flowers at the biennial well-dressing. A mysterious little figurine in the local museum may hint at older rites: Romano-Celtic or Romanesque, medieval or perhaps even modern, he (for it is indisputably male) has foxed experts for decades, ever since his discovery among items from Wenlock Priory sent to the museum at its opening in 1970. A 'child-pilgrim' like those found at Gaulish sacred springs? A Romanesque carving like those at Kilpeck? Who knows? Votive offering or talisman, he remains as mysterious as ever, inscrutable in his carved coffin or cradle, his bulging eyes staring out at the world beyond his glass case.

From the garden now I can hear the Mor Brook in spate, a subdued roar far removed from the gentle murmur (from the Old English *memere*) construed by earlier etymologists as the source of its name. It may come from the Welsh *mawr*, meaning 'big' – the Mor Brook being the big brook, as distinct from Tiddle Brook, the little brook. The Mor Brook rises as a dozen or more springs issuing from the side of Wenlock Edge. They well up in the long grass of Gorsey Dingle and Henchman's Coppice, in the woods of Spoonhill and Hawking Grove – sleek as an otter, silver-speckled as a brown trout – the Walton Brook and the Beggarhill Brook, the Beaconhill Brook and the brook from Shirlett, a conversation of streams, nattering their way from the Ash Bridge to The Lye, from The Lye to Harpswood Bridge, from the Marlbrook Bridge to the Hay Bridge, under the modern road-bridge at Eardington, swerving round the high brick vault of the nineteenth-century railway bridge, carving a channel deep into the sandstone where the children swing on a rope over the tree-hung cleft, and finally, with a flick of its wrist, diving under the little cast-iron footbridge on the towpath and out into the sunlit expanse of the Severn.

*

The noise increases as you walk across the Church Meadow until you stand, deafened, on the brink of the weir. Here the brook falls eight feet or more into the mill pool – today, after the thaw, a churning vortex of red soil-laden water. Wedding cakes of brown foam spin beneath your feet; twigs, branches, whole trunks jam up against one another in the roots of the overhanging trees. There was a leat that used to run from here down the long meadow beneath the hill to power the Lye Mill. The leat was filled in during World War II, when the meadow was ploughed up in the 'Dig for Victory' campaign. Now all that energy is pent up in the mill pool, grinding the red soil round and round, undercutting the banks, exposing the tree roots. In its time the brook powered a string of mills on its way to join the Severn – a thousand years of mills – sawmills, flour mills, fulling mills; turning the waterwheels at Callaughton Mill, Monkhopton Mill, the mill at Acton Round, Aldenham Mill, Morville Mill, the Lye Mill, Harpsford Mill, Eardington Mill; powering the bellows for iron forges at Hubbals Mill, the Hurst, the Upper and Lower Forges at Eardington. The Severn itself was too big and unpredictable to be harnessed in this way: it could rise from four to fifteen feet in a matter of hours, and fall just as quickly. Streams like the Mor Brook were the birthplace of rural industry, powered by charcoal and water power, hundreds of years before Abraham Darby discovered the application of coke to iron smelting at nearby Coalbrookdale – the conventionally accepted beginning of the Industrial Revolution. Every pound of water power was utilised, leats for the next mill often starting immediately below the preceding one. When the need for one commodity declined, a mill would simply be converted to the production of something else: to a silk mill or a paper mill, a cement mill or a cider mill, a mill for producing paint or oil, for crushing barytes, bark or bone. It was the coming of electricity

that sounded the death knell for water power. The last working
mill on the Mor Brook was Aldenham Mill at Muckley Cross,
which survived into the middle of the twentieth century as a
sawmill. Later there was a cement works there. And there's rural
industry there still: a small industrial estate and a metalworking
factory, demonstrating the old vitality, the old versatility, continuing the tradition. But the old mill sites are still there, their
stone footings streaming with green waterweed, waiting for a time
when the electricity and the coal run out.

When I reach the Vegetable Garden, I find that during the freeze
the winter greens have been reduced to skeletons – stripped by the
band of wood pigeons with their insolent English cry of 'Take
two cows, Taffy.' Like border barons, they rob and plunder,
taking all in the garden as of right, growing fat. (But we have our
revenge: they make fine eating.) Their gentler foreign cousins, the
collared turtle doves, come to the house to be fed almost like
domestic fowl; in pairs, they feed from the bird table among the
tits and sparrows, slim and sandy coloured, with their wistful cry,
'Where *are* you?'

It was Lady L who taught me how to distinguish them by their
calls – one of the tales she told me of her Shropshire childhood,
confided over tea at Dudmaston in the tall-ceilinged upstairs
sitting-room looking out across the terrace and the sloping lawns

to the Big Pool and the woods and the Severn beyond. By road, Dudmaston and Morville are six miles apart, separated by the road-bridge over the Severn; much closer by water, linked by the thin blue line of the Mor Brook, which enters the Severn opposite the Dudmaston estate; closer still as the crow flies. I met Lady L the first winter I was at Morville. Her real name was Lady Labouchere (though few stood on such ceremony). Her family had held Dudmaston since Norman times: half a hide of land, granted by King Henry I to Hubert Fitz Helgot of Castle Holgate in the Corve Dale, and by him to Harlewyn de Butailles, in a deed dating from before 1127. The deed is still there, in the house: a narrow slip of parchment, the language formal, convoluted, hedged about with provisos and conditions; the handwriting dense with contractions and suspensions; like an airline ticket to another world.

She was by then close to her eighties and already in failing health. For the next seven years I went to Dudmaston every Wednesday, crossing the black-and-white marble floor to work on the library in the mornings or to help her with her various historical projects at other times, and to sit with Sir George while she rested in the afternoons. There was lunch at one and tea at four, hot-cross buns at Easter, and steam whistles from across the park on Bank Holiday weekends – the sound of the Severn Valley Railway on the other side of the river. The big old sitting-room was piled with books, papers, letters, photographs, *Country Life*s and Christie's sale catalogues, half-finished embroideries and just-begun watercolours. There were generations of bone-china dinner services, centuries of accumulated gardening books; attics filled with clothes, pictures, furniture; photograph albums dating from the very beginnings of photography (a talent for photography ran in the family: Lady Charlotte and Lady Lucy Bridgeman, known to their descendants as 'the burnt aunts', were pioneer photographers who perished together in 1858 when their crinolines caught fire); drawers full of letters and whole family trees of diaries; and shelf upon of children's books, each inscribed by a different child – Wolryches and Whitmores, Darbys and Christies – favourite stories, reprinted for each generation, and new stories, each of its time. Together we plundered them all for exhibitions to explain the history of the house and its family.

For me Dudmaston came to be the epitome of the English country house, with its planetary system of sawmill, estate office, cottages and farms, its ranks of foresters, carpenters, cooks and gardeners with Lady L as its centre, its last and greatest chatelaine. She rescued the estate from near bankruptcy, filled the house with treasures, and gave it to the National Trust. Only in the eighteenth century did Morville attain that sort of stability: Morville's was a tale of lost heirs, heirs defrauded, heirs dead before their time; of childless couples, bachelor uncles; of a succession that zigzagged, backtracked, skipped generations; of a house eventually surplus to requirements, bought and sold; its library, archives, contents all scattered.

When Lady L died in March 1996, there occurred one of those curious incidents which country people tell about the death of a great personage. There had always been swans at Dudmaston, and Lady L took a keen interest in their welfare. In the days following her death, a pair of swans that had nested on the outlying Brim Pool began repeatedly trying to leave the pool and fly across the public road to the main part of the park and garden, trying to get nearer to the house. One of them eventually managed to take off, clearing the wire netting that ran alongside the road, only to be struck and killed by a passing vehicle. I came upon the scene shortly afterwards. The road was inexplicably white; there were drifts of – what? – snow? – paper? Feathers. White feathers, everywhere, caught in the high branches of the trees and along the hedges and in the grass of the roadside. One of the carpenters had already removed and buried the dead bird, but the other swan was still there, circling the dark waters of the Brim Pool, searching for its mate. Swans are said to pair for life. From Norman times onwards they were a symbol of prestige and royal favour; uniquely among birds they were perquisites of the Crown, ownership only granted to the greatest personages in the land.

With Lady L.'s death Dudmaston passed out of family hands for ever. She was survived by her husband, Sir George. The marriage had been a long and devoted one. In the days following her death, I would sit with him in the tall old room looking out over the Big Pool. We read *Gil Blas* together in French. 'I can't seem to find Rachel,' he used to say, wonderingly, 'but I expect she will turn up again quite soon.' Then he lapsed into a silence that remained unbroken until his own death three years later.

It was because of Lady L that the National Trust gave me the go-ahead for the garden. They were, not unnaturally, sceptical. I had never made a garden before. I had no horticultural training, no experience, no money and no income, and I was proposing, single-handedly, to fund, build and maintain a new garden – or rather a series of eight labour-intensive gardens – at a time when gardeners everywhere were converting to 'low-maintenance' regimes and many of the Trust's own walled gardens were still grassed over and being used as car parks. But Lady L believed in me. A passionate gardener herself, she had inherited from her Darby ancestors a dazzling collection of seventeenth- and eighteenth-century Dutch flower paintings – brilliantly coloured fantasias combining flowers of every description and season, posed in classical landscapes amid graceful ruins or spotlit against dark backgrounds with all the drama of portraits. Every Wednesday as we waited for lunch to be served she and I would study them together, continually finding in them something new or a detail whose significance we had not noticed before. When I went on research trips to London or Oxford, I would save up anecdotes about the books and libraries and people I had encountered to tell her over lunch the next day. When I started to source plants for the garden I would return from shows and from visiting specialist growers with armfuls of flowers to show her: striped auriculas, old double hyacinths, flamboyant tulips feathered and flamed like those painted by Rachel Ruysch and Jan van Huysum and Jan van Os. Before our eyes, the paintings began to come to life.

The Dower House already had a small area of garden in front and to the side, and to this I was proposing to add an adjacent field – in all about an acre and a half. Prior to my taking over the tenancy, John had been keeping cows in the field. Now, as winter turned to spring, the uncropped field began to turn into a wilderness. So John brought two of the Guernseys back – Pipkin and Paradise, neither of whom was in calf that year – to munch their way through it and reduce the herbage to a manageable height. Then I sprayed the field to eradicate the docks and nettles. By late June we were ready to burn off the stubble, stage-managed by Arthur – 'You've got to burn *into* the wind, to keep the flames from getting out of control.' The bulldozer was booked for the following week. But then the Trust called a halt. The terrain revealed by the burning was perplexingly uneven. Were these the remains of buildings? Was this the site of the medieval Priory, the vanished village? The regional archaeologist was called in to investigate. For a fortnight the garden's future hung in the balance as he and his assistant paced and measured and dug. Finally he reported that there was no stratigraphy – finds of different centuries were all jumbled up together, none later than the eighteenth century – that there was no pattern to the humps and hollows after all. It was 'made-up' ground, he concluded, subsoil tipped here by the cartload during eighteenth-century improvements to the Hall, then roughly levelled and grassed over. It seems builders could be cowboys even then.

The following week the archaeologist and his assistant returned with a posse of grandees from the Trust – the Historic Buildings Adviser, the Regional Director, the National Trust Gardens Adviser and his assistant – to look at my plans for the garden. Lady L told me afterwards that they had called at Dudmaston on the way to Morville: it was she, she said, who finally convinced them.

I got my go-ahead at last. When the bulldozer arrived to level the ground, half the village turned out to see what we were up to. As the turf was stripped away, the soil revealed was startlingly red and extremely stony: virtually no dark topsoil, no humus. The scene at the end of the first day was much as it must have looked when the ice first retreated – red raw, scraped bare down to the naked rock – with great mounds of wet red gravel heaped like the terminal moraine of a glacier. But by the end of the second day, with the gravelly subsoil redistributed and what topsoil there was replaced over it, the site for the new garden looked more promising: an acre of flat ground, sloping slightly back and up, away from the house, raked, like a stage, with the tall trees in the existing garden at either side like the wings of a set, the old pear tree centre-stage and a low terrace across the front like footlights – my theatre, my empty proscenium, waiting to be filled.

The National Trust Gardens Adviser had suggested that I put the whole of the new acre down to grass, and then each year cut out one or two new areas to be planted, rather than attempting to work on the whole area at once. It was excellent advice. So the first week in September, when John and his son Stephen came to plough and harrow the field, John brought with him a 'fiddle', a relic of the old days when crops were broadcast by hand. Then, taught by Arthur, I sowed the field, marching up and down, chest out, head up, for all the world like a toy soldier, eyes fixed on the marker at the other end. When it was done, John returned and rolled the field to ensure that the seed was firmly pressed into the ground. Early next morning I walked up into the garden, and found John and my next-door neighbour Dan already there, shaking their heads over the heavy tyre marks left by the tractor. It would have to be harrowed again. But John had no harrow fine enough for the job. The field would have to be raked by hand.

I raked for three days. Then with a storm brewing and time running out – the field had to be rolled again before the seed got wet, otherwise the seed would stick to the roller – all my neighbours, one by one, came to help: Arthur and Ian, Dan and John. Then, as the light failed, John switched on the tractor and started to roll the field, working by the beam of the head-lights, backwards and forwards, round and round, while the rest of us went on raking. We finished as the first heavy drops fell.

And when the grass germinated, the green seedlings came up in straight lines, like lines of text.

Necessary things for human life: fire, food, shelter (a home). Necessary things for plant life: earth, water, air (light). Necessary things for human growth: myth, legend, stories (history).

Septuagesima, Sexagesima, Quinquagesima – the names ring out like church bells, counting down to Easter: seventy, sixty, fifty days to go. On Septuagesima Sunday the vicar dons the purple vestments he will wear until Easter. It is strange that the colours of the liturgical year, laid down (one supposes) in the harsher climate of Rome or Constantinople, should sometimes mirror so closely those of an English garden: purple for Advent and Lent; white for the special feasts of Christ and his mother – Lady Day, Easter, Corpus Christi; red for the Holy Ghost and for the feasts of the apostles and martyrs; and green for every day – the green of the English summer – from Trinity Sunday all the way to the beginning of Advent again. Yet not so strange: our flowers came from many climes. What the country people call Lenten Roses are purple hellebores (*Helleborus orientalis*) from Greece and Turkey – ancient Byzantium. The *Crocus tommasinianus* which in January makes a shimmering ribbon of purple and silver and amethyst beneath the leafless roses comes originally from Hungary and Bulgaria – the Ottoman Empire. Even the reds of Whitsun – crimson peonies and the first red roses – have a whiff of the exotic about them: the red rose (*Rosa gallica*) and the European peony (*Paeonia officinalis*) both come from the warm south. The white of Easter, though, is of more homely descent: blackthorn, damson, pear, plum and cherry, wreathing the countryside with blossom in salutation of the day.

But there's a glow of yellow too, coming and going like a patch of winter sunlight, growing stronger and stronger as the earth turns towards the sun: winter aconites and yellow crocuses, marsh marigolds and primroses, crown imperials and daffodils. Even the butterflies are yellow, the first butterflies of spring: pale sulphur-coloured brimstones emerging from hibernation, flying their slow heavy flight across the grass of the Plat like detached pieces of sunshine. On sunny days the air is perfumed with the honeyed scent of the 'Cloth of Gold' crocus (*C. susianus*). The first big bumblebees are abroad, *Bombus terrestris* in their livery of yellow and black – queen bees who have slept the winter away in hibernation, prospecting now for nest sites in deserted mouse-holes where their larvae will spin cocoons of silk, hardening into golden-brown clusters like ripe hazelnuts. She feeds them pollen, gathered from hazel and alder, pussy willow and birch; my shoulders are yellow with it, brushed from the catkins as I make my way around the garden.

Red spells passion and intensity; white means purity. Purple is rich and sombre; blue, ethereal, the colour of Mary's robe. But yellow? The painter Wassily Kandinsky described yellow as 'the typical earthly colour. It can never have profound meaning.' In Tibetan Buddhism it is the colour of humility. In eighteenth-century England it meant not of the first rank: 'yellow admirals' were those passed over for promotion and not attached to any squadron (red, white or blue). There are long-standing connotations of jealousy, illness and ageing (yellowing paper), and more modern imputations of vulgarity (the yellow press), decadence (*The Yellow Book*) and cowardice (a sense not found until the 1890s). In the brighter light of summer, yellow flowers can look harsh and strident. (The gold of autumn days is another thing altogether – rich and mellow.) But in spring, as the grass begins to grow and the first leaves appear on the trees, yellow is exactly as it should be – young and fresh and uncomplicated.

Quinquagesima, Quadragesima – forty days to go, and between them comes Ash Wednesday, when the vicar burns last year's palms and the parishioners smudge their foreheads with holy ash. What shall we give up for Lent? The children at the school give up favourite TV programmes and answering back; the adults think of their waistlines and give up chocolates and alcohol.

Mothering Sunday, Laetare Sunday, Refreshment Sunday – three names for the same day, Mid-Lent Sunday, the fourth Sunday in Lent. Halfway to Easter now, and time off for a modest celebration. We go down to Hereford – the mother church of the diocese – for a concert in the cathedral: Bach's St Matthew Passion. The Bishop reminds us of the words of the Epistle for the day – 'Jerusalem . . . which is the mother of us all' – and tells us how people from every diocese used to make the journey to their own mother church on this day each year. It was a practice largely discontinued after the Reformation, though it lingered on here and there as a tradition of extended families returning for a feast in the parental home. And the Mid-Lent rejoicing is still there, giving the day its other name – Laetare Sunday, from *Laetare, Jerusalem* ('Rejoice, O Jerusalem'), the opening words of the Introit in the Latin Mass for the day. The name Refreshment Sunday comes from the miracle of the loaves and fishes, still the Gospel reading for the day in the Book of Common Prayer. On Laetare Sunday the Lenten rules of fasting and abstinence were temporarily relaxed. This was the day for eating simnel cake, with its layers of yellow marzipan and eleven marzipan balls on top, said to signify the twelve disciples minus Judas. The marzipan was, it seems, a latecomer to the recipe, and the Shropshire simnel preserves an older tradition in which the yellow colouring was provided by saffron and egg yolks. The yellow of marzipan, the yellow of eggs, the yellow of saffron: the colour of spring.

Paradoxically saffron comes not from a yellow crocus but from the brilliant red stigmas of a purple one, *Crocus sativus*. This is not the European 'meadow saffron' (also known as 'autumn crocus' or 'Naked Ladies'), which is not a crocus at all, but a colchicum, and is highly poisonous. *Crocus sativus* came originally from the

East. Its production there was jealously guarded, but by medieval times it was being widely grown around the Essex town of Saffron Walden too. Tradition has it that a native of the town, returning from pilgrimage to the Holy Land, smuggled a few precious corms home, concealed in his hat. Saffron is warming, reviving, sexy (the stigmas are the female sexual organs of the flower), exotic (the word comes from Arabic, and most of our saffron nowadays comes from Iran), laughter-inducing (Culpeper in 1649 warned that you might laugh yourself to pieces if you ate too much), even apparently aphrodisiac (Greek courtesans strewed saffron around their bedchambers, and Cleopatra is said to have bathed in it before taking a new lover). Ounce for ounce, it is the most expensive spice in the world. Just the thing for a celebration.

But nowadays we are more likely to celebrate Laetare Sunday as Mother's Day. Properly speaking, Mother's Day is an American import (celebrated there on the second Sunday in May) dating only as far back as an Act of Congress in 1913. In England the old ecclesiastical tradition of Mothering Sunday, celebrated on the middle Sunday of Lent, had by the nineteenth century become an annual holiday granted to live-in apprentices and young servant girls, so that they might visit their mothers once a year. Joyce, my oldest neighbour at Morville, came to work at the Hall in 1937 at the age of fourteen. Each year on Mothering Sunday she used to pick wild violets from the hedgerows to take home to her mother at Round Hill. They are not easy to spot in the wild: with their modestly bent necks and flowers hardly bigger than a fingernail, it is easy to see how they acquired the name 'shrinking violets'. But Joyce knew exactly where to find them, for she and her brothers had attended the village school at Morville, walking the three miles from Round Hill in all weathers, picking flowers, exploring the countryside. 'It took three-quarters of an hour to get to school and three hours to get home!' she said. 'We wore heavy boots which Dad cleaned with Dubbin. I hated children with patent leather shoes and ankle socks!' These are the sweet violets (*Viola odorata*) – not to be confused with the even tinier dog violets, which have no smell, or the opulent heavily scented Parma violets, which need the protection of a cold frame. Sweet violets bloom from February to May. The cultivated varieties have longer stems and old-fashioned names like 'Coeur d'Alsace' and 'The Csar'; I remember them on sale for Mothering Sunday in florists' and greengrocers' shops, tied up in tiny bunches. But I had never seen sweet violets growing wild, and without Joyce's directions I might have missed them altogether. One morning in March I went out to look, and there they were, exactly as Joyce remembered them seventy years ago: a thick clump of white ones clustered under a south-facing hedge in the Apple Orchard, each tiny white flower with a purple spur, and a glorious patch of purple ones scattered under a hedge on a high west-facing slope by the footpath on the outskirts of the village. And yes – I got down on my hands and knees to sniff – they still had that unmistakable perfume.

Prime is the hour when work begins in the monastery, and the whole temper of the Divine Office changes. The Hours from Prime to None are called the Little Hours, and the services are briefer and brisker, with fewer readings and hymns. Thomas Merton, the twentieth-century American Cistercian, described how he and his fellow monks would recite the Little Hours in the fields if they were too busy to return to the monastery. The tempo in the garden too is speeding up. In the Books of Hours the occupation shown for March is Digging, or Breaking Ground. In the Hours of the Fastolf Master one of the figures is cultivating the ground in a vineyard, swinging a mattock high above his head. In other Books of Hours, men dig with round-pointed spades made of wood, shod with iron. In the Earl of Shrewsbury's prayer book a man and a woman plant trees trained into fanciful shapes, while another woman heaves a heavy basketful of soil about. The illustrations are a treasure trove of tools: shovels, spades, mattocks, pruning knives, trowels, billhooks, sickles, scythes, big-toothed wooden hay-rakes and curving long-handled pitchforks. Their forms have not changed in five hundred years; any gardener today would recognise them. I still have a round-pointed spade – though mine is of steel – for digging planting holes in hard ground. But there are no digging forks in the illustrations. There are two-pronged hay-forks and three-pronged dung-forks, but these were essentially for lifting; digging forks were not introduced in Britain until the eighteenth century, when they were used for digging up root vegetables such as the new orange carrots (potatoes were still a novelty in much of Britain until the end of the century).

I have six forks: one with long narrow sharp-pointed tines which I have had ever since I began gardening; another with broad flat blunt tines, good for digging potatoes; my father's little 'Dreadnought', made in Wigan – a border fork (or, as people used to call them, a Lady's fork; he was not a big man), for digging between shrubs without disturbing the roots; my Irish fork, a relic of my days in Dublin, with a medium-sized head on a long shaft and no cross-piece or handle at the top, for digging without bending – a knack I never acquired; a fifth, enormously heavy one with a shaft reinforced with metal, which I use for levering up anything with a particularly tenacious root system; even one with knobs on – a broad scoop-shaped fork with knobs on the end of the tines which I'm told is for shovelling beets. Then there are my two old pitchforks, one with a short handle and one with a long handle, the wood polished smooth with use; and numerous hand forks. But in practice I use the sharp-pointed fork for nearly everything. (It is now minus a tine from using it to lever up a big stone.)

My father's favourite tool was his fireman's axe. He was a conscientious objector during World War II and served as a fireman during the Liverpool Blitz, driving a turntable ladder by night and looking after bombed-out families by day. Once, scrambled still half asleep when the bells went down, his fire crew discovered halfway across the Mersey en route for Birkenhead that they were going in the wrong direction; Pa claimed to be the only person who had ever turned a turntable ladder round in the middle of the Mersey Tunnel. He and my mother married in July 1942. She had won a worker's scholarship to Hillcroft College and thence to Liverpool University, where she was studying social sciences. They had a tiny one-roomed flat with a sofa-bed and a table and two chairs. From the window they could see the city burning. After the war, my father kept the axe and used it for practically everything in the garden: the down-curving point on one side for drawing out seed drills, the broad blunt point on the other as a mattock or cultivator; the flat iron shaft in the middle as a hammer to knock stakes into the ground. His way of turning swords into ploughshares.

A fork is better suited to this stony ground than a spade. When I dug the trenches for the yew hedges that first winter – a thousand feet of trench, three spade-widths wide and two spade-depths deep – I got tennis elbow in both elbows. And however many barrowloads of stones my neighbours and I dig out, however often we rake the stones to the margin of a seed bed, more stones rise to the surface after rain. 'I think your gardens grow stones,' says John.

But it's a good soil nevertheless. The clay makes it rich and moisture-retentive in summer; the stones help it to drain in winter and warm it up in spring. And over the years its stark red colour has mellowed to a warm brown as barrowload after barrowload of compost and manure have been dug in.

I like digging. I like the rhythm of it – foot shove, arm heave, shoulder turn, one pace sideways, start again – backwards and forwards across the plot like a typewriter. After the long immobility of winter – hunched over the computer or bent double over the roses, muffled against the cold – it's good to feel muscles working again, to feel the air and space around your body, hands holding the wooden shaft of the spade, thick pruning gloves exchanged now for lighter more flexible ones and then abandoned altogether; feeling the narrow top of the blade under the sole of your boot, the texture of your clothes moving against your skin, the movement of the air against your face. I have been cocooned in my own thoughts, shut up inside my head for too long – out of touch with the garden.

The sense of touch is a paradigm of connectedness. We talk of management being 'out of touch' or 'hands on'; people are 'hand in glove' or 'lose touch'. We have 'a firm grasp' of our subject, or tell someone who dithers to 'get a grip'. We speak admiringly of those who 'lend a hand', or who are 'not afraid to get their hands dirty'. Digging is about as close to nature as you can get in the garden; it's what the earthworm does, and the frost. Working the soil. I like the smell of it – the rich mouldy smell of newly turned earth. I like the sound of it – the thwack of the spade, the thump of the sods, the wingbeats of birds come to investigate. I like to feel the texture of the soil changing with the seasons and the weather and with my own activities. I like the satisfying look of a newly dug bed at the end of the day. I stand up and lean on my spade to ease my back, estimating how much done, how much more to do, and I watch the birds: a robin and a female blackbird with her bright round golden eye, come to see what I'm up to.

One of the people who came to lean over the garden wall the day the bulldozer arrived was Les. 'I used to dig that bit of ground,' he said, gesturing at the site for the Canal Garden. 'I used to grow vegetables there.' He had gardened for Colonel Cusack, he said, who lived in the Dower House during the war. 'You want to look under that old pear tree: he used to bury his gin bottles there.' (It was true – and not only gin bottles, but whisky bottles, beer bottles, bottles of every kind.)

Les was the gravedigger and sexton. From the garden I used to hear him tolling the bell for funerals. Some parishes toll only the number of years the deceased has lived. Les gave them half an hour at a solemn ten pulls a minute (the usual Sunday-come-to-meeting rate is sixty). How do you do it? I once asked. Do you count? 'I wait for the sound to go out of the tower, then I gives it another pull.' In his father's time, Morville funerals were marked by 'the joy bells' – several bells chimed in sequence rather than a single bell tolling. It was called 'ringing home'.

Today it's a big funeral, the Church Meadow full of cars, Les's old white pick-up parked respectfully behind the hedge. When the last mourners have gone, I walk down to the churchyard. 'Who is it?' I ask, and he tells me, standing on the coffin, chest-deep in the grave, his old tweed hat upon his head, puffing on his pipe. His hands are broad and flat as a mole's, made for digging. During the service, the clods of earth were discreetly covered with a tarpaulin; now the pile stands revealed, red and wet. Mossy, one of Les's neighbours at Morville Heath, has also dropped by. 'Where's old so-and-so?' he asks conversationally, wandering among the graves in his old green overalls, wellingtons and flat cap. 'Up by old so-and-so,' says Les, who has planted them all. 'Oh yes, found 'im now.' They use the familiar names they used of the dead in life. From time to time Mossy reads out an inscription: 'Never knew Booee was born at Broseley,' he says. 'Well, better get off.' 'Was that four o'clock striking?' I say, and we leave Les to finish planting Mr B – with Booee and Cyril and Ernie and Lenka, and Ernie's father and Lenka's husband and all the others, known and unknown.

Les was born just down the road at the Boar's Head Farm, and all his life he worked on the various farms and estates around the village – the furthest away was Home Farm at Willey, a distance of four miles. When I knew him he was back at Boar's Head, working for Clem Shaw. In bad weather I would find him there in his shed, mending tools or repairing bits of the beehives, surrounded by a lifetime of implements: the milk-bottle cardboard-cap putter-on (now propping open the door of the shed), which he used to put the caps on the milk bottles he delivered twice a day round the village at the age of twelve (in the days before refrigeration, the cottagers got one delivery a day, the Hall and vicarage two); the dock-digger, which he used before the days of chemical sprays to root out docks, with its foot-bar, its elongated claw beneath, and its round pivot at the back like a piece of wrought-iron scrollwork, brought in to have a new wooden 'stale' fitted; the enormous wooden bit made for a plough horse that had a sore mouth (in 1939 A. C. Walker's, where he worked then, had eight horses and one tractor; by the end of the war they had one horse and eight tractors, all sent on the American Lend-Lease scheme).

It was in his shed that they found him in the end, peacefully dead, sitting in his old chair as usual, among his tools. His own funeral was a splendid affair – his body carried to the church in a glass carriage, all painted in black with black upholstery, pulled by two black horses with black plumes, the undertakers walking beside it, and someone else now tolling the bell, waiting for the sound to go out of the tower before pulling each new stroke, ringing him home.

There are primroses now in the hedge bottom, and marsh marigolds in the boggy land by the brook. In the little Lammas Meadow to the east of the garden the wild daffodils are out – *Narcissus pseudonarcissus*, the pale Lenten lily, nodding in the breeze, and the stiff little Tenby daffodil (*Narcissus obvallaris*), taller, more upright, bright buttercup-yellow. I like the *pseudonarcissus* better. The Tenby daffodils seem immune to the buffeting of the wind, and March being the month of boisterous breezes it seems a shame that the daffodils should not dance in response. (Modern daffodil breeders, in their quest for ever larger flowers and long straight stems, have produced blooms so stiff and heavy that their stems snap at the first breath of wind: their place is on the show bench, not in the garden.) The Latin name for the daffodil comes from Narcissus, the beautiful youth of classical mythology who, stooping to drink from a pool, caught sight of his own reflection and fell in love with it. Unable to tear his eyes away, he sat gazing into the water, pining, until nothing was left of him but a daffodil, nodding its head over the stream. Our English word 'daffodil' is said to be derived from 'affodil', a variant spelling of 'asphodel', of which daffodils were at one time considered a form. The asphodel was the flower of the Elysian Fields, the heaven of the Greek and Roman poets where the souls of the dead strolled, but in the affectionate old English diminutive 'daffadowndilly' I fancy you can detect something cooler and brisker: the motion of a patch of *pseudonarcissus* tossing in the breeze of a chilly English spring. Of the two, the *pseudonarcissus* is the more intricate flower – you have to lift its head to look – with narrow outer petals, fragile and slightly twisted as if to catch the wind, cream with a thin stripe of greenish-yellow on the reverse, and trumpets of primrose colour, ragged at the mouth. It is shy to flower and prefers the damp shade, but where it is happy, as here, it will seed with abandon. The cool north-facing hillside above the garden was famous for them until the pasture land went under the plough during the last war. But the daffodils are here still, though higher up, in the secret places under the trees, and down by the streams and ditches, like Narcissus, admiring their reflections in the water.

I used to dislike daffodils. As cut flowers I hated them especially, with their stems tightly corralled in rubber bands, leaking that faint rubbery smell of theirs into the wet paper. Hilary Term at Oxford (named after that stern and abstruse theologian Hilary of Poitiers, whose saint's day falls at the start of the term on 13 January) was when one was always at one's lowest ebb, physically, mentally and emotionally, drained by the long winter, and this was precisely when the daffodils would appear in the shop across the road from the college where I worked, all bright colour and heartless gaiety. In the countryside they were even worse, lining the roads and roundabouts in stiff phalanxes of an unvarying shade of yellow. It was my Shropshire neighbour David Bromley, with his exquisite collection of old daffodil cultivars, who first taught me to love daffodils. Now I look forward to the first tiny tattered flowers of 'Rip van Winkle', waking up after the winter like a greeny-yallery hedgehog emerging from hibernation; to dear old double 'Van Sion', dating all the way back to the seventeenth century, sturdy, enduring, dependable – and always one of the first to bloom; to tall shining-white 'Beersheba', with elegantly fluted petals like a Fortuny pleated dress. I planted daintily drooping *triandrus* daffodils and wildly windswept *cyclamineus* ones; I filled the Wild Garden with waves of scented *poeticus*, their white perianths and red-rimmed coronas glimmering in the long grass – 'Actaea' and 'Old Pheasant's Eye', and the double gardenia daffodil with a perfume so heavy that it scents the whole garden. No: what's wrong with daffodils is people thinking that there's only one kind.

I came across the little nodding wild daffodils again in the flower-studded turf of the medieval *millefleurs* tapestries of the Musée Cluny in Paris, when I was researching plants for the Cloister Garden. I wanted this part of the garden to be a *Hortus conclusus* – an enclosed garden, divided into four like the Garden of Eden, like the paradise gardens of the East – surrounded by high walls of yew, a dark cloister where I imagined myself walking, looking out through the arches on to the sunshine and brilliant colours of the garden within. I had been looking at fourteenth- and fifteenth-century paintings in which I saw trellises interwoven with red and white roses, turf seats, trees clipped into quaint shapes, close-cropped grass enamelled with flowers. Now, standing in the Musée Cluny, I decided that I would stud the turf of my Cloister Garden with flowers like those in the tapestries – pinks, daffodils, daisies and violets; red and white campions, blue forget-me-nots, purple-and-yellow heartsease; orange marigolds, columbines, periwinkles and lily of the valley.

But the tapestries are a parable of Paradise, a fantasia of ever-lasting spring. There all of the flowers bloom all of the time, and the grass never needs cutting. In real life it's harder. My pinks and double daisies died; the lilies of the valley never came up; the annuals failed to self-seed; even the columbines dwindled away. Only the grass grew, ever richer and greener. In the 1980s and '90s English gardeners experienced similar problems with the New Perennial gardening style – a self-sustaining mix of perennials grown in a matrix of grass – developed in Germany and Holland. There the growth of grass was checked by the more extreme Continental climate. In this country the grass tended to swamp and eventually kill the flowers. Nowadays the grass in plantings like these is often replaced by gravel or mulches of bark, and the flowers augmented with swathes of ornamental grasses instead. The style of the flowery mead romanticised in the *millefleurs* tapestries is essentially Continental too. But gradually I discovered what would survive: cowslips and meadow scabious where the soil was poor, madonna lilies and peonies where it was deeper and richer.

Garden history can be seen as an alternation of prospect and refuge, a pendulum swinging back and forth according to the insecurities of the times, from the diminutive *Hortus conclusus* of the Middle Ages, walled or hedged about to keep its denizens safe from the perils of the world outside, to the confident outward-lookingness of the great Renaissance gardens, when man was the measure of all things; from the landscape parks of the eighteenth century, when trade and exploration were expanding to the furthest reaches of the globe, to the nostalgic inward-looking garden 'rooms' of the anxious war-torn twentieth. When Islamic terrorists attacked the Twin Towers of New York on 11 September 2001 the resulting shockwave spawned a whole new twenty-first-century generation of enclosed gardens, private refuges and inner sanctums.

The *Hortus conclusus* of the Middle Ages was a garden which existed at more than a merely horticultural level. It also functioned as a symbol of virtue or virginity, an analogy stemming initially from the Song of Solomon – 'a garden inclosed is my sister, my spouse; a spring shut up, a fountain sealed' – and hence of the Virgin Mary, who is frequently portrayed in the context of such a garden. By analogy too the enclosed garden came to represent the unattainability of the Lady of the courtly-love tradition, and key scenes of romance tales such as the thirteenth-century *Roman de la rose* would be played out in the setting of such a garden. Despite the sensuousness and splendour of the garden that surrounds the Lady in the series of six *mille fleurs* tapestries in the Musée Cluny known as the 'Lady and the Unicorn' series, her final act, having sampled each of the worldly delights in turn – taste, smell, sight, hearing and touch – is to renounce them all in favour of '*Mon seul désir*': Christ. But, heavily symbolic as such gardens were, there was real danger and a need for real walls. This was a world still full of wild animals – boars, bears, wolves – a world where politics was conducted by the sword, where the garden – whether secular or monastic – presented a real refuge from the horrors as well as the temptations of the world.

As it still does today. The enemies now are roads, concrete, noise, industrialisation, the destruction of the environment; the temptations commercialisation, trivialisation, homogenisation. But there's one difference. Our modern gardens are refuges not only for us, from the stresses and strains of modern life, but also – in a reversal of the medieval paradigm – for the wild creatures and flowers displaced by an increasingly man-made universe.

According to Saint-Just, theoretician of the French Revolution, 'The world has been empty since the Romans.' But in Shropshire, in one sense at least, the Normans were the natural inheritors of Rome. They built in stone: massive, heavy buildings with round-headed arches echoing the Roman remains of their native France. The Anglo-Saxons did not learn to build in stone until comparatively late; originally even their largest buildings such as palaces and churches (including perhaps the minster church at Morville) were made of wood. Anglo-Saxon remains are as a result relatively rare, though there is a little knot of stone-built late Saxon churches in and around Corve Dale, at Diddlebury, Stanton Lacy and Barrow. In contrast, the Shropshire countryside is littered with Norman churches and monasteries: a hundred or more parish churches, the Benedictine Abbey of Shrewsbury, the Cistercian Abbey at Buildwas, the Augustinians at Haughmond and Lilleshall, the Cluniac Priory at Much Wenlock, the Grand-montine Priory at Alberbury, the Benedictine Priory at Bromfield and the Priory church of Morville itself – all part of a Europe-wide revival of monasticism which took place in the tenth and eleventh centuries.

Hospitality was one of the duties laid down by the Rule of St Benedict, and horticulture was an important means to that end. The Benedictines in particular were noted for their horticulture – a role stressed by the Bishop of Hereford in 1138 when he permitted the monks of Shrewsbury to annex the church at Morville, on condition that they undertook the pastoral care of the parishioners and provided hospitality to travellers. The monks of the Benedictine Priory would have grown much the same selection of herbs and vegetables as their Anglo-Saxon predecessors, the canons of Morville, but they would have been able to add lavender and rosemary and other aromatics from southern Europe, as well as improved varieties of fruit like pears and vines. Plants would have been grown in a series of rectangular beds, one crop per bed, as in the pattern of the ideal monastery drawn up at the Benedictine abbey of St Gall in Switzerland, and though the Priory garden would have been too small to warrant dividing into kitchen garden and physic garden, there would certainly have been an orchard, which might well have doubled, as at St Gall, as a cemetery where the monks were buried, beneath the blossom.

But it was Norman architecture rather than Norman horticulture that fired my imagination – specifically the arcade of semi-circular Norman arches in the church at Morville. I liked their strength and simplicity, their stark contrasts of light and shade, the satisfying geometry of them, their simple horizontal and vertical planes, their views through. Down the road at Buildwas I could see similar arches supporting the enclosed cloister of the abbey there: strong and simple, like the Cistercians themselves, who sought a return to the original simplicity of Benedict's Rule (unlike the Cluniacs, whose elegant elaborate architecture I could see in the remains of the cloisters at Much Wenlock). Cloisters like these were an essential part of the monastery; a covered place for walking in and reading, with one side enclosed and the other looking out on to the cloister garth, a restful open space at the centre of the monastery. The cloister garth itself seems usually to have remained unplanted, consisting of a simple green lawn kept neatly shorn. But in large establishments such as Christ Church Canterbury there might be a second set of cloisters leading to the infirmary, and this smaller space might be planted with herbs for use by the monks who tended the sick. This was what became the model for my yew cloister.

I planted thirty yews, each about nine feet apart, in a line shadowing the hedge around the inside of the Cloister Garden, and I cut 120 hazel poles to bend into arches on which to train them. Gradually my cloister started to take shape.

Being ruled by the Normans was for the subject peoples of Shropshire – despite all the church-building and the apparent piety – like having a knot of vipers dropped into their midst, each head striking out at the others, thrashing about in a frenzy for land and power. Motte-and-bailey castles – defensive keeps on raw heaps of earth with protective compounds around them – dotted the countryside with all the visibility of modern watchtowers and barbed wire. Murder, conspiracy and rebellion were endemic. All five sons of Roger of Montgomery, the first Norman Earl of Shrewsbury, variously took up arms against the King, his successors, their neighbours, each other. The eldest, Robert de Bellême, was so notorious for his rapacity and unspeakable personal cruelty that he earned the name 'Robert le diable', long before it became attached to that other Robert, Duke of Normandy. (There is a rose of the same name, 'Robert le Diable', that grows in the garden here now, a dark red rose of peculiarly livid and unstable colouring, streaked with crimson and grey and purple like macerated flesh.) The mother of the clan was Mabel de Bellême, 'a little woman, sagacious and eloquent but bold and cruel', who shared her sons' taste for intrigue and murder, and was herself ultimately murdered by her enemies in Normandy. Robert de Bellême was, after the King, the most powerful man in the realm, inheriting from his mother a string of castles in Normandy, and by his brother Hugh's death in 1098 his father's castles in England too. Shropshire was Bellême's stronghold: here he was King in all but name. It had been granted to his father in 1071 as his personal fiefdom, as a buffer against the Welsh. Here no writ of the King had power except the 'writ close' addressed to the Earl himself, and in the event that the Earl should not choose to comply the King had no legal remedy. In 1102 such a situation occured. Twice the King summoned Bellême to court to answer forty-five charges of torture, murder and pillage, and twice Bellême refused, allying himself instead with the Welsh and the Irish, the King's ancient enemies. The King had no choice but to raise an army and march north to subdue him. Bellême had three castles on the Severn – at Shrewsbury, Montgomery and Quatford (where the castle controlled the old crossing place used by the Danes). Now he withdrew his forces from Quatford to Bridgnorth, refortifying the Lady Aethelfled's *burh* overlooking the Severn. But in an outflanking movement, the King crossed the river and marched up the valley of the Mor Brook to Underton to lay siege to Bridgnorth from the vulnerable west. The towns-people handed the town over without a fight: they held no brief for Bellême, and he, trapped at Shrewsbury and abandoned by the Welsh and the Irish, was forced to capitulate. Stripped of his title and English estates, 'boiling with rage', he was banished to

Normandy, where he vented his frustrated ambition on his countrymen in an orgy of torture, pillage and murder. It was nearly three hundred years before the Crown ventured to create another Earl of Shrewsbury.

The site of Bellême's castle at Quatford is a wild and brutal place, a sheer red-sandstone cliff the colour of dried blood, topped now with ancient oaks where rooks wheel and squabble in the wind. The cliff towers over the river and the flat land on the other side. I wanted to find the crossing that had played so large a part in Shropshire's history. I followed the long curve of the river below the cliff, looking for tell-tale signs – surely here, where the bank lowers, shelves, and the river widens? Here, where the smooth muscular surface of the water is irritated into a hundred tics and twitches: shallow water. I ask the fishermen with their rods and lines, the dog-walkers in their coloured jackets. Was it here? There are stones beneath the water, they say: in a dry summer you can see them. And there, looking across the river, I suddenly see what I am looking for: the track from the ford, curving away towards Morville and the Mor Brook, climbing the narrow fold between two steep little hills. I drive round to the other side of the river, north under the continuation of the cliff, the car radio crackling and wavering as the signal drifts along the waveband; then back over the bridge at Bridgnorth and south again, follow-ing the river to Eardington, looking for the other end of the track. It's an eerie place, silent and deserted: flat open land, bounded by the loop of the river, skylarks rising up out of the green wheat, the red cliff looming in the distance. By the side of the track three black rooks have been threaded through the wire strands of a fence as a warning to the others. Pressed almost flat by sun and wind, dried to bone and feather, they have assumed an almost

heraldic air, emblazoned on the fence like emblems on a shield. I
follow the track down to the ford. Beneath my feet I can feel the
hard stone of the old roadway under the cropped turf. And in the
silence, the creaking of wagons, the rhythmic clink of armour and
weapons, the jingle of harness . . .

The church at Quatford is a peaceful place, in contrast to the
castle. Built by Bellême's father, Roger of Montgomery, 'at the
desyre of his [second] wyfe, that made a vowe thereof in a
tempest on the se', it stands at the margin of the old forest of
Morfe. It still has a feeling of the forest edge about it, the
churchyard straggling up the hillside and into the trees, the
tombs not in rows but scattered here and there, each a little
separate from the others, like people sitting companionably
around at a picnic. A local variation on the story of its
foundation has it that Adeliza, Earl Roger's second wife,
was in peril of her life not at sea but lost in the forest, and
that she made a vow to found a church wherever she should
come to safety. The church used to stand in the bailey of the
castle, but a new road driven through the solid rock now
separates church from castle and slices the bailey in two, so
that the church stands alone on its own rocky promontory.
The church is of local red sandstone, sculpted by wind and rain
into fragile flaking pillow-shapes. This is eighteenth- and nineteenth-century work. The chancel, the oldest part of the
church, is built from big square-ish blocks of grey stone,
honeycombed with holes. It looks light, airy, fragile, but must
be surprisingly tough: it has scarcely weathered at all. I looked
it up when I got home. Tufa.

Tufa forms where streams saturated with calcium bicarbonate
bubble up from under freshwater limestone. The carbonate is

precipitated on to grass, leaves and twigs, gradually solidifying into a rock full of cavities and air-holes. In its soft and crumbly state it was an important source of lime. In its solid state it was valued as a lightweight and very durable building material. The Romans used it in the arched vaults of their bathhouses at Viroconium in place of timber, which would have rotted in the steam. The Normans used it in the high roofing vaults of their cathedrals at Worcester, Gloucester and Bristol, to lighten the weight. But why here?

Ann Scard had written a book about the building stones of Shropshire twenty years ago. Her telephone number was still listed in the phone book and, taking a chance, I phoned up. She is the daughter and granddaughter of master masons, and she told me that the tufa for Worcester Cathedral was probably brought by water from Southstone Rock, a large outcrop near the village of Shelsey Walsh in the valley of the River Teme, which runs through southern Shropshire and joins the Severn at Worcester. Tufa was used in the construction of the church at Shelsey Walsh itself and in other churches nearby. Perhaps the tufa for Quatford also came from the Teme Valley, brought upriver via the Severn.

But she rang me back later to say that the tufa may have come from much nearer at hand. The geological map for this part of south Shropshire shows an outcrop of tufa on the Mor Brook itself.

Of course: I should have guessed. The name of the bridge under which the Mor Brook passes as it nears the Severn is Marlbrook Bridge. 'Marl' is the word for the naturally occuring mixture of clay-ey soil and carbonate of lime – tufa in its crumbly state – which was spread on light sandy soils as a fertiliser. As the old rhyme says,

He that marls sand
May buy the land.
He that marls moss
Shall have no loss.
He that marls clay
Throws all away.

(Or coals to Newcastle, you might say.)

I went down to the Marlbrook Bridge to have a look. It's a tumultuous landscape, the ground on each side pockmarked with the grass-grown pits where the marl was dug. Marling is a practice older than the Romans. In Chaucer's time marl pits were so common that to fall into one was the equivalent of slipping on a banana skin: the medieval version of the pratfall (that, or falling into a heap of manure). Marl was also much used by the agricultural improvers of the seventeenth and eighteenth centuries to fertilise the land. It is a practice long discontinued now, replaced by imported lime and commercial fertilisers.

The tufa-bearing limestone occurs in a narrow band between two series of sandstone, 250 to 400 feet above the surrounding lowland. It seems odd to think of limestone in this red-sandstone landscape, a white bone protruding through the flesh – like a pterodactyl's wing or a mammoth's tusk. The outcrop runs all the way from Harpswood along the line of the Mor Brook, left down Corve Dale, following the skirts of the Brown Clee. It is the limestone that gives the escarpment above Morville its characteristic sharp profile. And it is the limestone, leaching into springs in the catchment area of the Mor Brook, that makes the soil around the village neutral or calcareous, unlike the soils of neighbouring brooks, which tend to be slightly acid.

*

As I stand and look at the tufa wall, with its rough surface texture and cellular structure, I become aware that wild bees are flying in and out of the holes. It's as if they too, like the tufa, are being born out of the limestone, frothing up out of the stone, transformed, metamorphosed, by contact with the air.

The ancients understood little about the biology of bees, though they were fascinated by their social organisation. They thought the ruler of the hive was a king and his armies all male. The bees' sudden appearance in spring and disappearance in winter was a particular mystery. In the Bible, Samson finds a swarm of bees issuing from the carcase of a lion (an incident engraved on the mind of anyone who spent childhood breakfasts staring at a Tate & Lyle tin). Virgil devotes a whole book of the *Georgics* to bees, including precise instructions for engendering them from the putrefaction of a dead ox. For Virgil the bees and their honey are a symbol of the Golden Age, their rebirth a signal of Rome's entry into a new Golden Age under the Emperor Augustus:

> At last they come pouring out, like a shower from summer clouds,
> Or thick and fast as arrows
> When Parthian archers, their bowstrings throbbing, advance to battle.
>
> *Georgics IV*, 312–14

It's an annual miracle. Unlike bumblebees, honeybees will not fly in temperatures below 48 or 50°F. All winter the hives in the garden seem silent and deserted. Early spring is when the honeybees are at their most vulnerable, dependent upon their last dwindling stores of honey for survival. This is when many colonies die. Then with the first warm day they come tumbling out of the hives as if newly hatched by the warmth of the sun.

I watch to see if they are bringing pollen back to the hive. The pollen of each plant species is unique – distinct in the shape and colour and size of its granules. As the workers alight on the landing board of the hive I can see the orange pollen of crocuses, the pale cream pollen of hellebores, the greens of alders and wood anemones. The pollen swells the pollen baskets on their back legs, vivid against their dark furry bodies. It is a good sign: it means that the queen is laying successfully, building up the armies of worker bees in readiness for the summer harvest.

Gardens and bees are inseparable. The fertility of our gardens – and of many agricultural crops – depends upon them. Only plants which are self-fertile or which rely (as most trees and grasses do) on the wind to disperse their pollen can do without bees. Without bees our gardens would be duller places and our bellies would rumble with hunger. But bees are now threatened by Varroa, a parasitic mite endemic in most countries, which arrived in the UK in the 1990s. The mites attach themselves to the bees, weakening and distorting their bodies. Varroa can be treated in domesticated bees by a variety of substances non-toxic to the bees, administered after the honey has been removed at the end of summer. But in wild bees, untreated, it can lead to the extinction of whole colonies. Until the bees develop their own strategies for dealing with the pest, they need our help.

Every garden of any size should have a beehive or two. I had a fancy to dedicate mine to six of the Muses, painting the hives ash-white, with the lettering picked out in blue – Calliope, Muse of epic poetry; Clio, Muse of history; Urania, Muse of astronomy; Melpomene, Muse of tragedy; Erato, Muse of lyric poetry; Thalia, Muse of comedy – imagining them as the muses of the garden. My friend Natalie Hodgson is more down to earth. She keeps a dozen hives on her lavender field at Astley Abbots, and her bees work for their living. But even she is unable to resist a bit of whimsy: her bees live in Pollen Row, with hives painted to represent cottages, church, school, shop, post office, BP garage and pub – the Beehive Inn.

The re-emergence of the bees in spring is marked by their own star cluster in the sky – the Beehive cluster between the constellations of Leo and Gemini, known to astronomers by the prosaic name of M44. (The 'M' prefix refers to a list of more than a hundred 'fuzzy objects' – star clusters, nebulae and galaxies – compiled by Charles Messier, an eighteenth-century astronomer.) Its classical name was Praesepe, or the Manger, and the two brighter stars on either side were known as the Asses, portrayed in old star maps as if feeding from the Manger. It lies overhead in the month of March, a misty patch visible to the naked eye, its disappearance on an otherwise clear night a sign of stormy weather to come.

The moles are on the move again too, heaving up their miniature castles in long Maginot lines across the lawn. When the ground froze in January they retreated deeper underground, following the earthworms. Now, as the soil warms, they abandon their winter quarters and move closer to the surface, spring-cleaning burrows which may have collapsed from disuse, pushing the soil out on to the surface with their broad white palms: fine, dry, friable soil – the best potting compost in the world. Later on in the year the young moles will emerge on to the surface and will live for a time in the outside world, in the air, among the grasses and flowers, looking for new territory of their own; when they find it, they will disappear again into the world beneath the surface – a world they will rarely leave for the rest of their lives. Adult moles are solitary beings, fiercely protective of their territory, each inhabiting its own subterranean world of tunnels and burrows, independent of others. They have underground larders where they store food, nests for sleeping furnished with leaves and dried grasses. They lack for nothing. They have no predators. I can understand Mole's affection for his home in *The Wind in the Willows*. It is a safe solipsistic universe, in which the senses in general need not be especially acute. But the mole has one sense of almost unimaginable sensitivity: touch. It is through touch that the mole experiences its underground world. Using its naked snout, the bristles on its face and tail, the fine hairs all over its body which brush against the tunnel walls as it moves, it gathers information not only from contact with solid objects but from such insubstantial sources as changes in temperature and vibrations in the soil and air. The snout in particular is exquisitely sensitive to changes in air pressure, to the slightest draught in the tunnels, the merest movement of the air – occasioned perhaps by the distant presence of another creature, by worms dropping into the feeding runs, by the soft fall of soil. In the pitch-darkness of its underground world the mole can detect solid objects and avoid obstacles merely from the compression waves set up by the movement of its own body.

If March comes in like a lamb it goes out like a lion. Now is the time of boisterous squally weather – of big winds, blue skies, white clouds and sudden storms of rain – the gales which occur around the vernal equinox on 21 March. Do the moles dream of the wind in the stillness of their tunnels? The tattered scrap of cloth caught all winter like a Tibetan prayer rag in the topmost branches of one of the trees now finally breaks loose and is swept up into the convection system, up and up, gaining height, higher and higher, until the whole countryside is spread like a map beneath, farms and villages, fields and woods, roads and rivers, striped with alternating bands of sunshine and showers as the weather fronts chase one another across the land. Down in the garden I clutch my hat to my head as the winds veer and back. There's a glint of gold as the weathervane on the Gatehouse changes direction. And down in Bridgnorth all the weathervanes of High Town – the nine weathervanes of St Leonard's on their nine crocketed red-sandstone pinnacles, the six-pointed star on the turret above the smooth grey brick of the Bluecoat School, the two golden pennants above the half-timbered Town Hall on its whitewashed arches, the wrought-iron shield with its cut-out date above the striped mock-Byzantine Market Hall with its multi-coloured brickwork – all swing in unison into the wind.

Spring is now so close you can almost smell it.

Terce

You can smell the spring even before it arrives, like a seafarer becalmed for months on the wide expanse of ocean, scenting land before he sees it. Caught unaware, stooping perhaps to collect milk from the step; one morning it is suddenly there, on the breeze, unmistakable after the long months of winter: a smell compounded of greenness and rain showers and damp earth; a hint of balsam, a rumour of hyacinths – pregnant with the ghosts of flowers-to-be, like Flora's breath. The clock strikes, the sound reverberating across the Church Meadow like ripples of water in the Mor Brook. Nine o'clock on a spring morning. How can you resist? The village is quiet; husbands, wives, children all despatched to office or school; hum of early morning traffic silenced; scrunch of postman's foot on gravel been and gone. Leave the mail unopened, the milk where it stands on the step. Follow your nose into the garden.

The scents of February and March were, like the violets, shy: you had to get down on your hands and knees to snuffle up the honey scent of snowdrops or the mossy green scent of the first daffodils. But now the foxy stink of emerging crown imperials comes bowling over the hedges to greet you. There's the pungent smell of wild garlic leaves trodden underfoot, the smell of newly mown grass and warm compost heaps. It's as if the tipping of the sun past the equinox had tripped a switch – as if those few extra seconds of light, that extra degree or two of inclination, had made all the difference. The air pulses with the sugar-sweet scent of Siberian wallflowers, the vanilla of *Clematis armandii*, choisyas and daphnes. Pure sex. Rooted to the spot, plants cannot walk around and look for a mate. Instead, they pump out these naked messages of seduction. Come hither, come hither. And the bees are only too happy to oblige, burying themselves headfirst in the flowers, nuzzling deep, drunk with nectar.

Even the rain smells different. April is the month of sunshine and showers, rainbows and reflections, of small, puffy white fair-weather cumuli which bubble up into cauliflower-headed cumuli congesti behind your back and take you by surprise. Intent upon some late pruning, I hear the rain before I see it, rattling on the leaves in a rising wind. 'Only a shower,' we say, sniffing the air. And it is: gone as quickly as it came, with ragged fragments of sky left in the puddles of the drive and a glaze of silver on the rose leaves. Falling from high altitude, short and sharp and heavy, the rain brings a whiff of ozone from the upper air, a hint of the sea; soon over, unlike the steady downpour of February. Indoors, a shaft of sunlight is reflected from the bevelled edge of a mirror and shatters into pieces on the floor: red, orange, yellow, green, blue, indigo, violet. In the garden there are scarlet tulips, yellow jonquils, blue and white *Muscari*. A rainbow spans the valley, one foot on Shirlett, the other on Meadowley: Iris, messenger of the gods. She bore a son, Eros, child of the rainbow, fathered by Zephyrus, the West Wind.

For it is – of course – a love affair, this passion for one's garden, and the very smell of it intoxicates, like the smell of a lover.

*

My mother's favourite painting was Botticelli's *Primavera*. A reproduction of it used to hang by her bed. The painting has been variously interpreted as a Christian – or Humanist – or political – allegory, the central figure as Venus or the Virgin Mary or even Dante's Beatrice, its subtext Lorenzo de' Medici's attempts to build a federation of Italian city-states, or the impending marriage of his second cousin Lorenzo di Pierfrancesco de' Medici in 1482. But it can also speak to us quite simply – of that moment in spring when the transparent veil of green which lies so lightly over the countryside is punctured with the brilliance of flowers for the first time; of love and passion and sexual initiation; of beginnings, awakenings. The right-hand side of the painting shows the pursuit by Zephyrus of Chloris, the virginal Greek personification of Spring (whose name shares the same root as 'chlorophyll', the green colour in plants), and her subsequent transformation into Flora, the Roman goddess of flowers – from the almost naked Chloris, clad only in a diaphanous veil of palest grey-green, into the richly ornamented figure of Flora, crowned and garlanded with blossom, her heavy robe embroidered with pinks and roses and cornflowers, her arms filled with flowers.

One of Botticelli's sources may have been a passage in Ovid's *Fasti*, written nearly fifteen hundred years before, in which Flora tells how, as Chloris, she was pursued and raped by Zephyrus; and how afterwards Zephyrus, repentant for what he had done, married her and made for her a garden full of flowers out of the fields which were her dowry, saying, 'Goddess, be mistress of the flowers.' Zephyrus was the son of Astraeus, the Starry Man, and Eos, goddess of the dawn. In Botticelli's painting he pursues Chloris, the two of them tumbling into the serenely ordered world of Venus and her acolytes in a whirl of wind-whipped drapery. Even the trees around them bend with the violence of their passing. Chloris flees

him in alarm, flowers tumbling from her parted lips – blue cornflowers, pink roses, the white flowers of strawberries. Theirs is the
only movement in this otherwise limpid tableau; all the other
figures seem arrested, self-absorbed. Even the three Graces seem
transfixed in time, as if waiting for the signal to begin their dance.
Only one character returns our gaze – Flora herself in her flower-
decked robe, holding the viewer in a cool regard and smiling
slightly, one heel raised as if to step out of the painting, one hand
poised to strew flowers from her arms. Now? she seems to say.

I look again at the first photograph of my mother. As she stands,
laughing, drawing the others around her, one heel is raised. It is as
if she too, like Flora, is about to step out of the picture. To begin.
She is even wearing a sprigged dress. Now? she seems to say.

My parents had known one another for three weeks when they
ran away together to Shropshire. She was selling newspapers in aid
of the International Brigade on Bolton Town Hall steps when he
first saw her. She came from a highly politicised and radical background, and was working at that time for the railway, as her father
had done before losing his job in the Depression. Pa was dazzled. It
was 1938, the year before the outbreak of war, and he was going to
Shropshire for a week with the local Unitarian minister, to stay with
the minister's aunt and uncle in their cottage at Ford, near Shrewsbury. It was agreed that the three of them should go together. But
then the minister couldn't go. And so, telling no one, they went
alone, walking the Shropshire hills all day, talking about everything
under the sun – literature, poetry, politics, music.

Is this why I came back to Shropshire – to rediscover that land of
lost content, to recover that sense of a beginning? With gardening,
every year is a new beginning, a fresh start, a clean slate. Garden-

ers have a lifetime of second chances (this year I *will* sow the celeriac in February), and each spring is a new beginning (this year I *will* weed the bittercress before it flings its seeds everywhere like grapeshot), each morning a clean slate (this year I *will* spray the roses before they get black spot, dig the tulips up six weeks after flowering, mow the long grass in the Orchard before the rain knocks it flat).

In Ovid's day Flora's feast was celebrated at the end of April. But Flora is much more ancient than Ovid's tale and her feast (as seems apt) was originally a movable one, for the flowers that cover her robe and wreathe her head and neck keep their own calendar; they bloom in accordance with nature's laws, not man's. One year we have primroses in February; the next, tulips in June. Global warming speeds some things up but slows others down. Zephyrus too is changeable, unpredictable – sometimes portrayed as impregnating and fertilising, at other times as a destructive force. In some versions of the story of the origin of the hyacinth, it was jealous Zephyrus who blew Apollo's discus off course, slaying the beautiful youth Hyacinthus, whom Apollo loved. Such was Apollo's grief that a flower sprang from the boy's spilled blood which bore the words 'Alas! Alas!' (thought now to be the *Scilla bifolia*, not the hyacinth, though our own wild bluebell is still called *Hyacinthoides non-scripta*, meaning 'not written upon').

April can be a treacherous month. Sometimes it comes with soft blandishments, sometimes whirling the plum blossom from the branches and keeping the bees mured up in their hives; now with honeyed words, now snapping the long incautious shoots of clematis and scorching tender growth of gooseberry and rose. The children from the village school come trooping across the Church Meadow wearing jackets and woolly hats to keep out the wind. They have come to rehearse their Easter play; this year it's Daniel in the lion's den.

Easter too is a movable feast (as Passover is in the Jewish tradition), both depending upon the moon. And from Easter is calculated the date of Septuagesima, of Sexagesima and Quinquagesima; the date of Ash Wednesday and Palm Sunday; of Ascension Day, Whit Sunday and Corpus Christi. Plant your potatoes on Good Friday, goes the old adage. But Good Friday can be as late as the last week in April or as early as the third week in March. I like this slipperiness of calendar and season. It reminds me to trust my instinct, plant when the soil is right rather than when the calendar says so; be guided by the weather, not the date.

Mankind has always had trouble with calendars. As human beings our personal experience of time may be infinitely elastic, but as societies we have always needed calendars, to fix future dates and record past ones. The earliest attempts may date back thirty thousand years. The trouble is that the natural markers of the passage of time – days, lunar months and solar years – are all incommensurables. Attempts to combine them in a single calendar inevitably run into trouble. Taking the day as 1, the lunar cycle is approximately 29 days, 12 hours and 44 minutes, and the solar year 365 days, 5 hours and 48 minutes. The seasons and the calendar have always had a tendency to drift apart. In our modern calendar the vernal equinox usually happens on 20 March, sometimes on the 21st, occasionally on the 19th. Under the ancient Roman lunar system of measuring the year, the calendar ran fast in relation to the seasons, so that eventually the spring equinox fell in the middle of summer. Julius Caesar corrected the misalignment in 45 BC, and switched to a solar system of measurement, but by 1582 the calendar had slipped ten days out of alignment in the other direction, so that the vernal equinox fell too early, on 11

March. That year Pope Gregory decreed that 4 October would be followed all over the Catholic world by 15 October, shifting the vernal equinox the following year back to 21 March. The Protestant countries – averse to being ruled by the Pope – refused to comply, with the result that two calendars (the Julian and the Gregorian) were in use in Europe at the same time for much of the following two centuries. For clarity's sake correspondents from different countries had to date their letters to one another in both systems, distinguishing the different dates as Old Style and New Style respectively.

There was disagreement too about the date upon which the new year began. Lady Day, 25 March, was when the church year began – the Feast of the Annunciation, the date on which Christ was nominally conceived – placed where it is in the calendar because it is nine months before Christmas, the ritual date of Christ's birth. Until the Gregorian calendar reforms it was also the date on which the numbering of the year changed. So from January to March each year, while France and the Catholic countries had moved on into a new year, Britain and the Protestant countries were still stuck in the previous one. By 1752, when Britain finally adopted the new calendar, the old one had slipped yet another day behind, so that eleven days had to be removed to bring Britain into line. There were riots in the streets, with people demanding, 'Give us back our eleven days.' At Christmas, crowds gathered in Glastonbury to see whether the famous Christmas-flowering Holy Thorn (*Crataegus monogyna* 'Biflora', said to have sprung from the staff of Joseph of Arimathaea when he brought the Grail to England after Christ's death) would conform to God's laws or man's, and bloom on the old or the new Christmas Day. That year it was reported to have burst into blossom on 5 January, 'thus indicating that Old Christmas Day should alone be observed, in spite of an irreligious legislature'. (In fact the thorn follows no one's laws but nature's, blooming in mild spells anywhere between November and March, as well as flowering again at the usual time in May.) The following Lady Day, tenants refused to pay rent, claiming they had lost eleven days of tenancy. To placate public opinion, tenancies were allowed to run for a further eleven days – which is why our modern tax year still begins on 6 April, eleven days after Lady Day.

And Lady Day is still one of the Quarter Days, the date from which many leases and agricultural tenancies run, so beginning the agricultural as well as the Church year. A better time for New Year's resolutions, I think, when seed is sown and life begins, than January, in the depths of midwinter.

On the first warm day of April I open the hives to see how the bees have fared during the winter. I use the sharp-edged steel hive tool to crack open the joints between crown board and brood super, brood super and brood box, puffing a little smoke between the layers as I go, to warn the bees that I am coming. The whole hive is glued together with the pungent dark red propolis (from *polis*, the Greek word for 'city') which the bees make from the sticky resin of trees such as pines, working it into gaps and crevices to stop winter draughts and keep out intruders. The propolis sets shiny and hard, like sealing wax. It is said to be the secret ingredient in the lustrous golden-red varnish developed by the violin-maker Stradivarius, and may be one of the reasons for the longevity and beautiful tone of his violins. It certainly contains an antibiotic that helps to keep the colony healthy, and before the advent of modern antibiotics it was much used in surgical dressings. Some beekeepers still make a point of eating a little propolis every day to ward off colds and flu.

As I delve deeper into the hives, the smell of the propolis becomes overpowering in the warm sunshine. I work quietly and gently so as not to disturb the bees, lifting out the brood frames one at a time, looking at each in turn. After the initial buzz of alarm and irritation, the bees settle back on to the frames, a shimmering mass of dark bodies and trembling wings. I peer down between the thick gold combs into the darkness. This is a good-tempered hive. Each hive is different, depending upon the temper of the queen herself. Everything depends upon her. Her smell – properly the 'queen substance', which can only be communicated by direct contact – is taken from her by the workers who feed her, and continuously passed from bee to bee, round and round the hive, reassuring them of her health and presence. A hive that loses its queen will know the fact within minutes and will roar its distress.

At this time of year the queen is building up to her egg-laying peak of two thousand eggs a day, working to restore the hive from its winter low of twenty-five thousand to a peak of eighty thousand by midsummer – necessary if the bees are to be able to make enough honey to feed the colony next winter. The whole enormous community, in all its dull complexity – nurse bees, guard bees, foragers and drones, cleaners and undertakers – is held together by a complex web of scents – one to guide the foragers back to the hive, another to keep the colony together when it swarms, a third to summon troops to the defence when the hive is threatened by intruders; a geranium smell, a lemon smell, a pear-drop smell – uniquely identifying this hive and this colony.

Walking down the garden afterwards, pulling my gauntlets off and unzipping the veil of my bee suit, I can see that the bees are working the early fruit blossom – sloe and damson and pear, the last of the myrobalan and the first of the plum, their shining white flowers filled to the brim with golden stamens. From late February to May the countryside around the garden foams with white; first the myrobalan or cherry plum (*Prunus cerasifera*), like an airy whirl of snowflakes caught in a gust of wind; then, three or four weeks later, the smaller denser flowers of sloe or blackthorn (*P. spinosa*), clenched to the thorny twigs like the rime of hoar frost on hedges still naked and black from winter; then the pear blossom like thick cream, clotting the knobbly fruit spurs of the big old pear tree in the middle of the garden. This is when the 'blackthorn winter' comes, often plunging the garden and the countryside once more into sub-zero temperatures. That first spring, when the yew hedges were no more than tufts of greenery and the whole garden just a billiard-table of grass, the temperature dropped overnight to –5°C, and we awoke to find the old pear tree, heavy with white blossom, a lone vertical in a frozen white world of horizontal lines.

I had the pear tree identified by the experts of the Royal Horticultural Society's fruit-advisory service. 'Forelle,' they said, 'the Trout Pear', a variety imported from Germany at the end of the seventeenth century. Pears can live for 250 years or more, and this one was probably planted here during the building works of the eighteenth century, on the newly 'made-up' ground, as part of a mixed orchard in which taller-growing pears would have nursed up smaller and shorter-living trees such as apples and damsons. I found the stumps and the last stragglers of nineteenth- and twentieth-century apples and damsons when I started work on the garden. The pear tree is now nearly forty feet high, tall and narrow like an English elm, stag-headed in places, its trunk twisted and chequered like a Roman mosaic, but still vigorous enough to bear heavy crops of sweet, white-fleshed, bright red-brown pears with the pattern of prominent dots that gave it its name.

Standard pear orchards were once the glory of the neighbouring counties of Herefordshire, Worcestershire and Gloucestershire, planted for cider- and perry-making. But Shropshire is really damson country. Like parts of Cheshire and Cumbria, the countryside hereabouts is full of old damsons, many of them planted by cottagers who were required by their leases to plant fruit trees in the hedgerows. Hardier than pears or plums, damsons have black angular trunks, their crowns broken and lop-sided, shattered by winter storms. They are notoriously brittle: the doctors hereabouts knew when it was damson-picking time from the number of broken bones they had to set. The fruit used to be sent in baskets to Lancashire for dyeing cloth, a practice continued even as late as 1950, when a Mr Hall from Bolton would come round the village with his lorry, collecting the cottagers' damsons; he paid tuppence a pound. The colour produced was not deep purple or yellow but khaki: it was the dye used for army uniforms.

I planted a plum and damson walk along the west side of the garden, giving 'Shropshire Damson' pride of place at one end, with reliable old 'Warwickshire Drooper' at the other – surely the prettiest in bloom, flowering right to the tips of the young red-brown wood, its long arching boughs bowed down as if by the weight of blossom – and, in between, the old purple gage 'Reine Claude Violette', 'Kirke's Blue' and 'Early Transparent' (more poetically known as 'Rivers' Early Apricot'), delicious dark 'Comte d'Althan's Gage' and the meltingly tender old greengage itself, 'Reine Claude'. In the Cloister Garden I planted sloe and myrobalan, the two ancestors of the garden plum. In the Vegetable Garden I planted two crossing tunnels of apple and pear trees, one-year-old whips to be trained into quadruple cordons, arranging them in order of flowering so that each tree had a pollinator. I planted standard pear trees, 'Catillac' and 'Jargonelle', in the hope that two hundred years hence they will have attained the stature and presence of the old 'Forelle'. And each spring as the garden foams with white I remember the soldiers who marched off to Gallipoli and the Somme with the khaki of Shropshire damsons on their backs.

There are few things in the garden that please me so much as these simple white flowers of spring: white damson blossom against a pewter sky, white sheets bellying out on the washing line, the pear tunnel flushing slowly with white blossom from west to east, from earliest to last, from 'Doyenné d'Eté' and 'Comtesse d'Angoulême', 'Louise Bonne of Jersey' and 'Hacon's Incomparable', 'William's Bon Chrêtien' and 'Fondante d'Esperen', all the way to 'Beurré Superfin' and 'Fondante d'Automne'.

Flowers came into the garden almost as an afterthought. I had conceived the garden first in black and white, as two-dimensional plan, as pattern; then in motion, as views in parallax, a series of pathways to be followed; then as a series of green rooms, all grass and hedges, as volume rather than colour. I hadn't thought about flowers at all. The first garden to be made was the Vegetable Garden: ten, then a further ten, interlocking beds of fruit and vegetables, with edgings of Pa's lavender. Then the Knot Garden, with its interlace of herbs – rue and germander and santolina – kept neat and flowerless by clipping. I copied into my notebook Albert Loos's dictum 'To find beauty in form instead of making it depend upon ornament, is the goal . . .' and noted beneath it a passage from Raymond Mortimer; 'Gracefulness, in things as in persons, results from an elimination of the unnecessary.' I was taking the long view, in space as well as time. I was preoccupied with vistas, shapes, form.

But as the garden grew up around me, and the yew hedges began to enclose and divide the ground, the perspective shortened. I began to want a foreground too. Inspired by Lady L's paintings I began to want striped tulips, scarlet anemones, gold-laced polyanthus, the strange forms of primroses beloved of the Elizabethans – pantaloons and galligaskins and jack-in-the-greens – everything that was intricate and old and beautiful. I joined the Hardy Plant Society and the Cottage Garden Society, sent off lists of requests to their seed exchanges, and received in return seed of half a dozen different species of hellebore, a dozen different columbines, dianthus and campanulas by the score. I joined the Wakefield and North of England Tulip Society and was given a dozen precious bulbs of English florist's tulips. I bought seed of white foxgloves and sweet white rocket from the Museum of Garden History. I pored over catalogues; ordered violas and roses and alliums by the hundred. And although I had no money, I had all the time in the world, so I read about propagation, discovered vernalisation and stratification, divisions and layers, pipings and cuttings, learned from my mistakes. Everything was new to me: most of the plants I had never grown before; many I had never even seen growing – I knew them only from books and paintings. And as they grew, each leaf was a revelation, each flower an epiphany. I saw how the purple foxgloves could be distinguished from the white by the colour of their leaves, even as tiny seedlings. I could trace the lineage of *Helleborus* x *sternii* back to the red-flushed stems of *H. lividus* and the lime-green flowers of *H. argutifolius*. Lady L gave me her mother's *Iris unguicularis* and the *Campanula lactiflora* from Uncle Wolryche's American border at Dudmaston. Jonathan Cook at Castle Bromwich Hall gave me plants of *Digitalis ferruginea* from the eighteenth-century Upper Wilderness there. My friend David Bromley gave me the precious double form of the wild blue *Geranium pratense*, explaining patiently that, being double, it set no seed, but because it set no seed its flowers lasted longer than the single kinds. Gradually the garden began to fill with flowers.

But with flowers come responsibilities. I fell in love with auriculas: light-centred alpines with creamy-silver centres and shades of mauve and lavender, violet and purple, burgundy and plum; gold-centred alpines in shades of rust, ginger, mahogany and cinnamon; edged show auriculas, chaste and exquisite with their white inner ring of 'paste', their black body colour and petals edged with green, grey or white; show 'selfs' in brilliant primary colours – red, yellow and blue; best of all, the 'dark selfs' with flowers the colour of bitter chocolate and leaves dusted with grey 'meal'. I loved the formality of them, their neatness, the concentric circles of jewel-bright colour set off by the paler central eye. Many of the auriculas in Lady L's Dutch flower paintings were the striped sorts favoured in the seventeenth century but later abandoned by fashion – until Allan Hawkes revived them in the late twentieth century. I wrote to him, and he sent me precious seed to start my own strain. I developed a yen for double auriculas too: bred largely from yellow sports, they have (yellow being the dominant gene) a more muted palette than other auriculas – old gold, sulphur, lemon sorbet and lime green; mushroom, pinky-beige, raw liver and an extraordinary greenish-grey like dead flesh. And 'Fancy' auriculas tickled my fancy too, in combinations of brown and green. But above all it was their smell which I loved: a secret honeyed sweetness with over-tones of incense or musk, often lost in the open air, but which given protection – on the showbench, in the greenhouse or indoors – was as overwhelming as it was unexpected. It seemed to originate from the white farina or meal, for the grey-edged varieties with their thick powdering on petals and leaves and some of the old border auriculas (the 'Dusty Millers' with their mealy leaves) seemed to smell best of all. I begged offshoots, spent money I didn't have, visited shows and nurseries, read books on their history and cultivation, planted them in three-inch clay pots with due attention to compost and drainage, watered, fed and fussed over them. And then lost them all, one after another. 'I think you should give up show auriculas until you have more time,' one grower said; another, more kindly, 'Grow border auriculas instead.'

April is the flowery month, and in the calendars of the Books of Hours the activities portrayed for April are Picking Flowers and Greenery. In the *Très riches heures du duc de Berry* – the most sumptuous of all Books of Hours – two ladies pick flowers while a pair of aristocratic lovers exchange rings and plight their troth before witnesses. In my woodcut Shepherds' Calendar a young gallant carries flowers and a leafy branch to his lady love who waits for him on the grass, weaving a chaplet of flowers. In the Hours of the Fastolf Master, the April calendar shows a gaily dressed figure wearing one green stocking and one red, and carrying a green branch. The mood is one of celebration, of flowers opening and new leaves sprouting.

One of my earliest memories of my mother is of her picking

flowers. When I was three years old, the family moved south and west, from the industrial north down to Somerset – at first to a flat in Wellington and then to a house in Taunton, where my father had been appointed minister at Mary Street Unitarian Chapel. My young parents thought they had died and gone to heaven. That first winter, Pa never wore an overcoat, and there were flowers in the hedgerows all winter long. They had never seen a horse chestnut in flower, or smelled a philadelphus. Here were avenues of chestnuts, their great boughs sweeping down to the ground, scattering the roadside verges with fallen petals; fountains of philadelphus filling the air with their perfume. I remember walking hand-in-hand with my mother through a meadow of tall buttercups, their golden pollen dusting my hands and face. There was purple clover heavy with the dark brown bodies of bumblebees, and white ox-eye daisies like spilled milk – 'Moon Daisies', she called them. There were cinnamon-coloured heifers, their bony legs like young tree trunks, bending their necks down to sniff me, liquid eyes close to mine, their sweet damp breath warm on my face – crowding close, jostling shoulder to shoulder – while my mother with her hands behind her back laughingly defended the flowers she had picked, only to find that the heifers behind had munched them anyway. In winter she took bare twigs from the flowering currant in the garden and brought them into the warmth of the house where they magically bloomed not pink, as they did in spring, but snow-white. In May she cut fragrant armfuls of double white lilac from the tree outside my bedroom window. On light summer evenings I used to climb into it in my pyjamas when sent to bed (too early, too early!). Betrayed by the neighbours, I pretended that I was walking in my sleep.

It was Pa's first garden. It was here that he carved our names on the speckled green sides of the marrows in the vegetable patch, parting the canopy of hairy leaves to show us how, as summer ripened into autumn, our names grew bigger and bigger. He planted potatoes, putting the tubers up to sprout on a sunny windowsill in February, and burying them at Easter, then showing us how to dig them up again, mysteriously multiplied, like treasure trove in July. He grew fruit: thickets of raspberries, briar patches of gooseberries, pale pink-and-gold stems of rhubarb forced from knobbly crowns under an old bucket. Like the small animal I was, I remember that garden chiefly by its smells: the sharp exciting feral smell of the flowering currant, beneath which I made a little den; the sweet-sour smell of raw rhubarb, pulled illicitly from its damp white sockets; the pungent smell of tomato plants that smelled like tomatoes right from the first tentative leaves they raised above the soil.

It is no wonder that smell has such a potent effect on us. The organs of smell are the only part of our brains that come into direct contact with the outside world. Molecules of gas dock with receptors in the mucous membranes of the nose and trigger signals which are transmitted directly to the olfactory bulb. In comparison, the data collected by touch have to negotiate dozens of synapses and chains of nerves before they reach the brain. Sight consists of mere images, projected on to a screen on the backs of our eyes. Hearing is mere vibration. Even taste, in comparison to smell, is relatively crude – little more than a way of distinguishing sweet, sour, salt. All the refinements of taste are due to our sense of smell. Smell is processed in the deepest, most emotional parts of the brain, the amygdala and the hypocampus, and it is smell, more than any other sense, which has the power to unlock memories. As I stand and sniff the white lilac in my garden now, I not only smell the lilac in that garden then but the flowering currant too, see the sunlight glancing through the leaves of the marrows, feel the crunch of raw rhubarb between my teeth, and recognise my tiny truculent four-year-old self.

Pa gave up the ministry ('Too many old people,' he said. 'I want to make a difference.') and went to work for the local Labour Party MP in the confident new dawn of the first Labour Government.

As the earth turns its face towards the sun, the colour of blossom warms from the chalk-white of blackthorn and damson to a hint of rose in the cherry trees across the Church Meadow. More stately than the myrobalan, more graceful than the damson, the wild cherry has the poise of a dancer on points, arms held aloft, fingers expressively drooping. It is the tallest of all the cherries, ancestor of the sweet garden cherries, its flowers pure white, its stems and sepals and emerging leaves just touched with blush-pink. Keep your Japanese cherries, with their big coarse leaves, their stubby shape and their 'improved' flowers, for city gardens. In the countryside only the wild white cherry (*Prunus avium*) will do. Slender, chaste, yet marvellously profligate, it is a native of the woodland edge and of woodlands throughout the British Isles, seeding itself around as well as suckering from the root, so that whole hillsides come into bloom at once. The blossom is short-lived, but while it lasts is astonishingly bountiful; and when it falls, it drifts down from the trees in a slow blizzard like warm snow. I take the train south to give a talk to one of the horticultural societies, and find myself travelling back in time through the cherries' flowering as it spreads from south to north, the tideline of blossom lapping against hills and down into valleys, from bud-break in Wolverhampton to one-third open, two-thirds open, fully open, beginning to fall, blizzard, fallen snow; and back, from

fully open, two-thirds open, one-third open, to bud-break again –
the countryside adrift with petals.

The cultivated double form (*P. avium* 'Plena') flowers slightly
later and lasts longer, but it is the wild cherry that is the subject of
Housman's most celebrated lyric:

> Loveliest of trees, the cherry now
> Is hung with bloom along the bough,
> And stands about the woodland ride
> Wearing white for Eastertide.

That 'hung' is just right: wreathed, draped, pendant, the flowers
and leaves droop from the branch like a bride's bouquet.

> Now, of my threescore years and ten,
> Twenty will not come again,
> And take from seventy springs a score,
> It only leaves me fifty more.

> And since to look at things in bloom
> Fifty springs are little room
> About the woodlands I will go
> To see the cherry hung with snow.
>
> *A Shropshire Lad*, II, 1887

Housman is right. Seize the day. The garden will be fine without
you. Now, after all the hard work of winter and early spring –
the pruning and muck-spreading and digging, the forking and
raking and sowing of seeds – now is the time to take breath, to
pause; to look and sniff and touch; to wander about and enjoy
the garden.

Sometimes I think we work too hard at our gardens. About four years into the making of the garden at Morville I was ill for the whole of the spring and summer. Neglected, the garden went its own way. Winter vegetables rocketed skyward and went to seed. Unweeded borders filled with seedlings and burgeoned into riotous growth. I wept to see it. But then the vegetables metamorphosed into flowers – leeks into glittering purple-and-silver globes hung with bees, endives into quilled sky-blue asters, salsify into huge shaggy mauve daisies. The self-sown seedlings revealed themselves as foxgloves, feverfew, poppies blown in from neighbours' gardens. The columbines crossed and seeded, producing a new generation of starry spurless double flowers like miniature dahlias. The blue love-in-a-mist grew horned seed heads and transferred itself from the Vegetable Garden to the company of the crimson roses in the Cloister Garden. Angelica seeded itself among the white roses, with its huge green leaves like umbrellas and hollow stems full of sweet sap. Bronze fennel strewed itself among pink roses and purple chives. The next year there were cardoons among the pinks; *Verbena bonariensis* among the seakale; huge grey woolly mulleins promising spires of yellow flowers among the purple artichokes; grey and plum-coloured poppies everywhere. The foxgloves positioned themselves at the front of borders where I never would have dared, the rose campions made silver mats of felted leaves under the dappled shade of the apples and pears in the tunnel. Colours were mingled with a breathtaking verve: golden buttercups among garnet-dark sweet williams (*Dianthus barbatus nigrescens*), purple foxgloves with last year's yellow scorzonera gone to seed. And as the garden grew, and the illness recurred, sometimes wiping out months and whole years at a stroke, this became the pattern of my gardening. Hardly anything was deadheaded. Little weeding was done,

except for the obvious suspects – bittercress, groundsel, shepherd's purse. And each spring I was lost in admiration: the plants
did it all by themselves. I had learned to stop worrying and trust
my garden.

It is St George's Day now, 23 April, and across the Church
Meadow the flag with its red cross on a white background flutters
from the flagpole on top of the church tower. Our national saint,
but an immigrant like so many of our best-beloved garden
flowers. His father was from Cappadocia in present-day Turkey
and his mother from Lydda (now Lod) in Israel, where he was
martyred for his Christian faith in AD 303. It's Shakespeare's
birthday too, our national poet. No actual record of his birth
exists but his baptism was recorded at Stratford on 26 April 1564,
an event which usually took place three days after the birth. (By a
neat piece of symmetry, he died at Stratford exactly fifty-two
years later to the day, on 23 April 1616.) But the real cause for
celebration is the arrival of the swallows, winging all the way from
Zambia in southern Africa to skim down the whole long length of
the Canal like a landing strip before banking right in a flash of
midnight-blue to avoid the overhanging branches of the big old
pear tree at the end, and off to check out last year's nests in the
trap shed. The first of the year!

> Merrily merrily shall I live now
> Under the blossom that hangs on the bough.

Summer cannot be far behind.

The old pear tree by the Canal is a survivor of the eighteenth-century enthusiasm for fruit-growing. But there was already an orchard here in the middle of the sixteenth century. When the King's commissioners came to value the property in 1545, five years after the dissolution of the Priory, they found 'houses, kitchen, pasture, barns, stables, buildings, etc. . . . one small garden, one orchard [and] four stews'. They valued it, together with the land immediately within the Priory precinct, at just ten shillings per annum. Of the 2,000 or so acres that had formed the endowment of the church at the time of Domesday, only 92¾ acres remained – 'arable, meadow, grass and pasture land' – which, plus the rent from two other houses (in one of which the Prior had been living) and the tithes of grain, hay and wool from the surrounding area, they valued at £29 10s 9d a year, giving a total of £30 9d. When they deducted the outgoings, there remained a net annual value of just £16 10s 10d and three farthings.

The Dissolution was a process that had been going on ever since the passing into law of the Act of Suppression in 1536. But the tide of history did not reach Morville until 1540. This was the last wave of ejections, when the bigger religious houses and those that were better run (against which no obvious charges could be brought) were finally bludgeoned or blackmailed into submission. Not that Morville Priory was grand or beyond reproach. Far from it. But being a dependency of the very much bigger Shrewsbury Abbey gave it a stay of execution until the fall of Shrewsbury itself in 1540.

The last Prior of Morville was Richard Marshall (also known as Richard Baker). He was appointed in 1529, having served the previous twenty-six years as Abbot of Shrewsbury. During his abbacy, debts at Shrewsbury had gone unpaid, accounts had not been kept and the buildings had been allowed to fall into a state of dilapidation; lands were being leased without the consent of the chapter, the infirmary was in ruins (the Subprior had been accused of carrying off the glass for the windows of his own chamber), and the room the monks slept in was without light and in poor repair. But perhaps Richard was weak rather than venal, ineffectual rather than self-serving. There is every indication that matters at Shrewsbury were handled no better under his successor. And so the King's Visitor came to Morville too, and the grand affairs of state were played out against the backdrop of hill and church just as they were in more august settings, and Prior Richard signed away four hundred years of history. Afterwards he went to live in Bridgnorth on a small pension, his parochial duties at Morville taken over by a curate. He died in Bridgnorth in early May 1558, and was buried at St Laurence's, just as the apple trees were breaking into blossom.

Pippins and pearmains, costards and codlins, leathercoats and russets; silver and white, rose-pink and carmine, pearly grey and apple green – the apple blossom of old England, now in flower once more in the gardens of Morville: 'Geneting' and 'Gillyflower', 'Calville' and 'Catshead', 'Quining' and 'Quarrenden', the branches clustered with flowers like posies carried by schoolchildren.

One small garden, one orchard and four stewponds: vegetables, fruit and fish. A good diet. The monks' fish ponds are still here – two of them, at least – behind the yard where we have our garden bonfires. But where were the orchard and garden, and where exactly the Priory buildings? I find myself becoming obsessed with this. I hunt through books and records, pore over maps, pester anyone who will listen. I find myself going over the same ground again and again. I clutch at straws, like the brief description of the Priory jotted down in notebooks by the antiquary John Leland sometime between 1536 and 1542: 'From Wenloke to Morfeld a village a 6. miles by sume corne, pasture and wood ground. I saw a little priory or cell caullyd Morfilde on the right hand as I enteryd into this village.' Leland had been commissioned in 1533 to scour the monastic libraries of Britain for 'forgotten monuments of ancient writers' in order that they might be brought 'out of deadly darkness to lively light' – a lofty Renaissance ideal in the context of 1533 but one which by the 1540s had become a policy of State appropriation, with manuscripts being removed wholesale to the Royal Library. Leland's real brief was to find monastic chronicles and ancient British histories with which to glorify the Tudor regime, demonstrating its ancient origin and bolstering Henry VIII's position as rightful King of England.

Leland was on the road for more than ten years in pursuit of his own antiquarian and topographical researches, as well as in search of books for the King. He wasn't the only one: other collectors were about the same business. They would have found no books at Morville, no library to detain them here, but there was a library at nearby Buildwas Abbey, and two books from it – William of Malmesbury's *De gestis regum anglorum* and Henry of Huntingdon's *Historia anglorum* – found their way into the hands of a rival collector, Matthew Parker, Archbishop of Canterbury. The books not earmarked for royal or archepiscopal libraries or scooped up by other collectors were simply abandoned to the holocaust unleashed at the Dissolution – pulled apart for their vellum pages, cut up, cannibalised as shoe-linings, used as stiffenings in later bookbindings. Medievalists now study the surviving fragments, trying to establish the texts, to identify the places where they were written, to reconstruct the lost libraries from which they were plundered.

Leland travelled compulsively, endlessly, restlessly – searching, noting, enquiring, writing it all down. He called it his 'laboriouse journey'. All other occupations of life were, he said, 'intermitted' to the cause of this one consuming passion. He planned to publish a great work that would make his name, 'Leland's *Britannia*', combining all his antiquarian and topographical researches into a single monumental volume. Ultimately he went mad. By 1550 he had been placed in the care of his brother, to whom the King granted Leland's three stipends to cover the cost of his maintenance. He died six years later in his mid-forties, his magnum opus unfinished, fragmentary.

I wonder what form Leland's madness took: mania or melancholia? Both, perhaps. I too feel that, like Leland, I shall go mad. Too many disconnected facts and too few answers. I have been writing this book too long. In one of my most manic phases I find myself invited to lead a retreat at the Benedictine Abbey of St Michael, at Belmont, near Hereford. The theme is 'The Hours of the Divine Office and the Hours of the Garden', the group a mixed bunch – mainly Catholics, but also several other 'fellow-travellers' like me. Attendance at the Hours is optional. The day begins with Vigils and Lauds at 6.30, then Mass at 8.00 and Midday Prayer at 12.45 (the 'Little Hours' of Prime, Terce, Sext and None compressed into a single office); then Vespers at 6.00 and Compline at 8.30. Gone is most of the Gregorian chant and the familiar Latin words of my childhood. But as the week wears on and I answer the summons of the bell to take my place in the Abbey each dawn, watching the colours of the east window move slowly down the vaulting and cross the stone floor as the sun rises higher, following the words of the prayers and psalms and readings through the day to the dying of the light in the tall west window at Compline, a kind of peace begins to descend.

One of the days of the retreat was devoted to an outing, and it had been suggested that the group might like to visit Morville and see the garden I had been talking about.

'We should look at the church too,' I said when we arrived. 'It was built by the Benedictines in the twelfth century.'

'Then we must certainly say a prayer,' said Father Brendan, leading us (to my consternation: surely we should ask permission?) into the church, where, standing in the aisle, solitary in his black habit, he led us in the 103rd Psalm:

> You stretch out the heavens like a tent.
> Above the rains you build your dwelling.
> You make the clouds your chariot,
> you walk on the wings of the wind.

When we came out of the church we found a dead swift lying on the path, its long back-swept wings – shaped like a discus, made for speed – pale with dust. The swifts arrive last of all our summer visitors, flying north over the Sahara from central Africa to arrive at Morville in late May. But they don't stay at Morville, unlike the swallows and house martins who return year after year to the same nests under the eaves or on the rafters of the outbuildings. The swifts are urbanites, boy-racers, party people; they cruise the sky above the Church Meadow, sieving the air for gnats with their wide-open mouths, but really they prefer the town, wheeling round the attics and the chimney pots of Bridgnorth in great shrieking mobs. Swifts are the natural acrobats of the aerial world. But once grounded they find it almost impossible to take off again. Their Latin name, *Apus*, comes from the Greek, meaning 'without feet'. In fact they have strong claws with which they cling to the vertical rocky surfaces of their preferred nesting sites, but it is true that their legs are small and weak, ill adapted for perching or walking. They eat, drink, sleep and mate in the air, returning to earth only to nest. Young birds may remain aloft for two or even three years at a time.

What must it be like to sleep on the wing, so trusting in the cushion of air to hold you up; so perfectly in your element that you are everywhere at home, with no fear of getting lost, no dread of arrival or pang of departure? Not like Leland, compulsively, obsessively, restlessly searching, but sublimely free, sipping from the rain clouds, dining on the plankton of the skies.

One of the group tenderly stooped to lift the dead bird out of the way. 'Oh! I think it's still alive,' she said. In the hope that it would still have enough strength left to fly, if only it could get aloft, we tossed it into the air. Silhouetted against the deep blue of the sky, the bird faltered, fluttered, fell and finally took wing.

After an absence of more than 460 years the Benedictines had come back to Morville.

In terms of the monastic day Terce is a pause, a break in the morning's work, just as May in the medieval agricultural cycle marked a pause after the heavy labour of spring ploughing and sowing, and before the summer harvest. In the calendars of the Books of Hours, this is the month for Courting and Making Mmusic, for Hawking and Riding, for wearing your best clothes and showing yourself off. Even today the month has more than its fair share of festivities, with a Bank Holiday at either end. And the gardener's calendar has surely also to make way for the secular feasts of Malvern and Chelsea, where the green-fingered worship at the shrine of horticulture. Holidays and regular rest periods are important for the health of mind and body, as the liturgy of Terce reminds us: *Concede nos famulos tuos, quaesumus, Domine Deus, perpetua mentis et corporis salute gaudere*, 'Grant us, we beseech thee, Lord God, continual health of mind and body.' Work and play. Mental and physical exercise. Proportion. Balance. I find that hard. I'm obsessive by nature. I boom and bust. Work my socks off, then collapse. To write in the mornings and garden in the afternoons is impossible for me: it's one or the other, all or nothing. Benedict divided the monks' day into equal periods of study, manual work and prayer: all things in moderation, he said. The message of the bells for me is: Stop. Think. Give thanks. *And do something different now*.

In the illustration for May in the Hours of the Fastolf Master an elegantly dressed man with a hawk on his wrist rides out on a white charger. In the *Très riches heures*, a whole company of riders threads its way through a forest, the horses gaily caparisoned, each rider dressed in gorgeous embroidered fabrics. I always associate Ivor with this holiday mood, whether Christmas or Maytime, first-footing or whenever England's winning at football or cricket. He appears out of nowhere, walking jauntily down the garden, his white ferret inside his coat, a handful of walnuts or a flower in his hand, an old knitted cap or a sparkly red-and-white Santa Claus hat on his head. His birthday is May Day, 1 May, that day of Jack o' the Greens and Green Men, the Celtic festival of Beltane. Ivor encapsulates the whole industrial history of Bridgnorth: he began work at sixteen on one of the farms between Morville and Bridgnorth; then, when farming shrank, he went to work in the carpet factory; then, when the carpet-making industry collapsed, into electronics, making televisions; then, when the electronics industry collapsed, into a period of pub work, odd jobs and unemployment. One long period of unemployment for Ivor coincided with the onset of my illness in 1994. So Ivor came to help. We were virtually the same age, though his was a childhood spent all in one place. He was born at Muckley Cross, a mile or so outside the village on the Shrewsbury road, one of ten children. The family moved into Morville itself when he was one. Ivor knew where the kingcups grew, and the oxlips. He showed me the buzzards and told me where the wren made her nest. 'I thought you two were supposed to be working,' said Arthur, walking past the end of the garden.

Eventually Ivor got a job at a small engineering works, the traditional staple of the West Midlands. He spends his days indoors now in the clangour of the guillotines and the arc and fizz of welding. But still it is Ivor who every weekend walks round the garden, stands and watches the bees, notices that X is out or Y is late this year, sits companionably in the steamy kitchen while the windows mist up with condensation – drinks a cup of coffee, smokes a cigarette, then 'I'll be off, then' – while I am mured up inside, enmeshed in things which matter less.

Today is 1 May. I get up early to greet the dawn and to take Ivor his birthday card. The sun is just over the horizon, glimmering through the black-and-white trunks of the damsons and silver birches at the top end of Arthur's garden. Behind its tall hedges my own garden is still silvery-damp with shadow. I cross the lawn from the house, leaving a trail of green footprints behind me in the dew. There are flowers everywhere: white daisies in the grass, blue periwinkles, drifts of bluebells, the ferny new foliage of lady's lace in the Wild Garden. I go up to the Iris Border to look at my new yellow tulips. Jack, the black cat, follows me, the shed scales of sticky buds from the horse-chestnut trees clinging to his coat. In the sunshine he is the colour of the 'Black Parrot' tulips in the Canal Garden, a rich auburn-black. There are more tulips in the Vegetable Garden, their stems green and straight above neat green mounds of feverfew and geranium. This is the tidiest my garden ever gets. Crimson and plum 'Couleur Cardinal', tall lily-flowered 'White Triumphator', darkest-of-the-dark 'Queen of Night', all standing to attention, bandbox smart. There is 'Arabian Mystery', deep violet with a pencilled white edge, 'Snow Parrot' and 'Shirley', stencilled with pink. There is orange 'General de Wet' in the Canal Garden and 'Ballerina' in the Side Garden, veined with crimson, giving off a faint sweet scent.

In the afternoon the garden is open for the annual village Flower & Garden Festival and the May Day Fête. The flower-arranging ladies have put the finishing touches to their creations in the church, the gardens are all mown and edged, the cakes baked and the maypole erected, the vintage car and the ponies polished to a gleam. There are families with pushchairs and old folk in wheelchairs, young couples in love and young couples who have fallen out of love, children in fancy dress and matrons who were Brownies when Miss Bythell was alive. In the middle of the afternoon the skies darken and everyone squashes into the white marquee where Joy and Sara and Hazel and Bridget are rushed off their feet to supply everyone with buttered malt loaf, halved scones piled with raspberry jam, egg-and-cress sandwiches, wedges of chocolate cake seamed with cream, and cups and cups and cups of tea, while the rain bounces off the gravestones and drums on the canvas. Then the sun comes out and everyone spills out into the churchyard once more, where there are stalls selling plants and home-made jam, booths for tombola and pitches for welly-wanging, and the jazz band starts up its playing again and the sodden wood of the lych gate steams in the heat.

May is also Mary's month. So many flowers are still named after her, even now, almost four hundred years after the Reformation. As children in Somerset we knew cow parsley as lady's lace, the harebell as lady's thimble, the mullein as lady's candle. The cuckoo flower (*Cardamine pratensis*) was lady's smock. Before the Reformation, we would have said Our Lady's candle, Our Lady's smock, and so on, but from the mid-sixteenth century such usage was discouraged and the names truncated. In Welsh many flower names survive with the suffix *Mair* (or *Fair* after a feminine noun), meaning 'Mary's': *Esgid Mair*, Mary's slipper, for monkshood; *Clustog Fair*, Mary's pillow, for sea thrift. Most of these names, English and Welsh, are only country names now, fast disappearing under pressure from standard English, in retreat from childhoods spent in front of computers and televisions rather than out in the fields. But as every gardener knows, *Alchemilla mollis* is still lady's mantle, and lady's bedstraw (*Galium verum*, said to be the straw on which Mary gave birth) is still the common name for that yellow-flowered, honey-smelling denizen of roadside places.

*

The bees are working the oilseed rape now. This is autumn-sown rape, flowering in May, four weeks earlier than if sown in the spring. When I open the hives, honey drips from fresh white comb. I take a super off the hive and replace it with an empty one. My clothes and gloves are sticky with honey. While the oilseed is in flower the bees can fill a super in less than seven days; thirty pounds, perhaps more, of honey. It's not an unmixed blessing: within a week or two the oilseed honey will have set hard enough to break your teeth. And the bees will travel three miles to get it, deserting the apples and the broad beans in flower in the garden, drawn by the overpowering smell. The garden is surrounded by it. There are brilliant yellow patches of oilseed all down the Corve Dale side of Wenlock Edge. In the early morning mist the patchwork of rectangular fields and sloping hedges shimmers like a skewed Mondrian painting.

I like it. I like that draught of pure colour, those acres of flowers, that dizzying smell of sex. For above all May is the month for lovers – for kissing is smelling, tasting, touching, all in one – and being tasted, smelled and touched.

In the Shepherd's Calendar a man and a maiden ride the same horse, she sitting side-saddle with her arm around him, he astride, the hawk on his wrist forgotten as he gazes into the eyes of his beloved. The Earl of Shrewsbury's prayer book shows a garden with two couples engrossed in one another: one woman perches on a man's knee with her arm around his neck; another man plays a lute while a second woman listens with her hand on his shoulder. Even the genteel company of the *Très riches heures* may be a betrothal party: the principal couple gaze into one another's eyes while musicians serenade them as they pass.

My mother fell in love with my father, she said, because he read poetry and went to concerts. The first time she saw him, she was walking down the street, arm in arm with Joe Moran, a returning hero of the International Brigade, with whom she was 'walking out'.

'I stole her from him,' said Pa, half proud, half shamefaced.

Pa was a millworker, twenty-three years old and already with the millworker's badge of a finger lopped by machinery. Every-one in those mill towns was missing a finger or two. When his was being sewn back on he had to choose between it being always straight or always bent; he chose to have it permanently bent so that he could still play the piano.

They used to sing together while he played 'Sheep may safely graze' or 'Jesu, joy of man's desiring'. He was born on the high moors above industrial Lancashire. His father had been killed in the Great War. At eleven he moved with his widowed mother and sister into the slums of Bolton. By the age of twelve he was working the early shift in a cotton mill, starting at 6 a.m., his schooling crammed into the sleep-deprived afternoons. His mother scrubbed pub floors for a living. By fourteen he was a 'little piecer', working barefoot ten hours a day in the din of the spinning mules, already practised in the art of lip-reading. At an age when others were graduating from university he graduated from 'little piecer' to 'side piecer'. He taught himself Greek, with his books propped up on the end of the mule, the whitewashed wall behind him covered in pencilled Greek words.

I went back to Belmont for Ascension Day, the fortieth day after Easter. The hymn at Mass is 'Love is come again like wheat that springeth green'. All week there has been no incense, no candles, only plain vestments. Now incense billows upwards, caught in the sunlight streaming through the open door of the Abbey church like the Lady's lace which lines the roadsides. There are clusters of tall white candles like the lit blooms of the chestnut trees, gold embroidery like the sleek pussy willows of Palm Sunday transformed into the lace and gold-wire of Ascension Day, their airborne seeds floating down like a benediction. 'God goes up in shouts of joy,' sings the cantor at Vespers. 'Alleluia, alleluia!'

All along the lanes the may blossom breaks over the hedgerows, long rolling waves peaking and cresting like the foam of Atlantic breakers. Myrobalan and sloe; damson, pear and plum; cherry and apple; now, last of all, the may. Its flowering used to coincide with May Day, its blossom carried in processions, woven into garlands, tied on top of the maypole. It blooms later now – since the reform of the calendar in 1752, more towards the middle of the month. And cold weather can delay it even further: 'Ne'er cast a clout til May be out' refers to the blossom, not the month. The blossoming of the may signals the shift from late spring to summer. This is hawthorn – the whitethorn as opposed to the blackthorn – universally planted as hedges by eighteenth- and nineteenth-century enclosers, and by twentieth-century road planners. It makes a dense, stock-proof barrier. The ease with which the hedging slips root gives hawthorn its country name of 'quick' or 'quickthorn', from the Anglo-Saxon *civice*, meaning alive or lively (as in the phrase 'the quick and the dead'). Its presence in the agricultural landscape is as old as agriculture itself. The Anglo-Saxons named the symbol for the 'th' sound in their language after it: 'thorn'.

The hawthorn has become domesticated. But for all that, there's still an edge in our relations with the may, a wariness among all the festivities. Its blossom is welcome, but never indoors, never used to decorate the church. To bring may into the house is unlucky; to cut a may tree down meant a death in the family. In the uplands of Britain – clinging to the sides of the Stiperstones and the Long Mynd, on Stapeley and Clee, as everywhere in the days before enclosures and bypasses – the may has a different persona, not as a hedge, but as single trees, stunted and wind-blown, scattered about the landscape: survivors, markers of ancient boundaries, faery trees.

Many old houses have a guardian tree at the north corner, usually a yew, to protect the house from harm as well as from cold winds. Here it is a big old hawthorn tree. North was always the unlucky side: the door of the church that was always kept locked; the side of the churchyard where no one wanted to be buried. The tree here is unusually tall for a hawthorn, in girth as big as two people holding hands with arms outstretched, its trunk knotted with tree ivy, home to half a hundred creatures. I can only guess at its age. It is as tall as the tallest chimney of the house. I look into its canopy from my bedroom window. It's a shape-shifter, a scene-stealer, a confuser of seasons: in December all midsummer-green and gold, its crown filled with billows of glistening ivy and swaying globes of mistletoe; in early spring, the first green buds so hardly there that they seem a trick of the light, a pale glaze like an enchantment, more a reflection of melting ice and lichened branches than green leaves; and in May, as spring opens into summer, I look out into tier upon tier of snowy blossom, a midwinter tree adorned for Christmas, its branches bowed down as if with weight of snow.

Whit Sunday, Pentecost: fifty days after Easter. There's no stop-ping it now: the tide of greenery is at the flood – a hundred shades of green, electric-bright or glassy-pale: parrot-green and verdi-gris-blue, pea-green and olive, sea-green and bronze. The grass is long and lush. My shirt sticks to my back as I mow. On Whit Monday we go out riding, the smell of leather and horse mingling with the heavy sweetness of the may blossom. The lilacs are out, thundery purple and white, bright crimson like spilled wine. There are red peonies in the grass of the Cloister Garden. At night the may-bugs hurl themselves at the lighted windows, their rough brown cases like the skins of raw unpeeled chestnuts, their clutching pincher feet . . .

In the interior of the church, the air is cool like the sea. It is nearly noon. As the flywheel spins in the dim, vertiginous void between vestry and bell chamber, the shadow of the church tower shrinks to an inky pool about its stone foundations. Slatted light filters through the wooden lattices in the narrow window embrasures of the tower, picking out the receding perspective of ladders above and below polished to mahogany by the passage of hands. The flywheel whirs to a stop, and the hawsers tighten across the great timbers of the bell-frame above, lifting the wooden hammer against the side of the tenor bell.

The clock strikes once more.

Sext

Just look at the rosebuds. Outside, each wrapped in a leafy calyx: five green sepals, lapped over one another, two outer, two inner, and one half-in half-out. Inside, the coloured ball of petals, unopened, unseen, as yet unexplored: the corolla. Together, the perianth. Some of the rosebuds have furry green calyces: the moss roses. Some have extravagantly ornamental calyces protruding beyond the tip of the bud like the heraldic mantling on a coat of arms: the damasks and the albas. Some are almost plain; smooth and round as a capsid bug: the gallicas. Every one plump and green and full of possibility, and quite new to me.

I'm all eyes. Mesmerised by the words, the new vocabulary; by the intricacy and variety of the buds themselves. An old riddle is running through my head:

> We are five brothers at one time born.
> Two of us have beards, by two no beards are worn
> While one, lest he should give his brothers pain,
> Has one side bearded and the other plain.

Carefully I peel a calyx apart. Five sepals: the outer two with leafy edges, the inner two plain, the fifth – its inner edge, tucked inside, as modestly plain as its two inner brethren – with an outer edge as triumphantly crocketed as half a miniature Gothic pinnacle or the velvet buds of a stag's horn.

The rose bushes are head-high now, and the back of the border is a secret place once more, damp and dim and tunnel-round, smelling of earth. Thick white roots of wood-sage dive beneath the leaf litter, pungent and pinkly brittle. Sunlight sifts through the canopy of rose leaves. Pale tendrils of clematis reach for the light. I stoop to gather the fallen leaves of giant cardoons, outgrown as the hollow stems rocket upwards, grey as aluminium, soft as felt. Out in the sun, iridescent flies, blue and green, bask. My fingers are sticky and aromatic from the calyces of the moss roses, bitter from the cardoons. The polished surfaces of the rose leaves wink in the sun. There's the sweet-sharp gooseberry smell of elderflower, crinkled bloom of medlars like crushed taffeta. The first wild roses trail in the long grass.

Don't blink. Beneath the wall the bearded irises are in bloom, the tall uppermost petals so gauzy, so delicate, that each bloom, once opened, lasts hardly longer than a day. Look, you can almost see through them. As fleeting as a rainbow, and with the same rain-washed colours, they were named after Iris, the messenger of the gods, who as a rainbow linked heaven and earth. It's the same derivation as the iris of the human eye, the coloured membrane which separates the inner from the outer chamber. Both have the same mysterious, shifting, shimmering quality, the colours depending on the viewpoint of the observer, one colour flecked by, veined with, shot through with another. These irises are pale blue, with a tracery of darker veins, their furled navy-blue buds rising out of translucent papery spathes, like new ballet shoes in tissue-paper wrapping. Later there will be rust-red ones and yellow ones, white ones and ones as dark as midnight. But these, the earliest, are the colour of summer skies, a clear pale blue, their shimmering standards like the crumpled wings of newly emerged dragonflies or the iridescent wings of the angel in Van Eyck's *Annunciation*.

The irises were given to me by the painter John Napper. They had formerly belonged to Chloe Gunn, the daughter of society portrait painter James Gunn. Now they were mine, a gift to the new garden. I spent a day digging them up at Steadvallets, the house John and his wife Pauline rented near Ludlow. I shared them out: some for me, some for Pru, some for David and Simon. I liked that – the feeling of passing them on, passing them down, from Chloe to John to me; from me to Pru, and David and Simon. Like a story, with different bits added here and there, elaborated or slimmed down, but essentially the same. These are old-fashioned varieties. They wouldn't be out of place in the border of a Book of Hours, along with the red roses and cornflowers and columbines, the pea flowers with their curling tendrils, the speedwells and carnations, the white flowers of the strawberries with their plump red fruit. Modern varieties of irises are bigger and brighter with stronger colour contrasts – plicatas and amoenas, bicolours and bitones – thick ruffled blooms which stand up to the weather. But now John had tired of his irises: he wanted blocks of brilliant colour – annuals he could change every year. He was always changing his garden. The beds were based on the abstract forms of Miró, sinuous, swirling. He used to plan it looking out from his studio window on the top floor.

It was John who first taught me how to see a flower, to really look. 'You have to see it from below, *against the light*. Do you see?' It was *Clematis* 'Huldine', growing near the house: an off-white, vigorous variety, useful because large and late-flowering.

But from above it was nothing. Against the light it was exquisite. Pale grey, with pale violet midribs dividing each tepal, and a frosted sheen like crisp sugar-icing. I planted it at Morville over an archway, where it could wander through a pale pink-and-white climbing rose.

And so I learned: about sepals and petals and tepals, calyces, corollas and perianths. But, more importantly, how to look. It takes time to look. And no one can be a gardener without really looking. And tepals? Petaloid sepals: a 'petal or sepal of a flower, where the calyx and corolla are not clearly distinguished'. Not everything is susceptible to precise analysis. We need to retain a sense of wonder.

Pass it on.

This is Sext, the hour when the sun is at its highest, the peak of the day, as June is the peak of the year. The message of the liturgy at Sext is one of joy: 'Then was our mouth filled with gladness and our tongue with joy . . .' Everything is perfect. The days are endless, the sky without a cloud. It's like the beginning of the school holidays and being a child again. *Magnificavit Dominus facere nobiscum* . . . 'The Lord has done great things for us, and we are made joyful.'

Every Trinity Sunday, in late May or early June, people congregate in the little church at Credenhill, near Hereford, to celebrate the life and work of the poet Thomas Traherne, the son of a Hereford shoemaker, who was Rector of Credenhill from 1657 until a year or so before his death in 1674. Traherne is one of the supreme poets of childhood, his work imbued with a sense of wonder and joy in God's creation. His poems are full of delight in the body with all its senses of touch, taste, hearing, smell and sight, especially sight, a recurring motif throughout his poetry. Here, in 'The Preparative', the infant has not yet begun to distinguish between itself and the world around it:

> Then was my soul my only all to me,
>   A living endless eye,
>   Just bounded by the sky,
> Whose power, whose act, whose essence was to see . . .

It is the infant eye with its freshness of vision that sees true. In 'Shadows in the Water' the child Traherne mistakes reflections in a puddle for other worlds beneath his feet, worlds he cannot reach although they are separated from him only by the seemingly insubstantial surface of the water – one of the 'sweet Mistakes' of 'unexperienc'd infancy', but which provokes in the adult Traherne the hope that perhaps

> Some unknown Joys there be
>   Laid up in store for me;
> To which I shall, when that thin Skin
>   Is broken, be admitted in.

One of Traherne's best-loved poems is 'The Salutation'. Here Traherne the child speaks of the magnificent gift of existence, of the wonder that he should have 'smiles or tears, / Or lips or hands or eyes or ears' at all:

> Strange all, and new to me.
> But that they mine should be, who nothing was,
> That strangest is of all, yet brought to pass.'

Strange too that Traherne's poetry should have survived. For two
centuries after his death he was known only as the author of
two minor theological prose works. Poets of his milieu wrote
poetry not for publication, but for private circulation among a
select coterie – in Traherne's case probably the religious community that centred around Susannah Hopton at nearby Kington,
under whose name his rapturous psalm-like 'Thanksgivings for
the Body' was published in 1699. Then in 1896 a volume containing thirty-seven poems in what proved to be Traherne's own
handwriting, together with another volume containing his acknowledged prose masterpiece, *Centuries of Meditations*, were
bought for a few pence on two London second-hand bookstalls.
Thereafter, fragments started turning up with increasing rapidity.
Shortly after the publication of the poems and *Centuries* (in 1903
and 1908 respectively), another manuscript with forty more
poems was identified in the Burney Collection in the British
Library (published as *Poems of Felicity* in 1910). Then the manuscript of a vast encyclopaedic work left incomplete at the time of
Traherne's death, entitled *Commentaries of Heaven*, designed to
show 'ALL THINGS . . . to be Objects of Happiness', was
rescued from a burning rubbish heap in Lancashire in 1967
and identified as Traherne's in 1982. Two further volumes were
discovered in 1997, one in America, the other by a Cambridge don
sheltering from the rain in Lambeth Palace Library: flicking
through a catalogue of unattributed works, he was intrigued
by the title 'Seeds of Eternity'; calling up the volume, he found
it to contain five additional unknown works by Traherne, including a remarkable extended prose passage in which the poet,
leaping the centuries to our own era of space travel, pictures a
'Celestial Stranger' to whom the Earth 'perhaps would be invisible . . . or seem but a needle's point, or a Sparkle of Light',

visiting the Earth and being amazed by its beauties, like the first astronauts on seeing our own fragile blue planet spinning in the depths of space for the first time – an image which, beamed back to Earth, changed everything for ever.

'Verily,' he says, 'this star is a nest of Angels!'

As the garden began to take shape, I started to keep a diary of the garden-making. At first just a record of things to do, things done, the rise and fall of the thermometer. But gradually it became something more. Writing for me became a way of seeing; the struggle to describe precisely became my way of paying attention. My husband gave me a camera – a Pentax with a zoom lens – and I used it to record the befores and afters, and to make a record of each of the plants. But the camera was no substitute for words. As a process it was too quick; as an image it was too limited. I like to take my time.

For one hectic summer I was employed at David Austin's rose nursery at Albrighton, near Wolverhampton, describing roses. Every day there would be a new list of which roses were coming into flower. A photographer and a retired perfumier were employed on the same project. ('Grapefruit?' the perfumier would ask, wafting a flower beneath my nose. 'Brown bread?') People came and went, the gardeners carried on with their work, the photographer snapped away, and every day I would stand, pencil poised – sometimes peering over dark glasses to deflect the white glare of my notepad, sometimes with the rain dripping from the brim of my hat – trying to capture in words the essence of each rose. What makes 'Alain Blanchard' different from 'Hippolyte'? 'Belle de Crécy' from 'Robert le Diable'? 'Duchesse de Montebello' from 'Duchesse d'Angoulême'? Trying to describe leaf, sepal, stem, thorn, habit, flower – single, semi-double, double; cupped, quartered, rosette, dome or globe; in truss or spray or cluster; in bud, in youth, in full flower, in age; from above and below; in the middle and at the edges; streaks and veins, tones and tints – rooted to the spot.

All the first roses I planted in the garden were white – but how many tints and subtleties are subsumed in that one word! – the paper white of 'Blanc Double de Coubert'; the ivory of 'Mme Legras de St Germain'; peachy 'Mme Alfred Carrière'; the carmine-streaked globes of Ayrshire 'Splendens', smelling of myrrh; the tumbling sprays of rosy-budded 'Félicité et Perpétue'; the brilliant red shoots and white cups of 'Adélaïde d'Orléans', brimful with yellow stamens; the hint of apricot in 'The Garland'; the apple-green freshness of 'Mme Hardy'; the heavy cream silk of 'Souvenir de la Malmaison', 'Sombreuil' like milky China tea. Then I made the Cloister Garden, and planted the old white albas and damasks: *Rosa* x *alba*, simplicity itself, pure as a dog rose; the lovely 'Alba Semiplena', taller than the type; 'Alba Maxima', the Jacobite Rose. I like white. Colour used to be as rare in my garden as it is on my person, but gradually colour is seeping in. Next came the blush roses – *Rosa* x *damascena* var. *versicolor*, dubbed 'York and Lancaster', with separate flowers of palest pink and white on the same bush; 'Great Maiden's Blush' and 'Blush Noisette'; the coconut ice of 'Félicité Parmentier'; the pale lilac of 'Narrow Water'; the soft pink of 'Céleste' and 'Fantin Latour'. Then the striped roses: carmine-and-white 'Rosa Mundi', paler 'Camaïeu', vivid 'Ferdinand Pichard', 'Variegata di Bologna' like blackcurrants and cream. It began with white roses, but now I have roses of every tint and shade from palest blush to darkest maroon: 'Black Jack', 'Emperor of Morocco', 'Black Prince'; slate-purples like 'Cardinal de Richelieu' and 'Nuits de Young';

intense dark red-purples with crimson and blue-purple lights –
'Russelliana', *R. gallica* 'Violacea', 'Robert le Diable', 'Belle de
Crécy', 'Hippolyte', 'Indigo'. Now chaste and chilly 'Comtesse
de Murinais' is wreathed in the prickly wine-stained embrace of
'William Lobb'; modest 'Blanchefleur' shrinks from roguish
dark-whiskered 'Capitaine Basroger'; the shamelessly Schiapar-
elli-pink 'Mme Isaac Pereire' flaunts herself beside muted and
matronly 'Honorine de Brabant'. In my garden there are now
purple roses, red roses, even yellow roses (though segregated in a
garden of their own). But not orange. I draw the line at orange.

'You can't see Venice twice for the first time,' Mirabel said. After
the first excitement of newness, will there always be the same
enchantment every year, watching the rose buds open, the irises
unfurl? It's the challenge that faces us all at some point, and which
faces me now, twenty years on from the beginning of the garden.
And it's true: you can change the colour of your tulips, you can
forswear roses in favour of dahlias, you can even move house and
make a new garden, but you can never leave yourself behind. For it
is the eye that becomes jaded – the mind, not its object. Even for
Traherne it was a struggle to retain that freshness of vision, to
protect it from the eroding sea of experience. As he constantly
reminded himself, 'I must become a child again.' But even if we
cannot see all anew each year, we can each time strive to see it
deeper, differently: the experience can be enriched, not impover-
ished. A rose at forty or at eighty means something different from a
rose at twenty; we naturally bring to it more associations, whether
personal or literary or historical, more 'back story'. And if we can't
see Venice twice for the first time, neither can we step into the same

river twice – the world is perpetually changing, renewing itself. See how different a single rose, a single petal can be, not only every year, but every day, and every hour of every day, as the world turns around it – in all weathers, in every season, bud and bloom, calyx and corolla. All we have to do is look.

I met Mirabel in 1989: Mirabel Osler, the writer and gardener, who had made a famously wild and romantic garden up in the Clee Hills and written about it in her wonderful first book, *A Gentle Plea for Chaos*. She had left the Clee after the death of her husband, and had just moved to a much smaller town garden in Ludlow, where there was no room for meadows of long grass or billows of wild roses, no tree house or stream. But as her garden shrank, so paradoxically it got larger, for Mirabel took to examining her flowers with a hand lens – peering deep into the purple-smudged heart of a cistus, the green eye of a rose, discovering there veins magnified to the size of the Zambezi, stamens as big as baobab trees. However small one's garden becomes, even shrinking at last to a flower on a bedside table, the whole of creation is there.

They lost the election, of course. The Labour MP for Taunton, Victor Collins, had been elected in 1945 due to the large numbers of evacuees there during the war. The war over, the evacuees drifted back to the cities and at the election of 1950 the country-side reverted to its old way of voting – leaving Pa, who had been Collins's election agent, out of a job. Eventually he found work as a clerk at a nearby army camp. Then he retrained as a probation officer, finding lodgings and a job three hundred miles away in the steel town of Scunthorpe, in the north of Lincolnshire. It was 1954. I was seven.

A frontier town, he called it: a weird architecture of slag heaps and cooling towers, a night sky scarred by the orange glow of blast furnaces, a population of everyone from nowhere, brittle, seething, the pubs overflowing with drink. She wept. But for us it was Paradise – our own private Amazon or Gobi Desert, our Himalayas or Hindustan. We were invincible. Traversing the high white slag heaps with their sides etched into deep grooves by run-off water and polished by our backsides and plimsolled feet into glassy slides that launched us yelling out into mid-air. Hurtling down the Z-bends of the Cut on roller skates, riding bicycles so big you couldn't sit on the seat. Browsing on earthnuts, the sweet knobbly tubers that grew beneath a special sort of yarrow; nibbling 'bread and cheese', the young leaves of the hawthorn; sucking the sweet sappy stems of flowering grasses pulled from their sockets.

The house at Bellingham Road was on the edge of the common – not an ancient place, but a scummy, scraggy, scrappy sort of place, a leftover strip of land between the council houses and the steelworks, populated by hedgehogs and rusty seeded docks and the Polish workers who lived in a hostel marooned in the middle of it. We were a tribe of two: dug dens in sandy soil and roofed them with bits of corrugated iron; made tentative alliances with other tribes; hunted the hedgehogs with our dog.

The steelworks ran twenty-four hours a day. A mushroom cloud of steam hung perpetually over the cooling towers. At night from the bedroom we could see the tipping – the sudden white-hot glare, muting to red, then orange. The windowsills would be black with smuts moments after they had been wiped clean.

She painted their bedroom apple-green, with one wall of apple-blossom wallpaper.

In the tunnel now, the apple trees are covered with thousands of tiny apples, no bigger than crabs. I have come with secateurs to thin them, so that the fruit will grow larger. But instead I am watching a dragonfly basking in the sun. Its transparent wings are fine as gossamer yet strong as steel, ribbed like a web of girders. I only see them on warm days: dragonflies are cold-blooded, grounded by cold weather; they need to absorb heat in order to fly. This places them back with the most primitive creatures on earth, millions of years old – back before the Ice Age, back before dinosaurs browsed, back when Shropshire was a tropical swamp and dragonflies with two-foot wingspans cruised the earth beneath colossal trees. Stealthily I creep closer to get a better look. It's a hawker dragonfly, with a long slim blue-banded body, storing up energy in the four wings it stretches out horizontal to the sun's rays. But it is far from asleep. From its perch it keeps watch for prey. Dragonflies are formidable hunters, quick and fierce. Their common names reflect that: hawkers, chasers, darters. Hawkers are the biggest, the most accomplished flyers; they roost in the trees at night and cruise the garden by daylight, in search of prey. Chasers are the ones with short muscular bodies. Darters are light and fast, returning with their prey again and again to the same perch. The damselflies are slimmer and slighter still, with narrower wings which they keep closed when they perch. Like hawks or sight hounds, dragonflies seek their prey almost entirely by sight. They have enormous compound eyes, making up almost a tenth of their body length, each eye with up to 30,000 facets, each facet producing its own image. The eyes meet on top of a dragonfly's head, giving it almost 360° vision. I have a sudden startling image of myself splintered into thousands of parts, blue shirt, white face, dark hair, multiplied sixty-thousand-fold in the darkness of the dragonfly's head, as in the control centre of some gigantic power station. Alarmed, half-queasy at the strangeness of it, I step back. And suddenly it's off in a whirr of wings, shimmering metallic blue-green as it skims over the rose bushes like the helmeted bikers who zoom past the end of the garden every summer weekend.

(It's a lovely road for biking, they say: long smooth curves, gently switchbacking up and down, the Clee on one side, Wenlock Edge on the other, all the way down Corve Dale. No traffic. I see them leaning into the Z-bends, sleek black and silver with a slick of red or blue, all steel and leather, part-man part-machine. I bought a motorbike too, but not for speed. I cruise the lanes and byways at hardly more than walking pace, sniffing the air, gazing over the hedgerows and into the fields, hardly disturbing the buzzard that flaps lazily away at my approach. My speed is 25–30 mph, max. The top speed, as it happens, of a dragonfly.)

In Scunthorpe my brother and I discovered a new hobby: collecting fossils. The soil was light and sandy. The town was expanding. Trenches appeared almost overnight for new drains, new electricity supplies, new roads. The cut sides of each new trench would be studded with fossils. On Saturday mornings we would scavenge the building sites for ammonites, the fossilised shells of mussels and oysters, caches of belemnites like spent bullets. In the garden where Pa grew shaggy white marguerites and Michaelmas daisies, 150 million years ago squid swam in the shallow coastal waters of the Tethys Ocean.

It was a new garden in a big L-shape in front of the house, and Pa set about filling it. But first he had to dig it. It was infested with horse-tail: *Equisetum*, a fearsome weed of agricultural land, with a ramifying root system that can penetrate thirty feet below the surface, throwing up plantlets from every node. We called it 'frogs' umbrellas', its leafless green jointed stems looking to us like the spokes of an umbrella blown inside out. Pa called it something else, less printable. Had we but known it, the frogs' umbrellas that Pa struggled to eradicate were even older than the fossils on which we lavished such care. In the Carboniferous era, when the coal seams that eventually brought the steelworks to Scunthorpe were being laid down, tree-sized horse-tails known as calamitids grew thirty feet tall. In the Jurassic era smaller species of horse-tails were the staple diet of herbivorous dinosaurs. One genus only survives, containing seven British species – twenty-five worldwide – including our frogs' umbrellas. They are un-related to any other living genus. (The very similar aquatic plant known as mare's tail, *Hippuris vulgaris*, is in fact no relation.) Ironically, given Pa's struggles, some *Equisetums* are now must-have plants for fashionable gardens.

It was in the garden at Scunthorpe that I first remember failing. I was 'First Year Girl Champion' at Ashby County Primary School Sports Day, 1954. Fast and fearless and top of the class. I had taken succeeding as a matter of course, so to fail came as quite a surprise. I was convinced that I could make silk out of the long silky seedheads of meadow grass – well, it was obvious you could, when you just *looked* at them – and had enlisted the help of a small schoolfriend with whom I laboured in vain all one Saturday morning, up to our arms in water, until she exclaimed in disgust, 'I thought you said you could *do* it!' I seem to have had an innate belief in the seventeenth-century Doctrine of Signatures: the idea that the appearances of plants gave a clue to their use. The spotted leaves of *Pulmonaria*, for example, were thought to resemble human lungs, and were therefore given as a remedy for pulmonary troubles (reflected also in its English name, lungwort).

I wonder if the grass I thought so silky was *Holcus lanatus* (meadow soft-grass) with its purple-pink plumes of flower heads. The word *holcus* is said to be from the Greek word for 'extraction', i.e. good for extracting thorns from the flesh. Useful for something then, even if I was wide of the mark in the detail. Its uses nowadays are more likely to lie in subtle landscaping effects than in first aid. I once saw it lit from underneath by lasers in a smart London pocket-handkerchief of a garden. Its other name is 'Yorkshire fog'. Less poetic than it sounds: 'fog' comes from the Old Norse meaning 'long, lank grass' – which is what happens to it at the other end of the season. I have enough of that in the Wild Garden here.

The principal image for June in the Books of Hours is Mowing – that is, haymaking (which is cutting grass) as distinct from reaping (which is harvesting grain): scythes (with long open blades) instead of sickles (with short, hooked ones). A line of men would work their way steadily across a field, beginning as soon as the dew had dried and working until noon. Then food and drink would be brought out to the field and the men would sleep for an hour through the hottest part of the day. Then they would begin work again and continue until dewfall. In the Hours of the Fastolf

Master a villager mows a meadow with a short straight-handled scythe. From his belt hangs a wooden strickle, which when dipped in grease and then sand would be used as a whetstone to sharpen the blade. A fresh supply of sand is probably contained in the bag which hangs from a nearby tree. The scythe has two handholds, the lower in the form of a projecting peg, the upper positioned across the top of the shaft in the form of a cross-piece, like the handle of a spade. The shape of scythes varied from locality to locality. The Fastolf Master, though he worked on occasion for English patrons, was French. The same pattern of scythe appears in the *Très riches heures*, and in the woodcuts of the Shepherds' Calendar, which also had their origins in France. English scythes of this period were longer and had two projecting pegs as handholds. Some Welsh scythes were straight, with a strap and only one handhold, designed to be used one-handed, with a crook in the other. Some Scottish scythes had a shaft or stale in the shape of a Y, one to be grasped by each hand. My neighbour Arthur gave me his father's old scythe, a typical English scythe of the Midlands, long and sinuous, with a sweeping S-curve and movable handholds which could be adjusted according to the worker's height. To 'set' it you stretched out your arm and held the tip of the blade in your left hand; the first peg should then touch the nape of your neck. I tried it, and it fitted: Arthur's father must have been no bigger than me.

Most people nowadays use a strimmer to cut long grass, and a petrol or electric mower for short grass. I bought a big petrol strimmer for the long grass of the Wild Garden and the Lammas Meadow. I learned how to balance its weight on the strap so that I could work all day with it, swinging it evenly from the hips, laying the grass in neat swathes. It was satisfying but noisy, and it smelled awful. Secretly I dreamed of the swish of the blade, the sun-warmed wood of the stale in my hands, the soft fall of the grass. But be practical, I said to myself. Besides, it's harder than it looks.

Mowing the lawn is purest summer drudgery to some, but I have always had a special fondness for my grass. At the beginning, I had too much of it: an acre and a half of grass with nothing in it except new hedges. Cutting the grass to different lengths was a way of reducing the amount I had to mow and making the task more interesting. I left some of it to grow long and mowed paths through it. I cut some of it once a month and made patterns in it. This was how the Turf Maze began. I tried other new garden layouts too by mowing them in grass first: the grid of beds in the Cloister Garden, the long rectangular shape of the Canal with its Dutch-gable ends, the sinuous lines of the New Flower Garden. After the black-and-white of pen and ink, my garden existed next in a green incarnation, sculpted in grass.

I like mowing. Up and down, backwards and forwards, each time a different slice of the garden, each time a slightly different view. Time to look. Time to consider. Would that penstemon look better over there? Would it be fun to cut a window in the hedge over here? And all the time that wonderful smell rising. And when it's finally finished and the shadows are lengthening, and you stand back to admire your handiwork, the swallows come skimming the smooth green surface of the newly-cut lawn like skaters on a vast green ice-rink.

I don't go in for 'lawn maintenance', though – all that weeding and feeding. I prefer my 'weeds': the clover, which keeps the grass naturally green with its nitrogen-fixing nodules; the daisy, opening and closing each day (its name comes from the Old English *daeges ēage*, meaning 'the day's eye'); the little blue-purple *Prunella*, known as 'self-heal', used to treat sore throats, mouth ulcers and open wounds – and still used in modern herbal medicine as an astringent for external or internal wounds. As Vita Sackville-West said, 'A weed is only a plant in the wrong place.' To which we should add: 'or one for which we haven't yet discovered the use'.

Grass is what we grow best in this country: foxtail, cat's tail, bent and brome; cock's foot, dog's tail, melick and fescue; quaking grass, oat grass, rye grass and barley; nearly 150 indigenous species, all told. The family of grasses is perhaps of all the plant races the most important to mankind, for it is from wildlings like these that our staple cereals are derived. Our mild climate and heavy rainfall favours grass. And British cows and sheep feed on the fat of the land. Miss Bythell's Guernsey herd won prizes in the 1960s and '70s. But in the days of skimmed milk and low-fat diets, when supermarkets started to sell milk for less than the cost of production, the rich creamy milk of Miss Bythell's cows was no longer wanted. In 2001 the herd was sold and the farm changed hands, the farmhouse sold off, the barns converted into dwellings and John, the farm manager, put out to grass.

In the long hot summer of 2006 John's successor, Mr Meredith, made hay in the Church Meadow, one man and a machine doing the work of a dozen men with scythes. First he cut the grass, dropping it neatly behind the tractor in long flat lines, then he returned a few days later to turn it. The sweet fragrance of mown hay wafted over the garden for days. That smell! – the smell of the sweet-scented vernal grass (*Anthoxanthum odoratum*), the first to bloom of all the meadow grasses – evocative of a thousand summer days, but now largely a thing of the past. Nowadays hay is much more likely to be cut for silage: cut, chopped and bagged in a single day. It doesn't lie in the fields at all, except in big black plastic bags. But this year Mr Meredith decided to make hay. A day or two afterwards, as the cut hay was lying in the field, a column of whirling grass and air suddenly rose up, hundreds of feet tall, moving at what seemed like walking pace down the windrow like some harvest demon stalking the field, come to exact his tythe. For a few terrifying moments it towered over the gardens. Then as suddenly as it had arrived it was gone – withdrawing up into the high blue sky, the stems of grass still whirling, but black now against the light, smaller and smaller, higher and higher, at first like a circling flock of crows – then swifts – then larks – then dots merely. I looked it up in a meteorology book: a phenomenon caused by intense heating of the soil, given a twist by the differential exposure to the sun of the rows of heaped grass and the stubble between. 'Whirlygigs, we called them,' said Ivor. He and his brothers used to chase them as children. 'We never caught one though.' Perhaps just as well.

Under the glare of the sun, I long for shade. Any new garden always lacks shade. Light and shade – what is the one without the other? I look longingly across the sun-bleached expanse of the Church Meadow at the church now bowered in trees within its picket fence. I think enviously of my friend David Bromley's garden high on the Ercall with the wind soughing in the tops of the tall trees around the house. When I began the garden I planted standard pears which will grow into fine large trees, standard plums and apples, sweet chestnuts and walnuts – but it isn't the same. So I took out the overgrown shrubbery of viburnum, variegated dogwood, Japanese maple, laburnum and forsythia that divided my garden from the house next door, and I planted a little spinney – too small for a wood, too wild for a grove, really hardly more than a thicket – of native British trees, with a top storey of pry (*Tilia cordata*, small-leaved lime), then field maple and wild service (*Sorbus torminalis*), then whitebeam and rowan beneath, and finally an under-storey of guelder rose, dog rose, spindle and eglantine (*Rosa rubiginosa*).

'Storey', our word for the different floors of a house, shares the same root as 'story', our word for a narrative. *Historia*, a sequence – of events, of details, of layers. History. Every piece of designed planting has its storeys, its layers of colour and texture and incident, just as every plant within it has a story. William Lobb was a Cornish plant hunter. The Duchesse d'Angoulême was the eldest child of the ill-fated Louis XVI and Marie Antoinette. The red and white roses entwined in medieval gardens symbolised Mary, mother of Christ, in her dual roles of virgin and mother – just as, centuries before, they had symbolised the qualities of innocence and experience in the goddess Venus.

The eglantine's name means 'prickly' or 'thorny', from the Latin *aculeus*, 'a little needle', by way of the Provençal *aiglentina*. Its other name, sweet-briar, comes from the sweet apple-like fragrance that rises from the leaves, especially after rain. In the sixteenth century the eglantine became a symbol of Queen Elizabeth I. Its leaves are small, crisp, bright green and glossy, and the whole plant thrives in the poorest of soils, flowering early in the year and producing a prodigious display of bright orange hips that lasts throughout the winter. So just as her grandfather Henry VII had adopted the device of the white rose superimposed upon the red (the Tudor rose) to symbolise the union through marriage of the two warring houses of York and Lancaster,

Elizabeth used the eglantine to convey her toughness and Englishness in the struggle against Spain – 'so green that the sun of
Spain at the hottest cannot parch it'. Its distinctive single pink
flowers with their white eye appear in many of her portraits; in
the British Museum's sumptuous Phoenix Jewel, eglantines and
Tudor roses twine together round Elizabeth's profile, enamelled
on gold, with a phoenix rising from the flames on the reverse.

At the Reformation the cult of the Blessed Virgin had been
suppressed, and the English people deprived of their special
devotion to Mary. Elizabeth's association with the rose and
her projection of herself as the Virgin Queen were both part
of a deliberate appropriation by Elizabeth of the external symbols
of the cult of the Blessed Virgin, an attempt to replace Mary,
mother of Christ, in her people's affections and to bind them to
her with an equal devotion. Gradually the whole garden came to
symbolise Elizabeth just as the *Hortus conclusus* had Mary, every
flower signifying one of her virtues and accomplishments: the
garden was England in microcosm, where poetry, music, the new
classical learning and the twin arts of horticulture and architecture
could flourish under the patronage of a new queen – no longer
Mary, the Queen of Heaven, but Elizabeth, the Virgin Queen.

Once Prior Richard had been ejected in 1540, the contents of the
Priory at Morville would have been confiscated or sold off, the
buildings stripped of everything saleable (timber, paving stones,
the tiles or lead of the roofs, even the stone of the walls, which the
King's men had a standing instruction to pull down to render
buildings uninhabitable), and what little remained would have
been pillaged by the local populace. By 1545, when the King's

commissioners came to value it, the property – 'houses, kitchen, pasture, barns, stables, buildings' – was all in a state of 'utter ruin'.

Such had been the volume of monastic property flooding on to the market in the 1540s that it had taken five years for a valuation to be given for Morville. But once the valuation had been given, the way was clear for the Priory to be sold. Events now proceeded with almost indecent haste. By the end of 1545 the Priory had been granted to Viscount Lisle, a man who had had his fingers in the monastic pie since as early as 1536. Weeks later, he sold it to Roger Smyth of Bridgnorth. Smyth was a self-made man, a burgess profoundly distrusted by his fellows, an energetic merchant with his eye on the main chance; that year he was one of the Bailiffs of Bridgnorth, the following year Member of Parliament for the town (an office he held again in 1552). In 1549 Smyth snapped up more church property, this time at Underton (the prebend of the Chapel of St Mary Magdalene in Bridgnorth, dissolved in 1548), granted to John Peryent and Thomas Reeve in December 1549 and sold to Smyth the following month. In 1557 he got his hands on a real plum: the Hospital of St James (a leper hospital on the eastern outskirts of Bridgnorth with an estate of 130 acres along the Severn as well as houses in Bridgnorth itself), granted initially to John Perrott and again immediately sold to Smyth. This was the straw that broke the camel's back as far as the town council was concerned: his fellow burgesses, having tried and failed in 1560 to wrest St James from him by legal means, in 1561 voted to ban him from the council as being 'not worthy to be burgess or Freeman of the Towne', citing the fact that he had 'prevented the Town of the Chaunterye of sainct Leonardes . . . that he hathe gotten into his hands the hospytall of sainct James . . . [and that] the said Smyth dothe occupy the Townes Land and holdeth the same with force'.

A man with enemies, then; a man on the make who took what he wanted and held on to it. A man without family: in terms of pedigree he could hardly muster a single generation. He remedied that by acquiring a coat of arms – 'Sable, a bend argent between six martlets argent' – and by marrying the daughter of an old landed family whose property adjoined his newly acquired acres at Morville: Frances Cressett, whose family had owned Upton Cressett Hall since the 1300s.

Then on 25 June 1562 Smyth mysteriously died, leaving under-age children and a hasty will dated the same day, shorn of all pieties and preamble, which left everything to Frances, appointing her one of the executors and her brother Henry one of the 'overseers' of the will, with a litany of witnesses which included her father, her uncle and her brother-in-law.

The Cressetts stood to gain massively by the will. They now effectively controlled through Frances all the property Smyth had amassed in the previous two decades. Within six months Frances had been married off again: a much better match this time, to John Hopton of Rockill, a member of a powerful old Shropshire family; both he and William, the eldest of the six children Frances was to bear him, went on to hold the office of Sheriff of Shropshire (in 1575 and 1591 respectively).

But Frances's story does not end there. By 1584 Hopton too was dead, and Frances had been married off again, this time into another even grander landed family, the Hordes, who had held the controlling interest in Bridgnorth politics for two hundred and fifty years, an unparelleled span of influence which was to last well into the nineteenth century.

Then the past caught up with her.

In 1584 a legal action was brought against her as executor of the will of Roger Smyth. The plaintiff was George Smyth, who had

been named in the will as Roger's son and appointed co-executor
with Frances. He seems to have been absent at the time of his
father's death, for when probate was granted on 5 February 1563
it had been to Frances alone (now the wife of John Hopton), with
Thomas Whitton (the other 'overseer' of the will, Henry Cressett
having died in 1562) swearing on oath that George had resigned as
executor. By the terms of the will Roger's daughters were to get
two hundred marks apiece when they married, and the boys
'fowre scoore poundes' each when the time came for them to be
apprenticed; 'my howse at Morefyeld . . . beinge the third parte
or there aboutes of all my hoole landes' went to Frances for her
lifetime 'towardes the preferment and bringinge up of my children', except for half of Roger's plate, which was bequeathed to
'my heyre'; all the rest – the other two-thirds, Underton and St
James, which the syntax indicates and the law might be expected
to dictate to go to George, his heir (together with the reversion of
the Morville property at France's death) – was left to Frances,
apparently this time absolutely. According to George, the will
was a travesty of his father's intentions. Had the Cressetts
tampered with the will in George's absence?

It seems likely that George was Roger's son by a previous
marriage (note the age gap: the other sons were very young, too
young to be apprenticed; the daughters were too young to be
married; George on the other hand was of sufficient age to be
named as executor of the will). Why else would the Cressetts take
such steps to disinherit him? But why then did he wait until 1584
to challenge the will? Perhaps because by then the major actors in
the plot were all dead – John Hopton, Frances's brothers Robert
and Henry, her father Richard – Frances herself being probably
no more than a pawn in their hands, a means of forging dynastic
allegiances with other, more powerful, families.

The will was produced in court, and after scrutiny by the judge was pronounced to be 'falsum, fictum et fabricatum'. George inherited all his father's property, including not only Morville itself but the Hospital of St James and the Underton property, which he went on to bequeath to his own descendants. As for Frances, she married one last time, this time, perhaps, for love: William Clench of Bridgnorth, formerly of Dublin, was the younger son of a family with scarcely more pedigree than Roger had had. Whatever else she was, she was a survivor.

Under Elizabeth the countryside was at peace, and her people prospered. They began to lavish money on trophy houses, parks and elaborate gardens. What sort of gardens would Frances Cressett have made in her time at Morville? The symbolism of the garden in Elizabeth's time might have changed, and its scale grown larger, but the ingredients would have been more or less the same as in the medieval *Hortus conclusus* – arbours, turf seats, trelliswork, roses, flower-studded grass – but with a new consciousness of the relationship between garden and house. For the first time too there might have been little pavilions, permanent garden buildings dotted here and there. Both were the legacy of Rome, part of the rediscovery of classical civilisation which we now call the Renaissance.

Much of Renaissance garden-making was modelled on the descriptions of Pliny the Younger's gardens contained in two of his letters. One striking feature of Pliny's garden was box 'cut into a thousand shapes or even letters, which sometimes spell out the name of the owner or that of the gardener'. Low clipped hedges depicting the coat of arms or badge of a garden's aristocratic owner first appeared in English gardens in Elizabeth's grandfather's reign. By her father's time these 'knots', as they were called, had become geometrical designs of great complexity – Cardinal Wolsey at Hampton Court had 'Knotts so enknotted, it cannot be exprest' – and, in accordance with the new idea of linking house and garden, they were now sited close to the house where their patterns could be appreciated from the windows above. The arrangement was usually in multiples of four, and this was a principle mirrored in the design of the garden at large, now based on a succession of squares divided into quarters by walks and *allées*, reflecting the architecture of the house and continuing its straight lines and proportions.

I went back to the Bodleian Library in Oxford to look at Elizabethan gardening manuals. The first surprise was that mid-sixteenth-century knots were made from sweet-smelling herbs and flowers such as lavender, hyssop, thyme, germander, thrift, 'gillyflowers' (in this context, pinks), marjoram, 'herb of grace' (rue), rosemary and sage. Grey-leaved *Santolina*, or lavender cotton, was still a novelty and only to be found in the gardens of the great. The dwarf form of box (*Buxus sempervirens* 'Suffruticosa') originated in Holland and did not begin to be used in England until the early seventeenth century – and even then it was deprecated as a constituent of knot gardens 'on account of its naughtie smell'.

So much for the planting. But what about the design? The Bodleian had a dozen copies of *The Gardeners Labyrinth* and another half dozen or so of *The Profitable Art of Gardening*, both by Thomas Hill. In essence this was a single text reworked and expanded, which appeared in various guises and many different editions over the period from 1563 to 1652. I called up all the copies and compared them. Inserted in many was a sheet of

suggested designs for knots and mazes which altered with each
succeeding edition. Sometimes the sheet was missing – as if
someone had taken it out into the garden to use as a guide in
laying out one of the designs and left it on the potting bench or
out in the rain. But those that remained showed the knot evolving
from a distinctive 'under-and-over' of interwoven hedges – the
typical Elizabethan 'closed' knot – into what became known at
the turn of the century as 'broken squares', in which the linear
design was carried by paths rather than hedges, dividing the area
up into innumerable little flower beds which were either hedged,
or edged with 'dead' materials such as tiles, shells or bones – the
Jacobean 'open' knot – then finally resolving itself into the blocky
arrangement of corner- and centrepieces characteristic of the
Caroline parterre.

The 'beautie and comelinesse' of the closed knot depended upon
the pattern of the hedges being visible: 'You must not plant
anything in it,' said the *Maison rustique*, another late-sixteenth-
century gardening manual translated from the French, 'or if you do
. . . you must see, that it be of a shorter stalke than that which
compasseth it about.' In contrast, '. . . the open knots are more
proper for Out-landish flowers.' This was Parkinson, writing in
1629. The late sixteenth and early seventeenth centuries had seen an
influx of 'Out-landish' (that is, foreign, mainly spring) flowers

which were to transform English gardens: new sorts of daffodil, fritillaries, hyacinths, 'Saffron-flowers' (colchicums and crocuses of all sorts), lilies (which would then have been understood to include crown imperials as well as martagons), 'Flower-de-luces' (irises), tulips, anemones and 'French cowslips, or Beares eares' (auriculas). These were the flowers you planted in your open knot, the point of which was that it was pierced with paths, so that you could wander through it and see these novel flowers at close quarters.

So I made a closed knot for Frances's garden. It is chaste and green but at the same time billowy and aromatic, soft and generous, not at all like the tidy parterres of clipped box which her descendants the Weavers would have preferred. Its beauty is in its interweaving pattern, which I look down on from my study window. The principal lines of the design are carried by wall germander (*Teucrium chamaedrys*, with its shining toothed dark green leaves), wild strawberries, thyme, marjoram, and purple and green sage. The spaces between are filled with rust-red crushed terracotta. I experimented with rue and *Santolina*, but the *Santolina* tended to perish in winter from the wet, and the fine blue-leaved form of rue turned out to be a nineteenth-century selection. All the way round the outside is a hedge of Pa's lavender, the grey-leaved 'Old English' sort (*Lavandula* x *intermedia*), with pots of 'stickadove' (the slightly more tender French lavender, *Lavandula stoechas*) and tubs of sweet-smelling myrtles. All summer the Knot Garden drowses away under the open windows of the house, softly green, wafting aromatic airs through the door which stands open all summer long, the cats sunning themselves against the panels of the raised woodwork, or sleeping in fragrant sheltered corners between the herbs, each curled within their own private compartment of the design. And then as a bonus – almost as an afterthought, when the rest of the garden is fading in late summer – the Knot Garden flowers in swells and washes of dusky pink germander and billows of violet-blue lavender. The lavender flowers almost at eye level so that the whole garden is seen through a swaying fragrant sea where bees swim like shoals of fish and butterflies dance like coloured sails. The tide of scent sweeps up to my study: the sweetness of Pa's lavender; the sharper, more medicinal smell of French lavender; the pungent lemony smell of germander; the warm aromatic smell of thyme.

In 1954 or 1955 my mother converted to Catholicism. During the time my parents were apart, she in Somerset, he in lodgings in Scunthorpe, she had been attending the local Anglican church. It was a new church, half-built. I remember the melancholy smell of wet plaster and its still-dusty concrete floor. Now in Scunthorpe she took me with her to Mass in the Catholic church, where the liturgy was in Latin and the sermon in Polish. I was sent to the Catholic school to be civilised by the Irish nuns. My best friend was Magda. I remember her mother, Mrs Wyslocki, beating her fist on a newspaper photograph of the faces of Khrushchev and Bulganin when they visited Britain. 'Butchers!' she shouted. 'Butchers!' It was April 1956. I was nine. I took my First Communion at the feast of Corpus Christi, wearing a borrowed dress made of heavy cream satin, trimmed with lace in a deep V from neck to waist, with more lace at wrist and ankle. We carried tall white lighted candles, wore wreaths of red and white flowers in our hair, with fluttering red ribbons down the back in honour of the day.

The nuns were fierce disciplinarians and fiercely academic. I learned to do drawn threadwork. I passed the eleven-plus.

*

And then, Houdini-like, they did it again. Having fallen out with his colleagues, Pa got a new job in the south of the county. My new school was Church of England, my new school badge blue and yellow, a pattern of trees and dappled sunlight. I started cycling to school, coming home each day for dinner and then cycling back again. On the way, there was a row of balsam poplars. Even now, that smell will instantly recall for me the crunch of bicycle tyres on gravel, the cold circularity of the handlebars with their rubber grips and three-speed, the straightness of the tree trunks slicing the sunlight into slabs of black and gold, the sound of their leaves in summer like pooling water, the heavy green-and-gold leatheriness of the leaf-muffled path in autumn. I started being late for school, my bicycle propped against a hedge, just looking. Looking at the buds of the first dog roses in summer, the way the hoar frost grew in winter, the way the beech trees' long scrolled pointed red-brown buds unfurled in spring.

Pa always used to plant trees. Wherever we lived, he always managed to leave a tree or two behind him. Ash, elm, oak, hornbeam – gradually the little front gardens would fill with trees. The next tenant almost invariably cut them all down. They were heroic, in their way, those gardens, a refusal to accept the confines of the everyday. They weren't sensible gardens, gardens grounded in the here and now: they were, I think, a dream of what a garden should be if only one had a little more room, a memory perhaps of the woods of Rivington, of the high moors and their steep-sided valleys overhung with trees, a lost Eden forfeited when he moved with his family into the slums of Bolton. On Saturdays Pa worked in Lincoln, twenty-odd miles away, following the raised causeway of Ermine Street, the Roman road which runs along the high scarp of the Lincoln Edge, the rich black soil of the fens lapping like an inland sea at its foot; and all the way he would sing or whistle – hymns from the *Ancient and Modern*, scout songs, the lilting love songs of John McCormack, 'The Star of the County Down' and 'She Moved through the Fair', bits of Handel and Bach. For my brother and me, Pa's trips to Lincoln were an excuse for an outing – showing visitors around castle or cathedral ('See the Lincoln Imp up there? There!'), handsomely tipped with silver sixpences quickly spent in the second-hand bookshops of Steep Hill; scrambling up the towers of village churches (which never seemed then to be locked) on the way back; and often Pa would dig a promising-looking sapling out of a hedgerow and take it home.

I remember the tree he planted outside my bedroom window when I was eleven, a tall and shapely young ash, dug from a hedgerow somewhere. Our black cat used to shin up its slender stem at dawn each morning to demand his breakfast from the level of my bedroom windowsill, the whippy top of the tree bending under his weight.

I took Pa back to Ford the summer before he died. We found the cottage where he and my mother had spent their summer idyll sixty years before. The cottage had been smartened up and added to, the corner where the photograph had been taken obscured now by a huge leylandii. But in the field beyond was an ancient blasted oak after which the lane was named – Kittyoak Lane. The cottage was almost unrecognisable, but 'Oh! I remember that tree!' Pa cried.

Stand still, and look at your shadow. The sun has yet to reach its zenith, which (as a result of bureaucratic tinkering) it will not do until one o'clock British Summer Time. But already your shadow is nearly six feet shorter than when you first entered the garden. It is 21 June, the longest day of the year, the day when the sun stands still. It is the summer solstice (from the Latin *sol*, 'sun', + *sistere*, 'to stand still'), when the sun reaches the most northerly point of the ecliptic, the imaginary line it describes in its apparent orbit around the earth. And just as a ball, thrown high up into the air, appears to hesitate for a moment and hang motionless at the limit of its trajectory before falling back to earth, so the golden ball of the sun appears to stand still over the Tropic of Cancer before 'turning' (hence the word 'tropic', from the Greek *tropos*, 'a turn') back towards the Equator.

The garden lies flattened by the heat and the light. Purple roses slowly bleach to cerise. The texture of leaf and petal, the articulation of surfaces, the linking of one space to another by the long shadows of early morning thrown across grass paths – all gone, evaporated with the dew. Not a breath of wind: no movement anywhere except the trembling of a white rose disturbed by the visitation of a bee. No sound but the buzzing of flies and the distant tapping of a thrush breaking a snail shell on a stone. Even the scents of the garden seem flattened by the heat, losing their high notes of citrus or spice, melding in a heavy bland sweetness. I am making a sundial. Struck dumb and blind by the heat and the light, only my hearing is alert. I am waiting for the clock to strike. In the centre of the maze is a straight-boled young elm which casts a shadow like a gnomon on the dial-face of the maze. It is a disease-resistant hybrid, *Ulmus* 'Regal', given by a friend when I began the garden in 1989. At noon Greenwich Mean Time the shadow of the tree will indicate true north – which differs from compass or magnetic north by several degrees. From this I can plot all the hours of the day.

But I have a dilemma: not only whether to abide by British Summer Time (BST) or Greenwich Mean Time (GMT), but whether to abide by either. Noon at Morville is ten minutes after noon at Greenwich. (The sun is overhead four minutes later for every degree west of the Greenwich meridian.) I like that. I like the idea of local time, a pool of time with the church tower at its centre, separate, remote from the outside world, ours. Church clocks used to be set from sundials, not vice versa. It was the coming of the railways which forced the issue of standardised time.

GMT is not even true for Greenwich. It is true that, in the summer months, the days are on average twenty-four hours long, but in September they last for twenty-three hours and forty seconds, and at Christmas for twenty-four hours and twenty seconds. Cumulatively the discrepancies build up until by mid-February sun-time is more than fourteen minutes slow in relation to clock-time, and in November just over sixteen minutes fast. This is because the apparent orbit of the sun is an ellipse, not a circle, and the plane of the orbit is inclined with respect to the Equator. GMT is based on a fictional sun travelling at a constant speed in an imaginary orbit above the Equator.

Now the railways are in retreat, and we have global time and atomic clocks. But time continues to elude us: even modern atomic clocks are out of step with solar time; without a 'leap second', in three thousand years the sun will be overhead at midnight instead of noon.

This is not a garden for the faint-hearted: here it's every man for himself. As the garden surges towards midsummer, delicate souls can be trampled in the rush – today the *Veronica* ssp. *incana* suffocated by the smothering embrace of *Galega officinalis*, the

Thalictrum delavayi 'Hewitt's Double' shouldered aside by the wiry stems of *Achillea ptarmica* 'The Pearl'; tomorrow (if I don't look sharp) my precious old violas, patterning the cool shady bed near the house with pools of blue and purple and amethyst, strangled by the too-rampant *Hedera* hibernica. And yet I would rather have my mountain of *Galega*, with its glaucous pea-like foliage and erect heads of pale lilac or white pea flowers like upside-down wisteria (one old name for it is 'French lilac'; another – less complimentary – is 'goat's rue') than that stingy little *Veronica* (pretty as it was), which never looked happy. I like plants that live life to the full. I admire their generosity and their exuberance. I also like a certain degree of self-help. If the *Veronica* was unhappy, it should have moved (it's no good relying on me). A plant that suits me better is *Verbena bonariensis*. Reputed to be not totally hardy – though here it has survived −10°C – it energetically self-seeds out of the unsuitable places where I put it and into various more congenial spots. One year it seeded itself into the asparagus bed, where its tall stems of tiny rose-lavender florets flowered at the same height as the asparagus – and with a low sun behind and the cloud of asparagus fern beaded with dew, who could claim that this was not the better place? Another year it moved to the head of the Canal, making a hazy purple screen between one part of the garden and the next. I like my *Achillea ptarmica* too – though many people would think it too invasive – with its sprays of small shining white double buttons and dark green matt foliage without a hint of yellow. It is a double form of our native sneezewort, but beware the seeds offered in seedsmen's catalogues, for seed-raised plants are almost invariably not fully double, and have a 'dirty eye' in the middle. The true pure-white double (I realise now) can only be raised from cuttings – too late for me, who finds this rude and robust imposter is already well

established everywhere. But I forgive him his subterfuge: together
with the white rose campion (*Lychnis coronaria* 'Alba') with its
mat of grey felted leaves, and the double and single feverfew
(*Tanacetum parthenium*), which came, like the foxgloves, as
uninvited guests and stayed to become old friends, they make
a foam of midsummer white.

In the Books of Hours the alternative occupation for the month of
June is Sheep-Shearing. Alike in both the Duc de Berry's *Très
riches heures*, portrayed in exquisite colour, and the plain black-
and-white woodcuts of the Shepherds' Calendar, groups of
villagers, men and women, sit on the ground, each with a sheep
on its back in his or her lap, shearing the fleece with an instantly
recognisable tool: the same one-handed shears that the Romans
used to clip their box. This time there seem to be no regional
differences: the one-handed shears are universal, appearing in all
the representations of shearing. They still use the same ones for
shearing the wild sheep of North Ronaldsay, the furthest-flung
island of Orkney. One summer I helped. The problem there: first
catch your sheep.

John Lane in retirement started keeping sheep in place of the
Guernseys: cross-breeds and big bone-headed Suffolks with long
lugubrious faces and lop ears, all mild as milk – except for the old
French tup who sent John sprawling more than once. In June, one

of the local farmers arrives to help with the shearing. He hooks up to a portable generator and makes short work of the shearing with his electric shears, the heavy fleeces coming away all in one piece, greasy with lanolin, still hot and pungent from the animals' bodies, before releasing the sheep again, dazed and relieved, suddenly all hip bones and elbows, like grizzled GIs astounded to learn peace has been declared.

Nowadays the sheep are shorn mainly for their own comfort and for hygiene. Each fleece fetches only 60p or so, hardly enough to pay for the shearing. But the medieval English economy – and the medieval English Church – was founded on sheeps' fleeces. Wool was our principal export, and the glorious parish churches of medieval England were built on the proceeds. Later, wool was replaced by cotton (and later still by man-made fibres), but sheep still had another contribution to make to the Englishness of the English landscape: the smooth swards of the eighteenth-century English landscape garden, which owed their finesse not to scythes but to sheep – nature's lawnmowers.

The image of sheep grazing has been associated ever since classical times with a golden age of peace and plenty, before wars and civil strife divided the people and urban civilisation corrupted them. It was a theme explored in the pastoral poetry of the ancient Greek writer Theocritus, whose *Idylls* Virgil imitated in his *Eclogues* in the first century AD. The same theme persists through medieval literature (the calendar illustrations of the Books of Hours are one form of pastoral) and into the Renaissance, where it culminates in the cult of Elizabeth I. In the late sixteenth century there was a great flowering of poems in the pastoral mode celebrating Elizabeth as 'the Shepherds' Queen'. Her accession was seen as the beginning of a new golden age, her England as a new Arcadia; her coming was seen as the end of winter, her reign one of perpetual summer. She was the 'Summer Queen', her motto *Semper eadem* – 'Always the same'.

Although pastoral was sometimes cast in the form of political panegyric – (Virgil's *Eclogues* praised the Emperor Augustus, just as Spenser's *Shepheardes Calender* was intended to flatter Elizabeth) – pastoral is essentially nostalgic and melancholic, containing an implicit contrast between the real present state of things and things as one would like them to be or as they once were. The word 'nostalgia' was coined at the end of the eighteenth century from the joining together of two Greek words meaning 'homesickness'. In terms of modern pastoral, this can be not only the longing for a lost time or lost innocence, but also for something which can never be found. Housman's *A Shropshire Lad*, with its cast of doomed soldiers, hopeless lovers, exiles and convicted criminals, is pastoral in that sense. Housman hardly knew Shropshire at all. For him it glimmered on the horizon, as it had done for me. He was born in Bromsgrove, near Birmingham, and those 'blue remembered hills' were less the real landscape of Shropshire than the landscape of the heart, the land of lost opportunities.

John Napper's late paintings are watercolours: large – sometimes very large – pictures with no shading, just flat unmodelled colour, with depth suggested by tone and a careful layering of elements which the eye interprets as perspective. There are still lifes, interiors, landscapes with figures. All are bathed in a calm and even light – a light that he once said had taken him seventy-two years to re-find. All his life, he said, he had struggled with oil paint. Now, towards the end of that life, he turned to watercolour, and to a light which he associated with the confidence and innocence of childhood. It was his resolution of the problem posed by pastoral, the achievement of a harmony between the light inside and the light outside (both literally and metaphorically), a harmony he said we must all find between ourselves and the outside world. Many of the scenes in his watercolours are played out with the distinctive profile of the Titterstone Clee (the view seen from the window of his water-colour studio) as the backdrop. He called one exhibition *37 Views of the Clee Hill* – 'One more than Hokusai!' he said. He and Pauline had spent most of their married life abroad, in London, Paris, the Far East, New York. In 1971 they settled in deepest Shropshire. Now it was as if the paintings were saying – after a lifetime of travelling – why would one need to go further? Everything I need is here.

John's final painting was one last view of the Clee. It was on his easel when he died: a wide landscape with sheep, facing east – to where the sun rose, and where the moon rose – not this time looking up towards the Titterstone Clee, but out from the Clee itself, a high viewpoint, high above a house which may or may not be Steadvallets, the valley below bathed in an ethereal light: neither sunrise nor moonrise but the light of eternity.

It is Midsummer Night. The garden holds its breath. 23 June, the eve of St John. Like Christmas Day and Lady Day and Michaelmas Day, St John's Day is one of the Quarter Days, the four principal Christian festivals appointed to coincide with the four cardinal points of the sun – winter solstice, spring equinox, summer solstice, autumn equinox. But like Christmas Eve, New Year's Eve, Hallowe'en (All Hallows' Eve, the eve of All Saints' Day), it is the eve, the vigil before the day, which is the most powerful, the magical time, when the hinge of the year stands open a crack, and the everyday world becomes permeable. It is the night of *A Midsummer Night's Dream*, when the lovers enter the forest and everything is changed. The night when maids cast spells to see the face of their future beloved. The night of the midsummer bonfires, protective purifying fires into which magical plants were thrown – St John's wort (*Hypericum perforatum*), mugwort (*Artemisia vulgaris*, known in Welsh as *Ilysiau Ieuan*, St John's plant), corn marigold, yarrow, vervain (*Verbena officinalis*). The night is never properly dark, the whole long expanse of the big field high now with wheat, suffused with pale starlight. Stand still: can you hear them? The badgers, leaving their sets, those meandering mazes of passages, galleries and chambers inhabited by generation upon generation of badgers, hundreds – even thousands – of years old, the badgers crossing the valley, rustling through the wheat.

Then, as the tanks rolled into Prague, there was a quarrel between my husband-to-be and my father. I hardly saw my father again for the next thirty years.

None

I hang like a water beetle in the meniscus of time. Pond skaters abseil down into the depths, each clutching a silvery bubble of air. Black diving beetles buzz and bump their way along the walls like wind-up clockwork toys. The stonework beneath the water is freckled with snails; on the bottom, curls of algae sway like submerged thoughts. I float between past and future. The dragonflies are mating, their bodies linked like brilliant red Allen keys. I feel the concussion of their wings as they pass.

None, the ninth hour – to rhyme with alone, stone, bone, hone. 3 p.m. Heat. Drought. Soil baked to pale terracotta. The garden is sliding from juvenility to senescence without the intervening stage of maturity. We teeter daily on the brink of disaster, the garden and I – horticulturally, aesthetically, financially, physically, emotionally.

The July/August gap yawns. I have too many bulbs, too many roses and nothing to follow. Where is my herbaceous border, my backbone of shrubs? There are too many white roses. They do not die well. In hot weather they brown on the bushes and refuse to drop. In wet weather they brown on the bushes and refuse to open. My sweet disorder of self-seeded plants is disintegrating into chaos. Blue and white self-seeded

campanulas totter. Hollow-stemmed *Galega*, all knees and elbows, capsizes over the path. The white ox-eye daisies, for a few
weeks a wonderful swaying sea of white, have collapsed into an
untidy straggle.

'It's Liberty Hall here,' I say to visitors. 'I'm only the referee.'
But wild scarlet poppies have appeared among the pinks and
crimsons of the Cloister Garden. Do I show them the yellow
card? What about the tall yellow mulleins and the waving
yellow froth of *Thalictrum flavum* ssp. *glaucum*, self-seeded, like
English mimosa, among the pink and white of the rose tunnel? I
like their foliage, grey and blue-green. Do I dare to let them flower?

I'm losing my nerve. Among the July saints is Doubting
Thomas – St Thomas the Apostle, whose feast day is now 6 July
(21 December in the Books of Hours and the Book of Common
Prayer). Poor Thomas, known only for his refusal to believe
unless he put his finger into the nail holes in Christ's hands, his
hand into the wound in Christ's side. He also appears in an earlier
episode in the Gospel of John where, upon learning that Christ
will soon be leaving the Apostles, he plaintively asks, 'We know
not whither thou goest, how know we the way?' But eventually
he found his way, to India and martyrdom, at Mylapore.

It's all going to end in tears.

The heavy, druggy scent of lilies fills the garden. The *Lilium
regale* in the borders of the Vegetable Garden, their white petals
glistening against rose-purple backs, their wide-open mouths and
lolling golden stamens an invitation to inhale. Then the white
Lilium longiflorum in their big terracotta pots, long fluted trumpets washed with green. Then the big white Oriental hybrids like
'Casa Blanca'. All white. I crave their dewy freshness like the
garden craves rain. The grass is crisp underfoot, dried to a crackle
brown, everywhere the whisper of drying seed heads swaying in a

hot wind. On the cliff face of the Hall, house martins line the moulding beneath the cornice like guillemots on a rock face, the air full of the wheeling of their wings and the twittering of their cries; swallows plunge in pairs, kissing and breaking apart within inches of the ground, banking suddenly with a flash of white. The pale margins of the variegated hollies in the Canal Garden scorch in the sun. In the New Flower Garden the cockspur thorn closes its leathery leaves to conserve water; the big heart-shaped leaves of the lilacs droop. Footings of vanished buildings and walls press themselves against the surface of the lawn like old ghosts.

15 July is the feast day of St Swithun, Bishop of Winchester and adviser of Egbert, King of Wessex. At his death in AD 862, despite his rank, Swithun asked to be buried humbly, outside the cathedral, 'where passers by might tread on his grave and where rain from the eaves might fall on it'. But in 971 his devotees decided to move his body to a great shrine which they had built for him inside. That day rain began to fall, and it fell continuously, day after day, for forty days and nights. The rain was interpreted as a sign of the saint's displeasure. He is still remembered today in the superstition that rain on St Swithun's Day means rain for forty days thereafter. But what I want to know is, does it work the other way around? We had no rain today, have had none since May. Does that mean another forty days of drought?

I water each night. Water left in the hose from the night before is as warm as dirty washing-up water. The pots near the house, the oranges in their tubs, wigwams of sweet peas, pots of white hydrangeas, lilies, agapanthus, further and further out into the garden, dragging the hose behind me. Then further out still, beyond the reach of the hose, filling cans from the tap under the wall at the far end of the garden, the water thundering into the cans, catching the light of the street lamp on the road beyond, backwards and forwards: new roses, a newly planted cherry, transplanted leeks dibbed in reed-thin in their puddled holes. Tall skeletons of cow parsley catch in my hair.

I retreat to the north bedroom in search of coolness. Whole days are lost: anything not done by nine in the morning has to wait until dusk; in the heat of the day the only tenable place to be is inside the house. I work on the computer, writing descriptions of roses. Outside, the temperature ratchets relentlessly up throughout the afternoon. Thunder rumbles round the bowl of hills. Rain falls – but not here.

At Mr Austin's the rose garden is deserted. The thunder rolls around the horizon like wooden balls on the floor of a bowling alley. The land is very flat, the rose fields stretching out on either side. It's still only mid-afternoon but already the light has the lurid quality of sunset. A crack of lightning, the wind rising, and I look up from the bushes where I am tagging and labelling roses. I can see the edge of the storm all around me, a black rim of cloud clamped low over the multicoloured rose fields like a lid. Directly above me is the great churning heart of the storm, a nuclear reactor towering hundreds of feet up into the air, hollow, the up-draught sucking in the hot humid air under the skirt of the cloud, feeding the storm in an accelerating chain reaction. A flicker of nervousness convulses my stomach. The wind speed picks up, making it difficult to stand. Lightning jags up from the ground to meet the cloud. I'm alone in the field, the flat land all around. I make a run for the car park and then stand again, transfixed, looking up. The rain when it comes makes me dive for the car, gasping. Within minutes the roads are flooded with red soil-laden run-off, water running off the fields, wasted, pouring across the tarmac and down the drains. I start to drive, slowly, the car shearing through water as if through a sea. In fifteen minutes I'm out of the storm. The garden when I get back is dry as a bone.

'You'll swing for that temper,' Ada said.

Ada: my grandmother Critchley, ruined beauty.

Time: the night I was born.

There are no photographs of the wedding. My grandmother, my mother's mother, had been against the marriage from the start. Now, on the night of my birth in the big cold bedroom in Accrington, my grandmother and my father had one final row, facing one another across the bed where my mother lay. 'You'll swing for that temper,' Ada said.

My mother turned her face to the wall.

I was a mistake, she said, too soon, too much, conceived scarcely six months after my longed-for brother's birth. Nowadays she could have – perhaps would have – had a termination: legal, neat, tidy. Nowadays too there would have been drugs to cope with the depression. She was given electric-shock therapy instead. She lost her memory; a common side-effect. When shown a photograph of my brother and me, 'Who are they?' she said. She was told she must never have another child.

While my mother was in hospital I was sent away to be looked after by my grandmother, a pattern that was to recur throughout my childhood. Once my mother begged her mother to be allowed to come too, to come home. Her mother refused. 'You have made your bed and you must lie in it,' my grandmother said.

As she had. Ada: she was devastatingly beautiful. Her vitality crackles like electricity in the few photographs I have of her. My mother used to cut herself out of any in which they appeared together. The only one to survive is the one taken eight months after my birth, in which my mother holds me and my grandmother stands by her side, holding my plump and shining brother and wearing the grimly satisfied smile of one who has been proved right.

She and her sister had been court milliners in the West End of London. An earlier photograph, around 1912: a big family wedding, she and her sister bedecked with ostrich plumes. Another photograph, 1916 or so: Ada at the Woolwich Arsenal, among the other female workers in their mob caps and shapeless overalls, like a jay among wood pigeons. 1917: no photograph, but a child conceived out of wedlock, a reluctant husband who drank and gambled his wages away on a Friday night unless pursued from pub to pub, the child left sitting on the pub doorstep in her nightgown while her mother went in to extract the house-keeping before it was all spent. There were no more children, and the child she had never kissed once in its entire life: my mother.

The bees are running short of flowers. In July, the nectar flow starts to dry up, and they have to make do with the purple heads of thistles and knapweed, still green among the bleached grass stems. The thistles' long taproots go down, searching out hidden water. The meadow-sweet is flowering in the damp ditches now too, its creamy corymbs heavy with sickly-sweet scent, its crushed leaves giving off a tang of carbolic. One of its country names is 'courtship and matrimony', from the sweetness of the flowers and the bitterness of the leaves.

I've been cutting up honeycomb in the kitchen, and have left the washed frames to dry on the draining board. The pool of sweetness that accumulates under them is found by a scouting party of ants, trekking across the veldt of the kitchen floor to scale the heights of the wooden worktop. These are the black ants (*Lasius niger*), opportunists who camp out in house walls. I watch them communicating the good news, one to another: a double file, one cohort going up, another coming down, delicately touching antennae as they pass. Outside, in the Lammas Meadow, the yellow ants (*Lasius flavus*) have been extending their huge domed metropolis. It is circled with a ring of satellite cities, exposed now as we hack back the long grass. Compared with the freebooting laissez-faire of the black ants, this is the world of a Fritz Lang movie. Here the trains certainly run on time. The pale yellow workers never see the outside world. Their eyesight is weak; they live out their lives in a perpetual scurry through a network of tunnels, milking the honeydew from the aphids that live on the roots of the grass, constantly moving the white eggs to optimum conditions of temperature and humidity. The network of tunnels reaches far underground: the mound of spoil above it – ten inches or more in height, and twice as broad – is only a pale reflection of its size. The mound is closed, with no connection to the surrounding environment, the outside world. Except once a year. On a single day in July or August, when the conditions are just right, the sterile female workers will pierce the mound and allow the young unmated females and males to make their mating flight. Nests all over the garden erupt together in an amazing display of synchronicity, their populations spewing forth into the air like Roman candles, wings flashing in the sunshine. For one day only. Then the young mated queen will tear off her own wings, rubbing them against a stone or some other hard surface, and spend the rest of her life – ten or perhaps fifteen years – confined in a single chamber in the centre of the nest.

'He can take the sun out of the sky before seven o'clock in the morning.' My mother: weeping over the breakfast pots.

His rage was volcanic, like a thunderstorm. And like a thunderstorm, soon over, and never directed at us – always because of some slight or other, not because he lacked patience or was easily frustrated – though we were always somehow implicated as if also having been slighted, the rage on our behalf. And after the tears of remorse the sun would come out again. But even on the best of days there was always an unease, a feeling of eggshells not to be walked on, of being always in disguise, of needing to conciliate, defend, protect. They took hostages, chose sides. My brother refused to play that game; absconded into juvenile delinquency, casual violence, a succession of schools.

'I only stay for you, dear,' she said.

In midsummer I find her watch, still set for winter time. The hour went on months ago but the watch, like a little chip of ice, brings with it a shiver of cold.

History is written by the victors, they say – or at least by the survivors. From the *Annals* of Tacitus and the Anglo-Saxon Chronicle to Leland's commission from Henry VIII, everyone has an axe to grind, a point of view. The information about the dedication of the stone church at Morville in 1118 comes from John of Worcester's continuation of the *Chronicon ex chronicis* – a Latin chronicle based in part on a now-lost version of the Anglo-Saxon Chronicle with a continuation from 1030 to 1141 by the monks of Worcester. It comes just at the point where John takes over the narrative from his fellow scribe Florence, who had died that year – an odd little local incident in the record of wars and rebellions, the deaths and successions of popes and kings. 'After the dedication,' he says,

> all who had come to that service set out to return home; but the air, which had been before remarkably serene, became clouded, and a great storm of thunder and lightning arose, and some of those on their journey back, being overtaken by it and unable to return, rested in a certain spot at which they happened to have arrived. They were five in number, three men and two women; one of the latter was killed by a stroke of lightning, and the other, having been set on fire from the middle down to the soles of the feet, perished miserably, the men alone scarce escaping with their lives. Five of their horses were also struck and killed.

Who were they, these two women, especially the one who 'perished miserably', her nether regions 'ab umbilico usque ad pedum vestigia' consumed by fire? Was this recorded as a judgement on women and their troublesome sexuality? A lesson to women not to meddle in Church matters? A sign of divine disapproval of the Bishop of Hereford who had conducted the service, or of the rival monks of Shrewsbury who had built the church? Or simply a meteorological record, an observation on the power and unreliability of weather, the wisdom or otherwise of sheltering during thunderstorms? Everything always depends on who is telling the tale. And who is reading it.

The badgers are digging holes in the soil of the churchyard now, hunting for earthworms. They are short of food. The earthworms on which they feed have retreated deep underground where the soil is still moist. Badgers are picked up by the roadside, dehydrated, undernourished. There will be few cubs raised this year. In some places the badgers are invading gardens, digging up lawns to find the worms. The advice to gardeners, broadcast in the newspapers and over the Internet, is to water your lawn late at night to bring the worms to the surface: save the badgers, save your lawn.

I sit on the grass path, picking blackcurrants. The sun is hot on my back but my head and arms are deep in the cool green jungle that surrounds the blackcurrant bushes. Despite the heat, the blackcurrants are cool and smooth to the touch. I sever the stalks with a thumbnail, gently rolling the berries between forefinger and thumb into a cupped palm before depositing them a handful at a time into a plastic bowl. It's a child's-eye view down here – or a cat's. I peer through a forest of the tall green stems and paddle-shaped leaves of horseradish, like so many miniature banana palms. Grace, the youngest cat, comes weaving towards me through the jungle, her pale fur slashed with sunlight. The blackbirds chink in alarm. She rubs against me and then just as suddenly is gone, off about her own business. I'm deeply envious of her subterranean existence in this green world of dappled shade.

The Church Meadow is full of cars: the children of the village school are holding their end-of-year service, when they say goodbye to the older children who are leaving to go to secondary school.

Above the big house, on the skyline, the hanging wood is rimmed with gold – a pale fingernail of ripening corn above the dark trees. In the Books of Hours the tasks for July and August are Reaping and Threshing, the tools are sickle and flail. The men bend, holding the stiff stems of the wheat or barley in one hand, the curved hook of the sickle in the other. The blade is crescent-moon-shaped, the handle short and straight. Threshing was done with a hinged leather flail, in Latin a *tribulum*, studded with nails – from the same root as the word 'tribulation'. The tasks are the same, only the machinery is different now.

In the Hours of the Fastolf Master the corn is being cut higher than in haymaking, producing short sheaves and a longer stubble. Only the ears of the corn were cut, with a short stalk. Afterwards, the poor were allowed to glean the fields for any leftover stalks, then Michaelmas geese and other poultry would be loosed on to the fields to fatten on any fallen grain, and then cows would be turned into the fields to browse the 'stover' – the long stubble, full of green cornfield weeds – or the stover might be cut and stacked for winter feed. Finally sheep would be folded on the fields to nibble what was left. The following spring the roots and the dung would be ploughed in together and, rotting down, would enrich the soil.

In the Earl of Shrewsbury's prayer book the cut is already being made lower: the men work on bended knee while a woman ties the stalks into long sheaves. By the nineteenth century the sickle for reaping had been almost completely replaced by the scythe, cutting the stalks right down to ground level. The land was then ploughed almost immediately afterwards.

Unthreshed grain was thought to keep better, so before mechanisation threshing continued throughout the autumn and winter, sheaves of corn being taken from the stack as and when grain was required. The heavy thump of the flails was the regular accompaniment to village life in winter. The men worked in pairs or fours, and it was said that you could tell how they were being paid from the beat of the flails: 'by the day, by the day,' for day-rate, and the brisker 'we took it, we took it, we took it' for piecework. Threshing was long, hard and laborious, and it was the first of the harvesting tasks to be mechanised, in the eighteenth and nineteenth centuries, at first using horses harnessed to gear wheels and later by steam-driven 'threshing boxes' which travelled from farm to farm. By the middle of the nineteenth century there were horse-drawn reapers to cut the corn too, and by the 1880s the reaper-and-binder, which not only cut the corn but tied it into sheaves. Eventually the combine harvester arrived in the mid-twentieth century, which cut the corn and threshed the grain all in one. At first the combines were followed on to the field by a mechanical bailer which gathered up the straw into rectangular bales, each as heavy as a man could carry. Now the bales are huge circular drums, spat out by enormous machines, the bales so big that they can only be moved and stacked by more machines. The depopulation of the fields is complete.

Once these would have been common fields, full of the comings and goings of the villagers and their animals. The harvest would have been a communal activity, the men working together, the women tying the sheaves, the children and dogs chasing the rats and rabbits that escaped from the corn. Typically, each village or hamlet had three large fields, two of which would be in cultivation at any one time, while the third lay fallow. Each field was divided into long thin strips which were shared out among the villagers. The strips were gathered into parcels or 'furlongs' ('furrow-long' in Old English, a rough measure representing the length of a furrow in the common field). It was a system as old as, perhaps older than, the Normans.

As I stand watering the garden each evening, I can see blocks of strips on the side of the hill opposite, beneath the pasture, high-lighted by the sinking sun: a pattern of furlongs and paths, the shadow of ridge and furrow. At Morville the open fields lay to the east and south of the church, their remains detectable in the field names on the nineteenth-century tithe map: Big Field, south of the Mor Brook, running down to The Lye; Middle Field, on the higher ground on the other side of the brook; Heath Field further round to the east.

Most of the open fields of England were swept away by the Parliamentary enclosures of the late eighteenth and early nineteenth centuries, but in Shropshire virtually all the open fields had already been enclosed before the start of the seventeenth century, by private agreement between neighbouring landowners. For the landowners and their farming tenants this often made good sense, as their holdings could be consolidated and rationalised, and new techniques of husbandry applied to the land. But before enclosure all the villagers had lived together in the village, cheek by jowl, making the daily trek to the fields together; now the new class of tenant farmers built new farmhouses, more conveniently placed out in the fields, away from the village. And for the landless cottagers and the smallholders enclosure spelled disaster: they relied on the fallow field and roughs as grazing for their cattle and sheep, and on the woods as places to gather firewood and to fatten their pigs in autumn. Now the woods were grubbed up and the land put under the plough, paths were blocked and streams diverted, the open fields dismembered and the new fields fenced and hedged to keep the cottagers and their animals out. Some landowners took the opportunity of enclosure to build or enlarge their parks, with walls around and gamekeepers to patrol them: when 910 acres of commons and waste were enclosed at Morville and the adjoining parish of Acton Round in 1625, 410 acres of it disappeared into the already existing park of John Weld of Willey.

The loss of freedom, the loss of a sense of entitlement, that feeling of exclusion, is something we recognise in the countryside even now, where right to roam is still a hotly disputed issue. Just as profound was the loss of the landscape, all the old familiar places extinguished, the reference points swept away, a whole culture grubbed out by the root. John Clare's 'Remembrances', though dating from the later Parliamentary enclosures, is a lament for a lost boyhood and a lost countryside, a litany of expunged places, which describes the effect of earlier enclosures too:

By Langley bush I roam but the bush hath left its hill
On cowper green I stray tis a desert strange and chill
And spreading lea close oak ere decay had penned its will
To the axe of the spoiler and self interest fell a prey
And cross berry way and old round oaks narrow lane
With its hollow trees like pulpits I shall never see again
Inclosure like a Buonaparte let not a thing remain . . .

Clare had lost his bearings, and he had lost the thread of his life. In the madhouse he imagined himself to be Lord Byron or the pugilist Jack Randall. He escaped from the asylum and walked all the way home from London to Northampton. But when he arrived, 'compleatly foot foundered and broken down', he found himself 'homeless at home', the people – and the countryside – unrecognisable to him.

There was something of the same sense of loss at the end of the twentieth century, when the reverse started to happen and hedgerows were torn up in order to combine the fields into agroprairie. Over the years the hedges had acquired new species of plants, become homes to dozens of birds, insects and animals, all now dispossessed. The fields themselves had acquired names, each name telling a story, so we too are dispossessed. Without the fields and the hedgerows the landscape is, literally, meaningless – robbed of its stories. For once this was a landscape of stories, each field telling a different tale about the place and its people. When you walked through the fields you could hear the story of the village – if you had ears to hear.

It's silent now. I walk down the brook towards The Lye, tithe map in hand. I read out the names of the vanished fields as I pass: Freezeland Piece, from the furze (OE *fyrs*) that once grew there – there's a patch of rough scrub still; Wiery Piece, from the weir at the head of the Mill Meadow – I can see the line of the weir in the water of the brook; Wollery Meadow, where the alders grew – and still grow; Gig Pit Leasow (OE *laeswe*: 'pasture'), where flax and hemp were retted in pits, and Hemp Piece further on. Beyond The Lye (*lye* or *ley*: temporary pasture) are Pit Leasow, where lime would have been dug in marl pits; White Ley, where the ground was speckled white with lime; Limekiln Leasow, where the lime was burned. Across the brook is Pound Leasow, from the pound where stray cattle and sheep were collected; further on, Gravels, where today huge machines dig sand and gravel for the building industry. North of the brook in the opposite direction are Cunnery and Conery Rough (*cony*: a rabbit, from the Old French *conil*, pl. *conis*), where rabbits (introduced by the Normans as a source of meat) were confined in their warren – the land here is potholed with rabbit burrows still; Hopyard Meadow, where hops would have been grown for beer; across the road Forge Meadow, one of many forges operating in Morville in the seventeenth century – the whole landscape full of people and activity. Now the men work alone in the fields, each in his cab, astride the giant machines, isolated by the radio and the noise of the machinery. In a single year recently 8,600 farmers abandoned farming, with a loss of 15,000 jobs. The fields now have numbers and change their names with every sale.

Who will tell our stories when we're gone?

*

Caring for my mother in her old age, me half-laughing, half-exasperated. 'No one's going to do this for me, you know.'

The old grammatical joke: 'I shall drown and no one will save me.' Tense: simple future. 'I will drown and no one shall save me.' Tense: future imperative.

I take the heaped bowls of blackcurrants and measure them out into preserving pans and big saucepans. It's already 9 p.m.; no matter how soon I begin to prepare – picking out the stalks, gathering up the jars and putting them to warm in the Rayburn, cutting out circles of waxed paper – it's always 9 p.m. before I start. I shan't be finished until midnight. Blackcurrant jam is easy, but this year I have left the blackcurrants so long that they are sweet and ripe enough to eat raw: delicious rolled in a crunch of granulated sugar. I find myself eating them by the handful, my fingers stained with the juice. But this also means the jam will take longer to set. It's nearly one o'clock by the time I finish and the whole kitchen is hot and sticky to the touch. I stand outside on the kitchen stairs, breathing in the night air. The sky is perfectly clear, full of stars, and yet empty at the same time: no recognisable constellations, no pattern. Only the dim veil of the Milky Way arching from horizon to horizon, like a torn scarf. It has been known as the Milky Way, or *via lactea*, since ancient times – a poetic path, a star road, a highway through the heavens. It takes an effort of imagination to see it for what it really is: the galaxy to which our solar system belongs, a vast flat spinning spiral 100,000 light-years across, seen edge on. My head spins with the knowledge, the vastness and emptiness of it all. Our solar system lies about two-thirds of the way towards the outer edge of the galaxy. Beyond is deep space, black, empty, dotted here and there with other galaxies . . .

When it was time to write his own will George Smyth left nothing to chance. After the shadowy figure of Roger, emerging out of nowhere, with no pedigree, no relations, no 'background' to flesh him out – whose children (apart from George) melt away with the insubstantiality of ghosts – here is a man of substance, a man of property, founding father of a dynasty. John, Richard, Walter, Edward, William, Leighton, Jane, Constance, Dorothy and Elizabeth; he lists them all and provides for each of them and for their husbands and wives in turn, disposing of the land and the money first, then each piece of furniture, each favourite horse, each suit of clothes: a white gelding and a mare called Overton to his second wife Elizabeth; his best bedstead and best feather mattress to his youngest son Leighton (then scarcely eighteen months old), together with two pairs of flaxen sheets, two pairs of hempen sheets, napkins, tablecloths, towels, a chest, twelve pewter dishes and the Turkey carpet from the parlour table; his second-best bed and feather mattress to his son Richard together with another chest, his best silver plate and 'one grey nag which is unbroken'; a grey mare called Tutbery and his third bed to his son-in-law Edward Bishop, together with his best doublet and all his best clothes and the iron tools from his 'work house'; a black horse called Hobbye to his servant Francis Barrett, together with more clothes; another two doublets and a pair of taffeta-drawn hose to his son Richard – and so on and so on, page after page, committing his soul to God, his body for interment in the chancel at Morville next to his father's, and his worldly goods to be divided between his children, his grandchildren and his household.

George's dynasty lasted just three generations. He was succeeded at Morville by his son John in 1601 and then by his grandson George in 1636. This George was admitted to the Bar at the Inner Temple in 1616 and was MP for Bridgnorth in 1623. He made a brilliant marriage to the daughter of Sir Hugh Brawne of Newington in Surrey and sired an heir, another John.

Then in 1642 Shropshire declared for the King. It was a war that was to divide the country for eighteen years, setting brother against brother, father against son, town against town. Charles raised his standard at Nottingham on 22 August 1642 and arrived in Bridgnorth – the second largest town in Shropshire after Shrewsbury – on 12 October 1642 with six thousand infantry, two thousand cavalry and fifteen hundred dragoons. He stayed for three days, pronouncing the promenade and view from Castle Walk 'the finest in his dominions', while he continued to gather recruits. Then he struck out south-east for the capital with the Parliamentary forces in pursuit, taking the flower of Shropshire's youth with him. The two armies met at Edgehill in Warwickshire on 23 October 1642. It was the first battle of the Civil War. Both armies were untried, half-trained, their ranks filled with raw recruits. Casualties on both sides were high. In some villages more men died fighting on the King's side in the Civil War than proportionately were to die from the same villages in World War I. And when the smoke of musket- and cannon-fire cleared over the field of Edgehill John Smyth, George's great-grandson, son and heir and only child of George Smyth of Morville, was one of the thousands who lay dead.

*

They were buried where they lay, in huge pits on the battlefield: five hundred here, a thousand there. The war dragged on for four more bitter years, during which Bridgnorth was held for the King by a garrison maintained at the town's expense. As morale fell and costs rose, relations between townspeople and garrison grew increasingly tetchy. The Town Hall and other large buildings on the High Street had already been razed by order of the garrison commander in order to improve the line of fire from the castle. Then, in March 1646, attacked by Parliamentary forces, the Royalists retreated from the town into the castle and fired the remaining buildings. The castle itself was virtually impregnable, defended on three sides by a sheer drop to the river. The Parliamentary forces settled down for a lengthy siege, stockpiling gunpowder in St Leonard's Church along the High Street. An easy target for the Royalist gunners. The explosion and resulting fire destroyed the church and what was left of the town. Three hundred families were rendered homeless. The garrison surrendered on 26 April 1646. Six weeks later the King himself surrendered.

The town remained in ruins until after the Restoration in 1660. 'The inhabitants,' said the Puritan divine Richard Baxter 'were undone and fain to lie under hedges til the compassion of others afforded them entertainment and habitation.' Cromwell ordered

the castle to be slighted to prevent future re-occupation, and walls
and buildings were demolished, but the foundations of Robert de
Bellême's keep proved indestructible to the end. Despite attempts
to blow it up the huge masonry shell of the keep remained, and
remains to this day, on its red rocky promontory high above the
Severn, leaning at an angle of 15° (more than the Leaning Tower
of Pisa), a symbol of the folly and futility of war.

The blackbirds are desperate for water. They have already
stripped the sour cherries from the trees, leaving the white stones
hanging like Christmas decorations, the ground beneath speckled
with red. The long strings of white currants, pearly-pink and
transparent, were eaten long ago. And now when I walk through
the garden the birds erupt from the raspberry canes in a clatter of
wings – autumn raspberries, fruiting early; much too early.

I don't net the fruit. Live and let live: in a good season there's
plenty for all; in a season like this I can do without. But this year
the gooseberries have been eaten too, which is a surprise. Not the
blackbirds, this time, who peck out the pulp and leave the tattered
skins still clinging to the branch. Gone, vanished, skins and all,
overnight. They are an old dual-purpose variety, 'Whinham's
Industry', a cooker when green, but sweet enough for dessert
when ripe. I had been waiting patiently for the moment when the
berries would turn from green to deep wine-red, their succulent
insides oozing with golden juice and translucent seeds, promising
a whole shelf-full of gleaming jars of bottled fruit for winter. But
when the day came someone had beaten me to it. A badger,
perhaps? For some days I had been finding large seedy droppings
around the garden. But badgers are fastidious creatures; they have

their own latrines. And then I remember Aesop's story of the Fox and Grapes, familiar from a thousand pub signs. I know that foxes eat rowan berries and other fallen fruits in autumn. My vine-growing neighbour Ian confirms that they will also eat grapes. And if grapes, why not gooseberries too?

I can't remember how Aesop's story ends, so I ring my husband at the bookshop and he comes home with an edition dated 1665 with parallel English, French and Latin texts, complete with a fetching illustration of the fox lusting after the grapes. The point of the story is that the fox, for all his wiles, can't reach the grapes because they are grown Italian-style up a tree. So he consoles himself with the thought that the grapes are in any case 'green and tart, not worth his stay'. Which is of course the origin of the expression 'sour grapes'.

News of individual casualties must have filtered back to Morville with agonising slowness. Perhaps John's death was not confirmed until after the King surrendered in 1646. George had already pre-deceased his son, in November 1641, but not before apparently having encumbered the estate with a huge mortgage. With both George and John dead, Morville reverted to George's sister Jane and her husband Arthur Weaver: a lawyer, a shrewd operator, an accumulator of much property in the district, a staunch Anglican at a time of Puritan controversy in the village. One of his first tasks was to set about repaying the money George seems to have borrowed.

Arthur Weaver originally came from Bettws in Montgomery-shire, just over the Shropshire border to the north-west, where the Weavers must have known Sir Thomas Hanmer, the noted gardener whose estate was on the Welsh side of the north Shropshire border not far away at Bettisfield. Sir Thomas certainly knew the garden of Arthur and Jane's neighbour Sir William Whitmore, at Apley on the other side of the Severn near Bridgnorth, and he was a close friend of the nurseryman John Rea at Kinlet, a few miles to the south of Morville. Hanmer's influence in the matter of gardens was considerable, though, as he confessed in a letter to his friend John Evelyn in 1668: 'Many gentlemen . . . have, upon my instigation and perception, fallen to plant both flowers and trees and have pretty handsome little grounds but nobody hath ventured upon large spacious ones with costly fountains . . . or great parterres.'

Bettisfield is in the parish of Hanmer, just over the fields from the present-day north Shropshire town of Ellesmere: flat, low-lying fields, a place of meres and mosses (the Shropshire word for a bog), rich soil, planted with barley then, sugar beet now. Sir Thomas had also fought on the Royalist side before escaping to France in 1644, and the estate at Bettisfield had been sequestered by Parliament. He had had to pay a heavy fine before he was allowed to return in 1653. Short of money and denied public office during the Protectorate, he devoted himself to his garden. It was in this period that he wrote his *Garden Book*, a record of what he grew, how he grew it, where he got it from (plants then were passed from hand to hand), and how well each plant performed in his garden.

By the middle of the seventeenth century flowers had ceased to be emblems of the Virgin Mary or Queen Elizabeth and had instead become botanical specimens. Ever since the end of the sixteenth century a flood of exciting new plants had been pouring into England from Southern Europe, Turkey and the Near East – Parkinson's 'Out-landish' flowers: tulips, hyacinths, ranunculus, crown imperials, anemones, auriculas and others – joined now by the first introductions from North America: the scarlet 'cardinal flower' (*Lobelia cardinalis*), the first lupins, the first Michaelmas daisies, sunflowers, vivid golden-red *Aquilegia canadensis*. It was the golden age of English flower gardening. Enemies on either side of the political or religious divide – Royalist or Parliamentarian, Puritan or Anglican – would swallow their differences to secure treasured plants and bulbs. Sir Thomas knew and exchanged plants with many of the noted plantsmen of the day, including Lord Lambert, the Parliamentary general, who was a noted tulip fancier. The philosopher Samuel Hartlib considered Sir Thomas one of the 'three most exquisite gardiners' in the kingdom, and John Rea in 1665 dedicated to him his great work, *Flora, Seu De Florum Cultura, Or A Complete Floriledge*. All these men would have described themselves as 'florists' – that is, flower fanciers, lovers of flowers, as distinct on the one hand from men of medicine or science (such as Nehemiah Grew, who in 1682, with the aid of one of the first microscopes, discovered the sexual nature of plant reproduction, or the Cambridge botanist the Rev. John Ray, author of *Historia plantarum generalis*), or on the other, those for whom flowers merely provided the backdrop to a fashionable lifestyle.

In France Sir Thomas had seen parterres 'of fine turf, kept low as any greens to bowle on – cut out curiously into Embroidery of flowers, beasts, birds or feuillages and small alleys and intervalls filled with severall coloured sands and dust with much art, with but few flowers'. He and his fellow florists in England, however, preferred something smaller, neater and more functional in which to show off their prized collections of tulips, auriculas, ranunculi, anemones and carnations – the five flowers that, with the subsequent addition of hyacinths, polyanthus and (much later) pinks, collectively came to be referred to as 'florists' flowers'. Sir Thomas's own garden consisted of rectangular beds which could be cultivated without stepping on to the soil, each bed edged with raised boards (in preference to hedges of box, rosemary or lavender, which would obscure the view of the flowers and rob the more favoured plants of nutrients) and planted up in rows, with a careful record being made of each bulb or plant, its position in the row and its provenance.

So in memory of young John Smyth, and of Arthur and Jane Weaver who succeeded him at Morville, I made a modest little garden of a dozen small boarded beds, and I filled them with Sir Thomas's favourite flowers.

It's a springtime garden, gay with brilliant colour – the blue and white of hyacinths, the red and white of striped tulips, the yellow of daffodils. Red cowslips, ancestors of our modern polyanthus. Scarlet 'star' anemones (*Anemone pavonina*). A row of mop-headed quince trees. In April and May it suits my mood. But by July the hyacinths and daffodils have retreated underground and the tulips are dried sticks, waiting to be dug up. It's as barren as I feel. In the seventeenth century there were few flowers that bloomed after midsummer. It seems Sir Thomas was content to leave his bulb beds largely blank for the remaining part of the year, although Samuel Gilbert, John Rea's son-in-law and (through Rea's daughter Minerva) inheritor of his collection of auriculas, advocated a sort of summer bedding to fill the blank spaces. Gilbert was the rector at Quatt on the Dudmaston estate, where he found time among his pastoral duties to write *The Florists Vade-Mecum*, published in 1682. He recommended 'Amaranths, Mirabilia Peruviana and Nasturtium Indicum' – all brilliantly coloured tender plants, raised on a hot bed with some protection from the weather, and then either planted out or plunged in the beds in midsummer. All were late sixteenth-century introductions from the Spanish colonies in Mexico and Central America. There were by Sir Thomas's time 'half a score' of new varieties of *Amaranthus*, including the long crimson tassels of 'Love lies bleeding' (*Amaranthus caudatus*) and the coral-like growth of the 'Cockscomb' (now classified in the genus *Celosia* rather than *Amaranthus*), red and yellow marvels of Peru (*Mirabilia jalapa*) and yellow dwarf nasturtiums (*Tropaeolum minus*, which he called 'Indian cresses'), as well as yuccas and scarlet cannas, known to Sir Thomas as 'Yuccoes' and 'Indian Canes'. But in this heat I have no taste for colour. I find the cockscomb curious rather than beautiful, Gilbert's combinations of crimson and yellow emetic rather than exciting. My heart's just not in it.

There is a window in the church at Morville that contains a small panel of medieval glass – the only medieval glass that survives in the church – apparently smashed, as so many other stained-glass windows deliberately were, during the Civil War, and put together again in a curious mish-mash. Local tradition has it that the pieces were hidden for safekeeping in the church tower, where they were later rediscovered. It is recognisably a representation of the Crucifixion, but mixed in with the figure of the suffering Christ are fragments of blue glass which seem to belong to another window altogether – to the Virgin Mary's cloak, perhaps.

Blue: the colour of possibility. 'Blue-sky thinking' is when the mind soars, 'blue screen' technique when the most amazing cinematic effects are possible. We escape into the wide blue yonder. The blue mineral lapis lazuli is the source of the most precious colour in the artist's palette. Medieval patrons would specify it for the Virgin's robe in their most luxurious Books of Hours. The mineral itself, brought by pack animal from a single mine in remotest northern Afghanistan, was used by the pharaohs to adorn their buildings. There are blue-glazed objects 6,500 years old, coloured with copper ores such as azurite and malachite in a process that became known as Egyptian faience – the oldest glaze known to man. The fragments of blue glass in the window of the church at Morville would have been coloured with copper and cobalt in a process unchanged from ancient Mesopotamia to the workshops of medieval England.

I try to lift my spirits with blue late-summer flowers: Cupid's dart, monkshood, the cool blue fireworks of *Agapanthus* exploding like sherbet on the tongue. *Agapanthus* was introduced into English gardens via the Netherlands in the middle of the seventeenth century, from the Dutch colony at the Cape in South Africa. The evergreen sorts, *A. africanus* and *A. praecox*, were the first to be cultivated. They came from an area of the western Cape where winter rains predominated and summers were hot and droughty, so they continued growing through the winter here, too, where their lush leaves were damaged by the cold. So English gardeners grew them in pots, standing them outside during summer and overwintering them under protection – at first just temporary shelters, often rigged up in situ over bigger specimens like *aloes* (also introduced in the middle of the seventeenth century from the Cape), but later, as the flood of tender evergreens increased, in new 'greenhouses' – specially built houses for overwintering exotic greenery, or 'greens'. These were not yet made predominantly of glass (that had to wait for improvements in glass-making in the eighteenth and nineteenth centuries), but had detachable shutters across the front instead which could be raised or removed in mild weather to admit light and air. The deciduous *A. campanulatus*, the principal ancestor of the modern hardy deciduous varieties, came later from parts of the Cape where summer rainfall predominated; they became dormant in winter and were therefore much hardier in our climate. As *A. campanulatus* and its offspring have narrow, grass-like leaves where *A. africanus* and *A. praecox* have broad strap-shaped ones, the width of the leaves is still a good indicator of hardiness in any new variety.

I breathe in their colours, counting off the shades – navy-blue, purple-blue, sky-blue, pale blue, rehearsing other colour names learned from Sir Thomas's *Garden Book*: 'grideline', from *gris-de-lin*, flax-grey, with tints of lilac; 'bertino', blue-grey; 'murrey', mulberry colour; 'watchet', sky-blue, the colour of childhood holidays by the sea. In the wreckage of my garden I cling to these fragments of blue like a shipwrecked sailor.

The name *Agapanthus* is a compound of two Greek words – *agape*, meaning 'love', and *anthos*, meaning 'flower'.

Agapanthus, the Flower of Love.

It crosses my mind that I too may be putting the fragments together all wrong. They were happy some of the time. After my brother and I left home my mother trained as a teacher and taught at the local College of Further Education. She studied Goethe and Mrs Gaskell, he Coleridge and Hazlitt. They went to conferences together on Wordsworth and the Romantics, took holidays in Dorset and Northumberland. Windblown and brown, they smile for the camera.

In the reign of Queen Elizabeth each parish had been made responsible for its own poor, the authorities alarmed at the quantity of 'sturdy beggars' thronging the roads, seeing them as a source of potential unrest. In Stuart England the problem was not so much one of beggars, those without any means of support – though there were plenty of them: the aged, the infirm, the orphans – as of the cottagers and the day labourers, whose capacity to earn – and therefore to feed their families – was now entirely dependent upon the season, the vagaries of the weather and the goodwill of employers. In the church at Morville there hang two large black-painted tablets, either side of the tower door, recording seventeenth-century gifts to the poor of the parish. Sir Edward Acton gave £100 to buy land, half for the benefit of the poor, half for the support of the parson; the land was probably that marked on the 1841 tithe map as 'Parsons Leys' on the hillside above the church, together with the four 'doles' (unfenced divisions of a common field) in Townsend Meadow below it. In 1689 Arthur Weaver left 'twenty and six shillings yearly for ever' to buy penny loaves for the poor, to be distributed every Sunday morning to 'six of the most aged Impotent and indigent'.

Poverty was endemic. It yawned like a chasm beneath the feet of every working man or woman. It was so easy to fall into it – through illness, bad luck, bad harvest, industrial depression. It meant chronic insecurity. You were never safe. And it was cyclical: if not you, then grandfathers, grandchildren, aunts and uncles, cousins. Until the middle of the twentieth century most working people had first-hand knowledge of poverty in their families. Or 'clogs to clogs in three generations', as my mother used to say.

When we speak of poverty now it is only relative: a question of the haves and have-nots in a materialist society. Pre-Welfare State, poverty was a matter of life and early death. I am a child of the Welfare State: free healthcare, free milk, free orange juice, free grammar school, free university education and subsidised housing in bright new council houses newly built on landscaped council estates made me taller, stronger, healthier, better educated, better off than either of my parents. In the early years of the twentieth century more than half the children of working men were reckoned to be in destitution – 'scrawny, dirty, ragged, verminous'. This was the world in which my parents grew up. Average life expectancy for a woman was forty-six; for the poorest it was still only thirty. Women could expect to bury at least one child in six.

Dennis Cooper was only four-and-a-half when his mother died. His sister Daisy was two-and-a-half, and his brother Les two or three months. Their mother was twenty-eight. 'Her face was as white as flour when he carried her out of the house. I knew I'd not see her again.' It was 1928. There was no National Health Service. There had been complications after Les's birth, and their father Frank had delayed too long in calling the doctor. 'He just let her lie.'

Frank Cooper was a farm labourer at Morville Heath. By twelve the boys were out at work, doing two-and-a-half days at school in Morville and two and a half days at A. C. Walker's farm. A. C. Walker farmed 400 acres at Morville, another 100 at Kite's Nest, 1,000 acres all told. He was one of the school governors, so when the boys were needed for picking or threshing there was no contest: they were fetched out of school. The farm grew potatoes, peas and sugar beet, and barley for beer. Beer was 2d a pint, so delivering the barley to the brewery in Wolverhampton was a much-coveted job: the waggoners got two free pints. The grain was harvested with an Allis Chalmers – one of the first combines. It came knocked flat from the United States on Lend-Lease. The first job was to put it together. It had a four-foot six-inch cut.

Dennis and his wife Joyce were the last recipients of Arthur Weaver's loaves. He was twenty-two, she nineteen. They married at Morville in February 1945. Joyce had come to work at A. C. Walker's as a landgirl during the war. When they married they moved into the toll house, a tiny cottage owned by A. C. Walker, built in 1723 to collect payment from waggoners on the turnpike through the village. They raised three children there. 'We couldn't get on the council housing list because we were in tied accommodation.' Then in 1970 the road through the village was straightened and widened and the toll house demolished. The family, now homeless, had by law to be rehoused by the council. Eventually they got a council house in Bridgnorth. Later, under the new 'right to buy' legislation, they managed to buy it. I visited them there. A comfortable house, a garden, a stake in the world; something to leave to one's children and grandchildren.

When Arthur Weaver died in 1689 he left Morville to his son, another Arthur. Arthur II was not the eldest son; that was Thomas, who had effectively been disinherited because he was still unmarried when the will was made. Arthur II had been canny enough to produce seven children already by his wife Maria Careswell of Shifnal, and so Thomas had to be satisfied with the lesser estate of Eardington (where the Mor Brook debouches into the Severn), together with the tithes of Quatford – unless he stepped up to the crease and got himself suitably married, in which case his father promised to find him a better estate. Arthur the elder had been busy on that score, purchasing estates all over this part of Shropshire, and he was able to settle estates on all of Arthur II's four sons: not only did fourteen-year-old John get his grandfather's patrimonial property at Tregynon in the county of Montgomery, but ten-year-old Edward, eight-year-old Arthur and five-year-old Thomas (the fifth and youngest, Anthony, had yet to be born) all had properties purchased for them in Corve Dale and Ape Dale, at Holdgate, Clee Stanton, Brookhampton and Longville.

Between them, Arthur II and his son John were to be in possession of Morville for nearly sixty years, Arthur II from 1689 to 1710, and John from 1710 to 1747: William and Mary, Anne; the first two Georges. John Weaver was MP for Bridgnorth from 1713 to 1734, the first member of the family to hold that rank for nearly a century, and became one of the King's Grooms of the Privy Chamber. The family was on the up-and-up again.

Fashionable gardens of the late seventeenth and first third of the eighteenth centuries were characterised by control: control over plants, through clipping and shaping; control over water, through the creation of elaborate fountains and waterworks; control over the topography of the garden by terracing – building retaining walls and reducing slopes into successions of level planes; symbolic control over the surrounding countryside, by ground plans based on military-style bastions with central vistas striking through the garden and out into the park like metaphorical sight-lines for cannon fire. The house on its platform dominated the garden, often as the centre of a *patte d'oie* (goose foot) of three or five radiating avenues cut into woodland or planted across open land, each with an eye-catcher in the form of some architectural detail at the end of the view.

The Weavers may have been on the up-and-up, but their gardening activities would have been seriously hampered by a lack of land contiguous to the house. Both Arthur I and Arthur II had bought land and tithes in Corve Dale and elsewhere, and the family still had considerable property in Bridgnorth, but their land at Morville seems to have been confined to a tiny enclave surrounded on three sides by land belonging to the Actons. In contrast to the Smyths, the Actons were already well established as landowners and country gentry by the sixteenth century, well placed to take advantage of the Dissolution of the Monasteries to acquire more land, and later to consolidate it by enclosure. They rose in the social scale: Sir Edward Acton was knighted by Charles I in 1644. By 1721/2 Sir Whitmore Acton owned 1,430 acres in the parish, much of it laid down to park. In comparison John Weaver's 'park' was no more than a field in front of the house. The big field above Morville Hall had its grand avenue, traces of which still remain, but the avenue was aligned not on Morville but (perhaps originally one of several) on nearby Aldenham, the seat of the Actons on the outskirts of the village. And it is from Aldenham that it would have been seen most dramatically, with the rising hillside behind; from the house at Morville the avenue feels uncomfortably askew. Ironically, however, it was John Weaver's son, Arthur Weaver III who, as fashions changed, got the blame for what by the middle of the eighteenth century had come to be regarded as a gardening solecism. Here is Thomas Percy writing to William Shenstone, poet, landscaper and garden theorist, on 29 July 1760:

When I saw you, you talked of giving a short History of false taste: I can furnish you with one or two real facts that are not unpleasant. Last year died a Mr Weaver, who had a Seat at Morville near Bridgenorth and who was possessed by the very demon of Caprice: He came into possession of an Old Mansion that commanded a fine view down a most pleasing Vale, he contrived to intercept it by two straight rows of Elms that ran in an oblique direction across it, and which led the Eye to a pyramidal Obelisk composed of one single board set up endways and painted by the Joiner of the Village: this obelisk however was soon removed by the first puff of wind.

Gardening has always been full of put-downs and pretension. Consider the gulf between the Chelsea Flower Show and the local garden centre, yew and privet, terraces and patios, the 'Yellow Book' listing of gardens open for charity and the world of television makeovers. But beware: what is 'out' one year may be 'in' the next. Red hot pokers (*Kniphofia* spp), once the Donald McGills of garden plants, are now cherished in subtle shades of green and cream; dahlias, once confined to suburban flower-beds now grace the smartest of upper-crust borders. What's next for rehabilitation: *Gladioli*? Lupins?

The new seventeenth-century greenhouses contained not only tender plants like *Agapanthus*, yuccas and aloes, but evergreen trees like oranges, lemons and myrtles. Sour oranges had been introduced into this country from Spain by 1595. Sweet oranges came later, in 1658, from India via the Dutch colony at the Cape: they had been planted by Dutch settlers on the slopes of Table Mountain in 1652. Nowadays few people bother to grow oranges in their greenhouses or conservatories; they buy them from the supermarket instead, imported by the lorry load and available all year round. But the sour Seville oranges still have an air of rarity about them. They appear in the shops once a year for only two or

three weeks in January, and making Seville orange marmalade is
still one of the milestones of my year.

I was making marmalade from Seville oranges the first January
we were at Morville and wondered idly whether the pips would
grow. They did. Eight years on, I had fifteen large and leafy trees
needing a suitable spot in the garden. (Thus are we led by the nose,
upon a whim.) A *parterre d'orangerie* seemed the very thing.

The word *parterre* had always been the French term for what
the English knew as 'quarters': (flower) beds, which might or
might not contain flowers, arranged in a variety of patterns
including those that the English called knots. Now in the later
seventeenth and early eighteenth centuries the word came to be
adopted in English to refer to the latest and most up-to-date forms
of parterre, specifically those which were without flowers and
elongated in shape, depending for their effect upon tightly clipped
box and coloured ground-covering materials such as crushed
brick or terracotta, iron filings or gravel. Whereas the geometry
of the Elizabethan and Jacobean garden was based on the square,
the gardens of William and Mary, Anne and the first George –
tugged by the general thrust of the garden outwards – were based
on the rectangle. The old-fashioned square knot, its pattern
symmetrical on both axes, became elongated into the swirl of
the parterre, outward-moving, asymmetric. The open knot, Parkinson's 'broken squares', became the 'parterre of cutwork for
flowers'; the closed knot (the *parterre de compartiment*) became
the *parterre de broderie*, with curling asymmetric scrolls of
embroidery-like box. The *parterre de l'anglaise* (first described
by Sir Thomas Hanmer) also made its appearance – the French-
man's homage to English lawns, its pattern carried by shapes of
smooth-mown grass. And round the outside, enclosing each
parterre, was the *plate-bande*: a long narrow bed – very narrow

in proportion to its length – edged with clipped box, mounded up into a ridge and planted along the spine with clipped evergreens above ranks of formally spaced spring bulbs: the proto-border.

The *parterre d'orangerie* was usually sited adjacent to the building in which the orange trees overwintered. The oranges were grown in special tubs with rings at the side through which poles could be inserted when the time came for carrying them into shelter. When the danger of frost had passed the oranges would be carried outside again and placed on a strip of sandy gravel or similar material incorporated into the design – either in place of the *plate-bande* or within the parterre itself. At the Bodleian I found John James's *The Theory and Practice of Gardening*, published in 1712 (a translation of a work by A. J. Dezallier d'Argenville, first published in Paris in 1709). These were exactly the years in which John Weaver came into his inheritance and was embarking upon his political career. James's pages are full of designs for parterres, including one for a *parterre d'orangerie*. This consisted of a central sub-rectangular *pièce d'eau* (which suggested the idea for my Canal), surrounded by a strip of hard-standing for the orange trees, with two small round lawns or basins at head and foot, each with a central statue (which I translated into a single round pond with a fountain) and flanking *plates-bandes*. I took 1,500 box cuttings, bought Versailles tubs for the orange trees, painted them sugar-bag blue, and called in a mechanical digger to dig the hole for the Canal before I could change my mind.

But where to find the stone to build the Canal? So far I had only learned about drift geology – the pattern of the soils and their origins. Now I needed to find out about 'solid' geology – the rocks beneath the soil.

*

Shropshire is a geologist's paradise. Of the thirteen internationally recognised geological periods, ten are represented in Shropshire's rocks, making it unique in Britain, probably also in the world. Shropshire place names – Ludlow, Wenlock, Caer Caradoc – have become standard terms worldwide for certain series of rocks wherever they occur. Shaped by cataclysmic forces – volcanoes spurting lava (the Lawley, Caer Caradoc, Helmeth, Hazler, Ragleth), sudden seismic upthrusts, waves of folding and faulting, catastrophic collapse – it's a place of unexpected juxtapositions. History cut and shuffled. It's where ages collide: Precambrian and Carboniferous, Devonian and Jurassic. The landscape is crazed with fault lines. To the west are the oldest rocks, Cambrian, Pre-cambrian and Ordovician, their names memorialising Cambria (the Roman name for Cymru – Wales itself) and the Ordovices, the last tribe to hold out against the Roman legions; to the north and east are the newest rocks, the New Red Sandstone of Bridgnorth and the North Shropshire Plain, the Carboniferous rocks that fuelled the Industrial Revolution; to the south is the Old Red Sandstone of the Clee Hills, with their volcanic intrusions of igneous 'dhustone', a hard, fine-grained dark-coloured stone, halfway between granite and basalt; and, in between, the rocks of the Silurian Age, when the great wall of Wenlock Edge, immeasurably long ago, was a coral reef in a tropical sea.

Here be dragons too: ancient Cambrian and Precambrian rocks that heave up through the younger layers like nightmare beasts from our collective unconscious – the great serpent-back of the Long Mynd, its tail in Ludlow, its jaws above Shrewsbury; the bony spine of the Wrekin like a sleeping brontosaurus, head under its paw; the spiky armoured stegosaurus-back of the Stiperstones. And across the middle of Shropshire, through the quiet Edwardian spa town of Church Stretton, runs a fault line as deep as the San Andreas.

At Morville we are on a narrow band of the Old Red Sandstone, running round the bottom edge of the Brown Clee. Five miles away and you are on the Wenlock limestone. Three miles the other way and you are on the New Red Sandstone, with its churches and public buildings of bright red, even-coloured stone. Six miles over the hill behind and you are on the dhustone. When the stone here was laid down Shropshire was 30° below the Equator – the present latitude of the Kalahari Desert – an arid environment where sandstorms raged alternately with flash floods, scouring the face of the land. The suitability of the sandstone for building is a function of the conditions in which it was laid down: much of the bright red stone was formed as windblown dunes, the sand grains becoming rounded as they were eroded by the wind, making for an unstable composition in the rock. The Old Red Sandstone was laid down in an arid environment of shifting river channels, the sand grains remaining more angular and tending to interlock, making the composition of the stone more stable. Its colour varies from village to village according to the minerals contained in it: ours is a greenish-grey, purple-banded stone, which extends to perhaps half a dozen villages. The purple and grey bands are due to the movement of iron from soluble ferrous to insoluble ferric: grey for ferrous, soluble in water; purple and red for insoluble ferric. You can see the swirl of the current still in the walls of the house.

The hard black dhustone endures.

The limestone yields, transforms.

The sandstone records. We have long memories here.

*

The stone for the house came from a stone-pit scarcely a quarter of a mile away on the hillside above, long overgrown, its lower slopes quarried now only by badgers. For months I sought a farmer close by with a dilapidated wall or outbuilding that we could quarry for stone. In vain. The Canal was eventually built with stone from a small quarry twelve miles away on the limestone of Wenlock Edge. Pale grey, not a bad match. There were seashells in it.

As we toiled away the rest of the garden went to hell in a handcart. Even when the Canal itself was finished, the turf all around had to be lifted and the soil levels corrected, the little box hedges planted and the hoggin paths laid. In the head, the turf curled and browned as my spade grew thin and bright, the backbone of the blade polished smooth.

The hoggin for the hard-standing came from Weeford, in Staffordshire, forty-odd miles away. Hoggin is a beautiful material, natural, cheap – available for hardly more than the cost of transport. Technically known as 'bound gravel', it is a naturally occurring mixture of gravel and clayey sand which, when repeatedly wetted and rolled, sets hard. Like the sandstone, the colour of hoggin varies according to the source. The hoggin from Weeford quarry is a lovely soft pinkish-grey, a little like new plaster. It is sold 'as raised', but I had it put through a three-inch screen to remove the very biggest cobbles. In laying the hoggin, we followed the method outlined in John Reid's *The Scots Gard'ner*, published in 1683. Place the larger pebbles in the bottom of the path to a depth of about six inches, and then add three or four inches of progressively finer material, until a smooth even surface is produced:

> . . . and so Rake, Tred, and beat; and when compleatly levelled, beatt well with the Timber beaters, while moist, then Roll

soundly with the Timber-Roller, and afterwards with the Stone-Roller, especially in Rain, for which the spring and Autumn is best; but if dry weather, you must dash water on the Roller (continually in Rolling) with the watering pott . . .

We did it in a heatwave . . .

In August the garden begins to run out of steam, and so do I. These are the dog days, the days about the heliacal rising of the Dog Star, noted from ancient times as the hottest and most unwholesome period of the year, a period when malevolent influences were thought to prevail. A sort of inertia sucks at my heels as I walk through the garden, slowing my progress to a reluctant crawl. I visit the garden less and less, becoming a stranger – visit the far reaches of the garden not at all. Seed heads dry and shake their contents on to ground baked hard by the sun. The roses in the Long Border begin to repeat and I almost wish they wouldn't. This second burgeoning of leaf and bud seems almost indecent. Let them die in peace. The peas bloom grey mildew in the heat. Pots go unwatered. The turf seats in the Cloister Garden turn brown and dry. There are flashes of silent summer lightning on the edge of the garden, like the twitch of a nerve, but still no rain.

Now is the time for beekeepers to beware the hives, when the nectar flow ceases and the bees are bored, restless, irritable; when the female workers expel the now-superfluous drones and, tearing off their wings, leave them to die. Wise beekeepers here shut the bees in their hives and transport them up on to the Long Mynd, where they can gorge on August heather. The heather honey is dark and viscous and strong-tasting, unlike the light clear honey of early summer – the bright yellow of dandelion honey in April and May, the pale greenish-straw of lime-flower honey, tasting of mint, in early July.

I heard of a man stung to death by his bees after a long feud with a female neighbour about land rights. He had cleared the trees from the banks of the common stream where the kingfishers flew, planted suburban flower-beds in the midst of the sheep pasture, with his ride-on mower mowed to neat lawns the tall grasses of the meadow. Some say he irritated the bees by mowing too close to the hive. Who knows? Perhaps someone whispered to the bees . . .

It's payback time. *Dominus iustus concidit cervices peccatorum . . .* 'The Lord, who is just, will cut the necks of sinners . . . Let them be as grass on the housetops, that withereth ere it be plucked up. Wherewith the mower filleth not his hand, nor he that gathereth sheaves his bosom.' This is the Hour of None: the hour of just retribution, the time when the chickens come home to roost. *De profundis clamavi te, Domine: Domine, exaudi vocem meam . . .* 'Out of the depths have I cried to thee, O Lord: O Lord, hear my voice.' After the red-letter days of May and June, the days of lilacs and roses, the elation of Ascension Day and summer solstice, these are my *dies mali*, my bad-luck days – not in the cold damp days of winter, but now, under the hard bright sun of summer. I wish, like some butterflies, I could aestivate – sleep right through it, wake in the dew of September.

The garden becomes a quarry for self-medication: feverfew for migraine; valerian to make me sleep; chamomile to calm me down, St John's wort to cheer me up.

In the calendars of the Books of Hours every month has, in addition to the horticultural and agricultural activities of the year, its sign of the zodiac. The sign for August is Leo, the lion – my birth sign – his great mane and breast a sickle-shaped curve of stars riding high over the house in March and April, sunk now in the west like a pale question mark.

My mother's grandfather was a trade-union organiser; he had sided with the millworkers against his own father and been exiled from Leeds to London. One of my mother's first duties as a small child was sitting upon her grandfather's knee to read the political speeches to him from the newspaper. At ten she stole the cane the teacher used to beat the children with, took it home and put it in the dustbin. At eleven she won a scholarship to the grammar school; she did well. At fourteen her father was put out of work; they existed on the dole, her mother taking in washing; she had to leave school without School Certificate or Matriculation. At twenty-two she met my father, won a scholarship to complete her education at Hillcroft, an adult education college for women; she refused him the first time. She did well; they offered her a second year; she refused him the second time. She won a TUC scholarship to Liverpool University; she excelled; won the Lundie Memorial Essay Prize for an essay on the Beveridge Report; won the only distinction in Social Sciences granted that year; would have gone on to finish a degree had not the war made that impossible: only two-year Certificates were allowed. She got married. She started work as an industrial social worker; got pregnant 'by her own wish': my brother, born on VE Day. Got pregnant again: me.

I search the sky for portents: August meteors, the Perseids, debris of the comet Swift-Tuttle, burning up as they enter the atmosphere. The meteor shower reaches a peak around 12 August each year. To see one on my birthday, 17 August, would be special. Not out of the question, for the shower is broad, lasting for up to a week either side. They radiate from the constellation

Perseus, low down on the northern horizon. Not much chance before midnight, but maybe then.

After my mother's death her spectacles were returned to me by the undertaker. I didn't know what to do with them, had a superstitious dread of looking through them; couldn't throw them away, but couldn't keep them. Eventually, sorting her clothes for the charity shop, I slipped them into one of the pockets, as if she had left them there, by an oversight. I don't want to see the world as she saw it.

After I gave up my job in 1988 I managed to live and to finance the garden by editing, designing exhibitions for the National Trust and advising libraries on conservation. Then in 1993 I fell ill, poisoned by toxic crop-sprays in the run-off from a flooded field that Easter while helping a friend dig her garden out from under a mudslide. I thought it was flu, but couldn't seem to recover. The symptoms: joint pains, disturbed sleep, vivid dreams, constant headache, exhaustion. By Christmas I was out for the count. One day's activity meant three weeks recovering in bed. I was diagnosed as having ME. The illness lasted for five years. I lied through my teeth to prospective clients and employers, feigning other work commitments when really I was in bed; arranged dates for a time when I calculated I might be up again. Only close friends knew the truth.

As the grim prognosis began to sink in, it became clear that I would need more help in the garden. Ivor was replaced by Tony, a burly bear of a man from the stone quarries who in an hour could dig a planting hole for a rose that would take me all morning to complete and all day to recover from. With his help and the help of friends and neighbours, I continued to garden. Dan (nearly eighty even then) helped me plant apple trees ('An ounce of help is worth a pound of pity,' he said); his cousin-by-marriage Wilf planted roses in the tunnel ('but don't you tell anyone, or I shall have to garden at home'); Ruth from Ireland, with her pale Irish skin, weeded the gravel under a blistering sun. And one raw New Year's Day when I languished, incapable, indoors, Arthur (unasked) finished the trench I had been struggling to dig for the new land-drain under the tapestry hedge: the best New Year's gift I ever had.

Gradually my recovery rate improved: to two weeks, one week, three days, eventually to one day on, one day off. By 1997 my financial position was critical, but I was feeling more confident that I would one day be better. Confident enough to tackle the Canal. Our bank manager was Mr Davies. His father had had a hill farm on the Brecon Beacons – forty acres, four hundred-plus sheep. He died at fifty-seven when Ioan was twenty-one and had just been posted elsewhere by the bank. In Ioan's absence the farm was sold up. 'I felt really bad about that, losing the farm,' he said. Now sixty per cent of his customers were Welsh hill farmers, with the countryside in the grip of the worst farming depression since the 1930s. He helped them, listening to their stories, supporting them where he could, seeing them through until times got better. All over the country, farms were going under. There were business failures, suicides. Many of the sheep farmers at this time were also struck by ME, triggered by exposure to organo-phosphates in sheep dip. Mr Davies stuck by them, refusing to be transferred elsewhere. And people survived.

My husband and I made a change for him, he said – my husband with his bookshop and me with my garden. 'You are so lucky, you enjoy what you are doing,' he said. When I said that it was really not a sensible thing to be doing, to build a canal when one had no money, 'Oh, but it gives you pleasure,' he said, 'and I have faith in you!'

What gave him pleasure was driving heavy goods vehicles. He had always liked heavy goods vehicles as a child, when his mother's brother, a lorry driver, had taken him everywhere on his runs during the school holidays. As bank manager, he drove the school bus as back-up emergency driver before work in the morning, and spent his holidays driving heavy goods vehicles for a local haulage firm. In retirement, he restored his own 1950s charabanc.

And once the Canal was complete I filled it with water from the spring, drawing it in stages so as not to leave John short of drinking water for the cattle or us short of water for the plants. And as the level rose, the Canal began to attract to itself all the creatures of the garden: Grace the cat, with her pale sandy coat, leaning down to drink like a lioness at a waterhole; a pair of grey woodpigeons, dipping their beaks, tails in the air; black-and-white wagtails strutting their stuff on the hoggin; clusters of bees sipping from the dampness at the edge like a shifting, tasselled fringe. The water was colonised by dragonflies and damselflies, water beetles, pond skaters and water boatmen. The beetles and the pond skaters and the water boatmen are amphibians; they have wings and arrive by flight. But how did the water snails get there? Browsing the stones on the bottom in their hundreds of thousands, speckling the walls like pores, it was as if they had been released from the limestone itself, precipitated out like fossils after millennia of desiccation, unlocked from the stone by the lapping of the water.

After decades of estrangement from my brother I went back to Lincolnshire to look after him and his family after they had been involved in a car smash. The youngest was in traction in hospital; my brother and his wife both had broken bones, were unable to drive. Blood is thicker than water. I had very effectively cut myself off from that part of my life, hadn't been back for years. Now, wandering the streets, I found to my surprise that I could navigate my way through the town, knew what was round the corner, that if I turned here I would find a curving street and that if I turned there at the end of that street I would find the church on my right with a square of grass in front of it. It was an odd sensation, to find the memories still there after all those years. As if they were someone else's memories, implanted, not mine at all. I was at that time studying the seventeenth-century Poor Rate in the City of London, mentally following the progress of the rate collector as he moved from house to house, alley to alley, street to street. Each day, as I left the Guildhall Library, I found I could negotiate my way – to a theatre, a restaurant or a bar – through twentieth-century London via streets I had never visited before, as if following a submerged mental map of seventeenth-century streets. As if then was now and now was then. These memories of Lincolnshire, supposedly mine, were no less strange to me than the streets of London which I found I could negotiate with such confidence. But there they were, like a pattern of drowned fields; and there was me, swimming to the surface.

On the clay bottoms where the soil is heaviest the corn still stands, but further down Corve Dale some of the sloping fields on the valley sides and on Wenlock Edge are already ploughed, the soil a patch-work of rose-pink and terracotta, the hillsides sculpted by the lines of the plough into great sweeping curves and folds. They plough early now. Artificial fertilisers and two crops a year: maximise your investment. The whole landscape becomes an art form, a canvas on which the giant machines doodle, their tracks running up from the road, doubled or quadrupled in repeating patterns, looped at the top where the machines turn. In the stubble fields monumental bales of straw are strung out across the hillside, their flat pale faces and circular outlines articulated by the low sun into planes of light and shadow, abstract art, a modern version of standing stones.

I relent and decide after all to fill the boarded beds of Sir Thomas's garden with scarlet *Lobelia cardinalis*, vivid red nas-turtiums, crimson cannas, all raised in pots and now plunged in place already in flower, just as Samuel Gilbert had recommended. I add the latest black-and-red dahlias: 'Dark Desire' and 'Ragged Robin'; 'Rip City' and 'Chat Noir'; dusky 'Arabian Night' and vivid 'Bishop of Llandaff'; and as their sappy green stems begin to thrust upwards I can feel my spirits start to rise.

And then at last it rains. Rain at last – rain falling in the dusk on the parched garden – rain on the drooping roses and the un-watered pots, on the brown grass and the prematurely autumn-tinted trees – soft, gentle, healing rain. I stand in the doorway at midnight. Salty smell of wet earth and lavender. The gravel glistens in the beam of light from the half-open door.

Vespers

Colour is seeping back into the garden. Leaves sparkle, washed of the dust of August. The grass is greening up again; the red of the dahlias vibrates against the glossy evergreens of the tapestry hedge. The angle of the sun is lower now, making the light redder and less intense, enhancing pure reds and their complementary greens.

I sit in the sun in the west-facing arbour of the Cloister Garden, one of the cats on my knees. The sun moves down the sky. I feel no inclination to read or work; I merely sit. It is paradoxical that, as the days grow shorter, I should feel this sudden expansion of time. Yesterday we finished clipping the yew hedges. There are stray fronds still scattered about the grass. Now, nearly twenty years after the garden began to be made, the hedges are seven feet tall, wrapping the garden round, lapping it with green in this bleached, post-harvest landscape.

The wound-up watch-spring of summer is winding down. The days fill with rounded golden light, like a rich old Sauternes, full and sweet. Sugars caramelise in the leaves – tones of butterscotch, cinder toffee, treacle tart; quince paste, marmalade, toffee apple; Beaujolais, cassis, Lynch-Bages. The hedgerow shines with great plates and bunches of glossy berries like so many jars of jelly and jam ranged on a larder shelf – scarlet hip and crimson haw; red bullace and yellow crab; purple elderberry and blue-black sloe. Trees blaze, as if a reverse photosynthesis were taking place, green chlorophyll turning back into pure energy.

The swallows are gathering in a row on the loop of telephone wire that runs down to the house. All summer they have been restless silhouettes, dark against the sky or outlined against the water as they sweep low over the Canal; now they sit for the first time, companionably burbling like a huddle of pashas smoking hookahs – discussing travel plans? – close enough for me to see the blue sheen of their wings, the red of their throats, their white breasts. The swifts are long gone, heading south over the Sahara and down into central Africa. And the water boatmen and pond skaters too have gone: shipped their oars and flown away, leaving the Canal vacant like an end of season lido. But the swallows, like me, seem to have all the time in the world.

I wander the garden, browsing on milky-white hazelnuts, ripe yellow plums, crisp crimson apples netted with russet. I lay my ear to the beehive and feel the bees' warmth. Idly I compare the cobnuts one with another, sampling first 'Butler' and 'Ennis', then 'Cosford' and 'Merveille de Bolwiller', 'Fertile de Coutard' and 'Gunslebert', 'Kentish Cob', tastiest of all, with slender, thin-shelled, oval nuts rolled in their green calyces like Cleopatra in her carpet. Despite its name, 'Kentish Cob' is not a cob but a filbert. Cobnuts belong to *Coryllus avellana*, our native species, and have short helmet-like calyces (*Coryllus* from the Greek *korys*, a helmet; the Anglo-Saxons had the same thought: our modern word 'hazel' comes from the Old English *haesil*, a head-dress). They have broad round nuts or 'cobs' (from the OE *cop*, meaning head – the reverse process giving us 'nut' as a slang term for both heads and testicles). Filberts on the other hand are derived from *C.*

maxima, a species native to south-eastern Europe that has longer, slimmer nuts, with calyces that protrude beyond the end of the nut, sometimes enclosing it altogether. The word 'filbert' is often said to be a contraction of 'full-beard', but more plausibly is an anglicisation of the Norman word *philibert* (short for *noix de philibert*), from the time of their ripening on or about St Philibert's day. St Philibert was the founder and first Abbot of Jumièges, the greatest of the abbeys of Normandy, and his feast day is 20 August – which would of course, before the reform of the calendar, have fallen eleven days later in the season, at what is now the beginning of September.

I like the wordplay of 'nuts' and nuts, the association of calyces with beards and helmets and head-dresses: anthropomorphic, but it works the other way too. We speak of *jeunes filles en fleur*, green inexperienced youth, hearts of oak; we say someone is blooming or has withered; we too spring up and die down. Ruskin would have called this sort of thing neither true nor useful, an example of what in poetry he called the Pathetic Fallacy, the product of 'an excited state of the feelings, making us, for the time, more or less irrational'. But it is a useful way of understanding the world. I feel a little like a herbaceous plant myself.

> Who would have thought my shrivel'd heart
> Could have recover'd greennesse? It was gone
>   Quite under ground; as flowers depart
> To see their mother-root, when they have blown;
>   Where they together
>   All the hard weather,
>   Dead to the world, keep house unknown.

> . . . And now in age I bud again,
> After so many deaths I live and write;
> I once more smell the dew and rain,
> And relish versing: O my onely light,
>   It cannot be
>   That I am he
> On whom thy tempests fell all night.
>
>   George Herbert, 'The Flower'

Herbert was born in Montgomery in 1593, a man of the Marches like Traherne – and like Henry Vaughan too, who 'saw Eternity the other night / Like a great Ring of pure and endless light'. Is there something about the Welsh borders, the Marches, that breeds metaphysical poetry? Something to do with the landscape, the juggling of identities, the feeling of being between, that prompts the philosophical speculation, the precision of language, the yoking together of like and unlike in striking metaphor, the metrical irregularity? Something that grows out of the soil, the weather? A large part of the poetry of Herbert and Vaughan explores the dynamic of a personal relationship with God, the transformation of a heart as stony as flint (Vaughan's second collection of poems was entitled *Silex Scintillans*, the 'flashing flint', from which God strikes fire) through spiritual awakening, expressed by images frequently drawn from the natural world – Traherne's puddle, Herbert's flower, Vaughan's vision of Eternity, with Time 'in hours, days, years' moving beneath it 'like a vast shadow'. Vaughan was born at Newton-upon-Usk in Breconshire in 1621. John Donne knew the Marches too: 'Good Friday, 1613. Riding Westward' was written as he rode across England into Wales to stay with the philosopher-poet Edward Herbert (later Lord Herbert of Cherbury), the oldest of the seven

Herbert brothers. Donne always wrote best on horseback, he said, for then his mind was 'contracted, and inverted into myself'. He dedicated his Holy Sonnets to the Herberts' mother, Lady Magdalen Herbert, and it was he who preached the funeral sermon in London after her death in 1627. At his own death George Herbert gave the manuscript of his poem sequence *The Temple* to his friend Nicholas Ferrar, founder of the religious community at Little Gidding, requesting that the poems be published only if Ferrar thought they might do good to 'any poor dejected soul'. They went into thirteen editions in less than fifty years, and continue to be in print today.

I pick the hazelnuts when they are firm and white and milky, with something of the texture of fresh coconuts about them – ripe, but before the shells turn brown. This is when the nuts are at their most delicious. But picked like this they do not keep, so I pack some in bags at the bottom of the refrigerator and leave the rest to ripen on the trees. If I want to get the best crop of nuts I know that my hazels need to be grown on a 'leg', and that I must ruthlessly cut out any branches that spring up from the base, aiming at an open goblet-shape of eight or a dozen branches, annually tipped to about six feet for ease of picking. But then I lose that fountain of arching many-stemmed growth which is what I love about hazels – the way they transform that corner of my garden into a little chantry with clustering columns and fan-vaulted roof, dim, cool, set apart from the colour and motion of the rest of the garden. For their sake I have come to accept, even to love, the business of coppicing which at first seemed so brutal – the five-year rhythm of cutting all the stems back to a 'stool' no more than six inches high, promoting new growth, clearing out the old trunks, letting in the sun and air. If the hazels remain uncoppiced, the plants of the woodland floor – snowdrops and snowflakes, bluebells and oxlips – gradually dwindle, the bulbs making leaves but no flowers in the deepening shade. Plants like the oxlips and wood spurge vanish altogether, surviving as buried seed, biding their time. They can wait like this for decades, even a century or more. Then, when the hazels are cut and light is let in once more, there is an explosion of flower, the whole woodland floor 'recovering greennesse'. The products of coppicing are useful too: nothing is thrown away, the hazel branches bent into arbours or arches, cut into bean-poles or tent pegs, the thicker trunks added to the wood pile to keep us warm in winter, the brash shredded into mulch, the twiggy bits used as pea-sticks or bent over the emerging peonies. And the cut stools spring up again into straight new wands which will in time make a new roof, the nuttery growing once again secret and chapel-like, until the bulbs are once more extinguished and the cycle begins all over again.

By the side of the hazels is an old damson tree, its crown shattered by storms now but still fruitful. The most luscious fruit hangs out over the beehives. To pick or not to pick? Damson trees are famously brittle. Shall I wear my bee suit and fumble and sweat as I pick the fruit, or risk death from a thousand stings if I fall? Either way I risk breaking my neck. I opt for a middle course, fetching a stepladder but dispensing with the bee suit, hoping the bees won't bother me if I don't bother them.

Gradually the basket fills with blue-black fruit. I can see the bees flying in and out of the hives beneath. The sun is pleasantly warm, the dappled light soft – not too bright – as I peer up into the tree. Clear amber extrusions of resin glow in the sun along the older branches. Once the tears of Phaethon's sisters, now – how myths change! – the legendary repository of dinosaur DNA. In

Ovid's story Phaethon's sisters, weeping for their brother, were turned into trees, their tears solidifying as amber. Ancient amber, such as that from the Baltic, is the fossilised resin of prehistoric conifers (gymnosperms, probably pines). But since more recent times – the Eocene, say, rather than the Early Cretaceous – some flowering plants (angiosperms), like the poplar and the damson, have also exuded gums. Amber has been prized for jewellery – for its colour, its warmth, its lightness – since the time of the Romans and long before, though the pieces that command the highest prices now are curiosities, those which contain the trapped bodies of prehistoric insects. As I pick, I disturb a harvestman – slow, short-sighted, mainly nocturnal creatures which emerge at the time of the harvest – his thistledown body carried as if on springs. With his immensely long thin legs he delicately palps the oozy substance. Spider yet not a spider: a future fossil?

Phaethon, like Icarus, aspired too high. He thought he could drive his father Phoebus Apollo's sun-chariot. But as soon as the horses started to climb into the sky the chariot careered out of control, singeing the earth and the heavens, melting the ice caps and boiling the rivers dry. The chariot was eventually brought to a halt by a well-aimed thunderbolt from Jove:

> Phaethon, hair ablaze,
> A fiery speck, lengthening a vapour trail,
> Plunged towards the earth
> Like a star
> Falling and burning out on a clear night.
>
> Ted Hughes, *Tales from Ovid*, 1997

Ovid's subject in the *Metamorphoses* is change: transformation, transmutation. But it's one-way traffic, like sedimentary into metamorphic, caterpillar into butterfly: they don't come back, Ovid's cast of characters. Phaethon, consumed with ambition, becomes a comet, burning up as he enters the earth's atmosphere. His sisters, consumed by grief, unable to move on with their lives, become trees, rooted to the spot. Daphne, fleeing in panic and terror, pursued by Apollo, becomes a laurel (*Laurus nobilis*, the bay tree), wreathing the brows of victors. Philomela, raped by Tereus, her tongue ripped out so that she cannot tell of the deed, is transformed into a nightingale, filling the forest with her song. Her avenging sister Procne, dabbled with blood, becomes a swallow. Cyparissus, distraught with grief at accidentally having killed a sacred stag, becomes a cypress tree, the emblem of grief. (His story survives in the botanical nomenclature of the genus that bears his name – *Chamaecyparis*, the dwarf cypresses – though Daphne has found herself reclassifed into a genus of flowering shrubs.)

These are ancient tales which seek to explain how the world came to be as it is – how the swallow got its red throat, why the daffodil nods its head. In Ovid's hands they become, as Ted Hughes observes in the preface to his own version of the *Metamorphoses*, explorations of human emotion pushed to its utter limit, the moment when passion 'combusts, or levitates, or mutates into an experience of the supernatural'. But they are also about the permeability of the human world by the natural world: how, in the extremes of passion or grief or terror, the boundary between humankind and nature dissolves, becomes transcendable. They are affirmations of our relationship with the natural world. Shooting stars, trees, birds. The wild is in us, and we are in the wild.

I have never left the damsons so late on the tree, and their emerald flesh is succulent and sweet beneath their blue-black coats. When

I later turn them out on to the kitchen table, the heap of shining black fruit with their matt powder-blue overlay is flecked with narrow pale gold leaves. What a colour scheme for a room! My little study perhaps? How lovely to paint one's rooms the colours of the fruit in the garden. What about the apples? 'Egremont Russet' for the hall – a smooth sulphur- almost lemon-yellow base, overlaid with cadmium tints of reddish orange and a net of matt brown-russet. The sitting-room in the shining pink and gold of 'Cornish Aromatic'. The upstairs corridor the dark claret of 'Norfolk Beefing'. The spare room the pale apricot-tan of 'Cats-head' with its undertones of chartreuse. Why stop there? The bedroom in the deep yellow of ripe quinces, with a bedspread plumply quilted like the dumplinged base of the fruit, folded and tucked as if with the imprint of a cook's thumb, and soft muslin bed-curtains like the white down that coats its ample curves. I go up the garden to look at the apples ripening in the tunnel for inspiration. All of the sixteen trees – each one trained into four perpendicular cordons – are laden with fruit. These are not the flawless spherical fruit of supermarket shelves, but the Quasimo-dos and Cyranos of the apple world, humped and bossed, flat-round and oblong-conical, with basins ribbed, puckered and russeted, eyes open and closed, skin flushed, striped, spotted and seamed, flesh redolent of acid drops and honey, pear drops and strawberries, pineapples, hazelnuts, aniseed and cloves. Some of them are gaudy as peacocks, gleaming yellow as egg yolks, green as grass, crimson as the eye of Mars. Others, subtle as scholastic philosophers, hide their exquisite flavours beneath dun exteriors, like 'Ashmead's Kernel' and 'Court Plat Pendu'.

Taste and flavour are not the same thing. Taste in itself is a blunt instrument, our taste buds capable only of distinguishing salt, sweet, sour, bitter. The detection and analysis of flavour is a much more complex matter than taste alone, involving the interplay of all five senses: texture (which the experts call 'mouth-feel') – whether crisp or smooth, juicy or granular; smell (how tasteless food seems when we have a bad cold!); sound – masking the crunch of food, removing its appetising snap, crackle and pop, removes much of food's appeal, as does playing around with the look of it (pale-yellow orange juice, for example, is perceived as being less sweet than 'orange' orange juice). Our emotions play a part too. Serotonin and noradrenalin, two brain chemicals which control mood, also affect our perception of salt and bitterness. Someone who is depressed has lowered levels of serotonin or noradrenalin, and may put more salt on their food because their ability to detect saltiness is impaired. Workers who are anxious or stressed may crave salty snacks and be able to drink cup after cup of coffee, oblivious to its bitterness. A similar mechanism – an inability to taste the sweetness in food – may prove to be the reason why some depressed people binge on sweet things.

I'm a Twiglets, pretzel and olive sort of depressive, myself.

Apples are easy to pick: a gentle lift and a twist, and if they come away in your hand you know they are ready. The ripening of the apples in the tunnel is like a long ripple which starts in late August with the raspberry- and strawberry-flavoured apples of summer; then the first russets and the big green 'Lord Derbys' which cook to a perfect froth in time for Harvest Supper; then the crisp and scented apples to eat at Christmas and Twelfth Night, the rich and nutty New Year dessert varieties and the long-keeping cookers; then the biffins which will last us through to Easter. The racks in the fruit store gradually fill with tray upon tray of gleaming fruit. It is the perfect environment in which to store them – cold, frost-free, dark. The racks recede into the gloom, their coloured contents glowing in the darkness, smooth, shining, cold to the touch.

The trouble with pears is that they have to be picked unripe to complete their ripening in store. And try as I may, I never quite get the timing right. All too often, brought to the table, a perfect exterior will hide a rotten or 'sleepy' core. My pears are a mystery to me. We just don't speak the same language. Whereas my apples are all English and masculine – 'Edward VII', 'Lord Derby', 'Lane's Prince Albert' – their names recalling great country houses or English counties – 'Devonshire Quarrenden', 'Cornish Aromatic', 'Norfolk Beefing' – their highest accolade 'crisp', my pears are feminine and French and difficult: 'Duchesse d'Angoulême', 'Marie-Louise' (Napoleon's second wife), 'Josephine de Malines'. Even my one and only English pear, 'Hacon's Incomparable' (Hacon apparently to rhyme with 'bacon', raised by Mr J. G. Hacon of Downham Market in Norfolk around 1815), sounds better said with a French accent. *Beurré* and *fondante*, *bergamotte* and *superfin*, I need a dictionary to decipher them. *beurré* is a pear that is buttery in texture, rich and smooth; a *bergamotte* is one which is short and broad in shape, like a bergamot orange; *fondante* is a pear that is melting in texture, one which, according to the doyen of dessert Edward Bunyard, should dissolve upon the palate 'with the facility of an ice'.

In April the pears' foaming curds of white blossom are one of the delights of the garden, but by midsummer they have gone all sultry and sulky on me, impenetrably aloof. With their creamy flesh, their curves, their ripe juicy plumpness, they are like voluptuous heavy-eyed French Empire beauties who demand absolute obedience from their acolytes. It is said that there is only one day – a single moment – when a classic dessert pear like

'Doyenné du Comice' is at its best: real pear afficionados sit up all night in case they miss it.

Pears apart, the language of fruit is one of ripeness, perfection, wholeness, good humour. We speak of a peach of a girl, a plum of a job, of life being just a bowl of cherries; of plans coming to fruition, of being the apple of someone's eye. It's the language of hilarity and cheerful ribaldry: you lose your cherry, blow a raspberry, skid on a banana skin, don't give a fig. A well-tuned car runs as sweet as a nut. The best ever is a vintage year, the future a juicy prospect.

  In 1989, the year I started my garden, my neighbour Ian planted a vineyard on the south-facing slope of the old kitchen garden here – rows and rows of 'Madeleine Angevin' and 'Müller-Thurgau', neat as a pin. Despite the comments of Tacitus about the unsuitability of the British climate for wine production, there have been vineyards in these islands for nearly two thousand years. There was one near Bridgnorth in the eighteenth century producing a hogshead (sixty-three old wine-gallons, equivalent to fifty-two and a half imperial gallons) of wine a year. According to Ian you don't need sunshine to grow grapes; you just need the right varieties. Aspect helps: Ian's south-facing slope at Morville is ideal. And soil: the glacier that scooped out the steep-sided valley in which the Mor Brook runs deposited the perfect combination of soils – a good loam over a clay subsoil with a deep layer of pebbles beneath. The clay gives richness and body to the wine; the pebbles ensure good drainage and give finesse and elegance. And now we have a second vineyard in the village, further round the same south-facing slope: Richard Rallings's Morville St Gregory to Ian's Mor Valley. Richard thinks his soil may be even better than Ian's – lighter and sandier, quicker to warm up in spring, but still with the same clay subsoil and the same layer of pebbles beneath. He won't know for sure until he tastes his first vintage.

Harvesting and Treading Grapes are the activities portrayed in the Books of Hours for September. In the calendar of the Earl of Shrewsbury's prayer book, a man stands up to his thighs in a vat of red must. His sleeves are rolled up as he reaches out to scoop the last remaining grapes from a basket brought on the shoulders of a second man; a third man with a full basket waits his turn. Three more men strain to lower a hogshead of wine into a cellar. Round the corner, the new wine is already being broached by a tapster, and a group of men stand drinking. Ian makes his wine in a little slate-roofed winery in a corner of the garden next door. He presses the grapes by hand, using a small wooden screw-press filled from plastic buckets of grapes. I stand in line with Ian's parents Pat and Arthur, each with our bucket, taking the chance to chat and to ease our backs. The juice runs out, sharp and green and fruity, into a plastic tub. From time to time Ian decants it into large glass jars to await fermentation. Gradually the shelves fill with jars, while the pale wedges of pressed skins, turned out like sandcastles behind the winery, mount into tottering piles. They make the most wonderful compost.

The buildings here have cavernous cellars, dark and deep as badgers' sets. Here Ian stores his wine in a vaulted chamber beneath the Hall. Slab-tables of slate or quarry tiles range around the walls. Here beer and cheese would have been stored, hams salted, vegetables steeped in vinegar or brine. We get a glimpse of the domestic economy of the Hall in past times, of the products of the 'buttery, Larder House, mylke howse, Kytchin . . . Brewehowse [and] kyllhowse' enumerated in the will of George Smyth in 1600. The cellars beneath my house were once a kitchen, two semi-basement rooms equipped with a bread oven, a vast open fireplace for boiling and roasting, windows to see by, a well in the corner and a doorway through into the big house beyond; a third room is deeper, older, with arched recesses for vats and beer barrels. I put buckets of flowers down here to keep cool before the Wakefield Tulip Show in May; bowls of blue hyacinths in autumn to bloom in time for Christmas; pots of endive in winter to force for chicons, the tender new shoots blanched pale pink and gold under an upturned pot.

The cellars must date from the earliest phase of the buildings' construction, between 1546 and 1562. Although the first description of the house comes from George Smyth's will of 1600 (at which time it included a hall, a best chamber, a parlour, 'the chamber where I lye', a 'brusshing chamber' and at least three other bedchambers), there are features extant today – the great hall (into which a first floor was subsequently inserted), the E-shaped plan of the central block with projecting wings, the twin staircases in the angles, the use of exterior buttresses – which when taken together, appear to indicate a mid-sixteenth-century date, suggesting that it was his father Roger, not George himself, who built the house (though the ornate emblematic plaster ceiling installed in what is now used as a kitchen may well date from George's time, as moulds used in the design appear to be identical to moulds used at Upton Cressett Hall, his mother's family home, in the 1580s).

The house that Arthur Weaver III inherited in 1747 was essentially that built by the Smyths two hundred years before. Evidently a fashionable young man, he lost no time in commissioning substantial alterations and improvements. In 1748 he retained the services of the architect William Baker of Audlem, who was responsible for the addition of two identical pavilions, each with cupola and ornate weathervane, either side of the original E-shaped block, to which they were linked by curving walls of rusticated stone. The south pavilion housed the stables, with the horses entering and exiting through the front door; the north pavilion housed the staff, with a sham front door to match the stables, and the staff entering and exiting discreetly out of sight, at the rear. And enclosed between them – pavilions, walls and central block – was a spacious semicircle of perfect lawn.

Arthur Weaver III was born into an era of stability, prosperity and confidence. England was enjoying the fruits of peace after seventy years of civil strife and foreign war. It was an age in which people could afford to take the long view in their approach to gardens: time for trees to grow and mature, time for the scars of earth-moving to heal. Whereas the gardens of Arthur's father's and grandfather's generations had been small in scale, relying on the immediate effect of bulbs and flowers against an unchanging background of clipped hedges and evergreen topiary – controlled, contained – the new style displayed a confident assumption of continuity within which change and development could be accommodated. It was the moment when, in the words of Horace Walpole, William Kent 'leaped the fence, and saw that all nature was a garden'. It was the age of what came to be known as landscape gardening.

The vital underpinning for the new style was the ha-ha. The earliest ha-ha in England was constructed at Levens Hall in Cumbria in 1695. Within fifty years landowners everywhere were adopting it as a means of achieving the seamless transition from garden to park that was an essential prerequisite of the landscape style. Prior to this, most large houses would have been fronted by an enclosed court, paved or of rolled sand, with a central gateway. Did Arthur Weaver III build the ha-ha at Morville? Given that it forms the long straight side of his great semicircle of lawn, and seems consistent with the building of the pavilions, it is likely that he did. He probably also oversaw the rearrangement of the approach to the house, with its grand gate piers and new drive from the north. Perhaps this too was when the old village was swept away, to improve the view from the house. In 1761 the 1st Earl Harcourt became notorious for having removed the village at Nuneham Courtenay near Oxford to make way for his landscape improvements. Unfortunately for him, the poet Oliver Goldsmith happened to be travelling along the turnpike on the day the villagers were turned out of their old homes; appalled, he wrote the incident up in 'The Deserted Village':

> The man of wealth and pride
> Takes up a space that many poor supplied;
> Space for his lake, his park's extended bounds,
> Space for his horses, equipage, and hounds.

The Earl had built new houses for the villagers beside the Oxford road, but for Goldsmith that was hardly the point: they had been turned out of their homes to gratify a rich man's caprice. By an irony of fate, the 1st Earl died after falling down one of the wells left on the site of the old village. His heir was a republican who refused his title. A follower of Rousseau, he had already in his father's lifetime created a Rousseau-esque flower garden in the newly landscaped grounds; one of his first acts upon succeeding to the estate was to obliterate the 1st Earl's vistas with new planting and institute a custom of taking tea each week with one of the villagers.

The ha-ha at Morville is still here, fulfilling its old purpose and some new ones: as a conduit for storm water between the drains and the stream; keeping the cattle from straying on to the front lawn; as a hunting ground for the cats who now patrol its stone edge on the lookout for prey; occasionally as a car park for the unwary drinker. One morning we woke to find a red sports car upended in it, its bonnet pointing to the sky.

And when he was done Arthur commissioned a painting of his splendid new house and garden: the house still with its Elizabethan turret stairs and dormer windows, but altogether grander now in scale with the two pavilions splayed out on either side of the new lawn, upon which various figures are shown sociably grouped. The figures are probably no more than a conventional device, inserted to enhance the scale of the building and give a sense of movement to the painting, though it is tempting to see in the lively central group – which includes an elegantly dressed woman, her back turned to display the drapery of a sumptuous golden sack-back dress, and a man in bright red frock coat and breeches luxuriantly trimmed with gold, sitting on the grass playing the newly fashionable oboe, his music spread out beside him – a representation of Arthur and his new wife, Susannah Papillon.

Their idyll lasted less than five years. They married at St Margaret's, Lee, in Kent in August 1754. Susannah's family, of Acrise Place, near Folkestone, were of prosperous Huguenot descent – military engineers, international traders and MPs. But her father, David Papillon, seems to have had a sinister reputation which still lingers among villagers in the vicinity of Papillon Hall, the strange octagonal house near Lubenham in Leicestershire where he lived prior to 1717. By 1754 Arthur had resigned his seat as Member of Parliament for Bridgnorth and by April 1759 he was dead, his body brought home to Morville from his house in Hammersmith to be buried in the churchyard alongside his father and grandfather. It was his cousin Arthur Blayney who found the will sealed up at Morville – an old out-of-date will, much altered, dating from before Arthur and Susannah's marriage, which left everything to Arthur's father's oldest surviving brother Edward. There was no mention of Susannah. Either she had pre-deceased him, or the marriage had broken down. I looked the Papillons up on the Internet. The motif on their coat of arms was a *papillon*, a butterfly. I wondered whether Susannah was a butterfly, broken on the wheel of Georgian society, or whether like Frances Cressett she was a survivor. But there the trail goes cold.

There is a curious coda to the story of Arthur Weaver III and his garden. Thomas Percy's letter to William Shenstone continues:

> In view of one of his windows grew a noble large, Spreading Ash, which tho' the spontaeous gift of Nature, was really a fine object: and by its stately figure and chearful Verdure afforded a most pleasing relief to the Eye; you will stare when I tell you that Mr W. had this Tree painted *white*, – leaves and all: it is true the leaves soon fell off, and the tree died, but the Skeleton still remains, as a Monument of its owner's Wisdom and Ingenuity.*

> * This painted Tree I saw with my own eyes a few years ago.

I stand on the lead roof of the church tower, looking down on Arthur Weaver's pavilions, the ha-ha and the semicircle of lawn. The clock strikes the quarter hour on the bells beneath my feet.

The bells date from 1759, the date of Arthur Weaver III's death. Perhaps one of the bellringers' first tasks was the melancholy 'ringing home' of his body. The bells were cast by Abel Rudhall of Gloucester, and were probably brought upriver on the Severn like the tufa for Earl Roger's church at Quatford, each bell inscribed with its maker's initials and date, and a message that reflects that prosperous confidence with which Arthur Weaver began his tenure at Morville: 'Peace & Good Neighbourhood', 'Prosperity to this Parish', 'Fear God & Honour the King'. And yet the England of the three Georges was not a golden age for everyone. There was widespread unrest in both town and country. In the absence of a police force or proper custodial system capital offences multiplied six-fold, almost all of them offences against property: the penalty for poaching a rabbit or stealing a sheep, picking a pocket or slitting a throat, was all one – hanging or (after 1787) transportation. The rate of enclosures accelerated, this time sanctioned by Acts of Parliament. At Morville the last of the commons and wastes were enclosed in 1773. The suffering of the squatters, the very poorest people who had built cottages on the fringes of the commons, pastured a few animals there and re-claimed a bit of ground, was far worse than the position of the cottagers and smallholders affected by earlier enclosures. There had in the past been occasional prosecutions of squatters for encroachment, but their activities had, by and large, been toler-ated. Now they found what few rights they had entirely extin-guished and themselves rendered homeless into the bargain.

I spread the tithe map out on the stone balustrade of the tower and look to the north and east of the village. I can tell the later enclosures from the earlier ones by their larger size and straight boundaries, by the broad roads of regulation width, the regimen-ted single-species hawthorn hedges. The earlier enclosures down by the brook are smaller in size and more irregular in shape, still following some of the old boundaries. The later fields, high above the village, scalp the land, close to the sky.

Down in the garden, butterflies swim in the viscous golden air, their wingbeats slowed to a sleepwalker's pulse. Shoals of tortoiseshells sip from the late-blooming lavender, their fox-coloured wings barred with silver and turquoise, like Navajos wearing necklaces. One or two golden-brown commas sun themselves against the yew hedge, their wings burnished and mottled like walnut marquetry, the edges deeply lobed and indented – the colour and shape of oak leaves in winter. Peacocks open and close their wings on steeples of ginger-eyed Michaelmas daisies. No painted ladies – perhaps they have already departed, following the swifts back to North Africa – but an occasional Red admiral floats lazily about in his red, white and black uniform, too lazy to follow the fleet back to the Mediterranean. Will he find a snug berth here for the winter? The small tortoiseshells and the peacocks and the commas will hibernate in the house or the toolshed (waking sometimes to flutter against the windowpane; and always the dilemma whether to let them out or not – will they damage their wings if I don't? Is it too cold out there if I do? Will they starve in here if I don't?).

They are beautiful airheads, the butterflies, homeless but unconcerned, who sleep wherever they happen to find themselves, wander the world with nothing more effective for defence than painted owl-eyes to scare away predators; who store up no treasure, build no homes. (The bees know better. The workers are sealing up their city, making it warm and draught-proof against the onset of winter, laying in stores. By day they work the ivy flowers for pollen and nectar. Even at midnight there is a subdued din in the hive as they beat their wings, driving off the water and turning the nectar into honey.)

But, despite their apparent fragility and ephemerality, butterflies are great survivors. They know how to adapt. When food is short in winter they close down and hibernate. (A whole colony of bees, active all winter, may die of starvation in a cold spring.) And, eclectic in their tastes as any gourmand, adult butterflies will feed on whatever nectar-rich flowers our gardens offer, English butterflies developing a taste for *Verbena bonariensis* from Brazil, *Buddleia* from China, Michaelmas daisies from North America. They live longer than either bumblebees or wasps, who expire at the end of summer. And, unlike honeybees, they have no intention of working themselves to death for the sake of the next generation (butterflies lay their eggs and depart; a worker bee in summer dies from exhaustion in five weeks).

Many butterflies react to summer heat and drought by aestivation – going to sleep for a month. Their response to a changing climate is simply to migrate. They can fly vast distances. Millions of butterflies annually complete the two-thousand-mile return journey to Britain from North Africa and back again. Monarch butterflies, powerful migrants from Central and North America, have now reached the south-west coast of England via New Zealand, Australia and the Canary Islands.

As I watch, the red admiral alights on some overripe fruit long fallen into the grass – a yellow plum spotted with red – lazily opening and closing his wings as he sips. In our warming world with its chaotic weather systems it is creatures like these, fragile as they are, which will survive. Time should be running out for the red admiral. But he acts as if he has all the time in the world. Perhaps he has decided to change the habit of generations and stay for the winter after all.

Watching him now reminds me of an earlier time, a time when I was no higher than the Michaelmas daisies that grew in Pa's garden in Scunthorpe. I must have been about seven or eight years old, and I suppose from their height the Michaelmas daisies must have been old *Aster novi-belgii* varieties like 'Climax' or 'Colwall Beauty' – at any rate they were lavender-blue with ginger-gold eyes, and they were covered with tortoiseshell and peacock butterflies all through September and October. Pa used to grow them with large clumps of white daisies – my mother called them 'marguerites' – probably shasta daisies (*Leucanthemum* x *superbum*), with their big white flowers and dark green toothed leaves. Looking at Michaelmas daisies now I see their frailties – the need to stake some of them, their susceptibility to mildew or drought, the way the bottom leaves brown and wither – and I still cannot like the pinks and purples or the washed-out greys, but for me those huge, unfashionable lavender-blue flowers have all the glamour and self-confidence of a world where everything was possible and the summers went on for ever.

In the garden they are a second chance, a re-blooming after the droughts and despairs of August. They derive their name from Michaelmas, the feast of St Michael and All Angels – 29 September, the third of the four Quarter Days. Michael is the archangel of Revelation, the slayer of demons, the dedicatee of churches built on pagan sites to Christianise them. Glastonbury Tor is one such place, an eerie almost artificial-looking mound projecting from the watery flatness of the Somerset Levels like a sacrificial altar or a landing pad for aliens. We used to climb it as children in the old days before there was an easy path to the summit, scrambling up, grabbing the tussocks, hand over hand in a tearing wind, to the chapel of St Michael at the top, where Pa would tell us how the body of King Arthur was brought here, to the Isle of Avalon, and how he sleeps here still, the once and future King, awaiting England's call in her hour of need; and how Joseph of Arimathea came to Glastonbury and drove his staff into the soil of Weary-All Hill, where it took root and flowers still on Christmas Day; and how at the time of the Dissolution the last Abbot of Glastonbury was dragged on a hurdle from the Abbey gates all the way through the town and up to the top of the Tor to be executed on the summit. And hovering above it all I would imagine Michael as a Burne-Jones warrior-angel, all scaly armour and shades of blue steel, trampling the Devil underfoot.

Pa had his own demons, which he would exorcise by climbs like these, trampling them under foot with his heavy walking boots, or by long hikes alone in the hills, like the day he drove all the way to Scafell and, having scaled it and come down on the far side, set off to climb Helvellyn on the same day – coming down late into the dark, having finally succeeded in conquering them. After he gave up walking they doubled as gardening boots. I have them still. In 1969 he went back into the Unitarian ministry. An arrogant twenty-three-year-old, I taxed him with preaching rules he himself could not keep. 'You have to have religion or a code of ethics,' he said, 'even if you fall short every day – otherwise we are no better than beasts.'

One last photograph: Pa the same age as I am now, on a high hill somewhere, his tweed jacket blowing open in the wind. He laughs into the camera. He looks like someone I might have fallen in love with.

In the agricultural year, Michaelmas – and all of late September and early October – was the time for 'wakes', for time off, time out, celebration after the hard work of the harvest; the time for Harvest Suppers, Michaelmas fairs, the dedication feasts of parish churches; for feasting, drinking and dancing. A goose, plump from feeding on the stubble fields, was the traditional Michaelmas dish. The Nottingham Goose Fair (to which as a teenager I was forbidden to go) still survives, its reputation as rowdy and raucous as ever, though the geese are no longer driven through the lanes in great white honking flocks, walking themselves to market on their own webbed feet.

The Morville saints are an odd lot, mostly distinguished by their absence. St Gregory is the dedicatee of Morville itself, the mother church, but Monkhopton is not sure: they think theirs is St Peter, though there are clues in the stained glass that he may share the honour with St Paul. Aston Eyre's may be Gregory or Benedict or St Thomas of Hereford (not the doubting one), the Church of Christ or even something to do with Palm Sunday, while the church at Acton Round has lost its saint entirely. But come Michaelmastide each church has its own Harvest Festival and Harvest Supper, a celebration of community life and harvest safely gathered in.

The tradition of a communal meal after harvest stretches back to medieval times at least, whereas Harvest Festival is a

nineteenth-century innovation, devised by the vicar of Morwen-
stow in Cornwall in 1843 on the model of the Anglo-Saxon
festival of Lammas. In Morville parish church the windowsills
will be piled high with fruit and flowers: Sara will bring apples
from her orchard and black grapes from the greenhouse at the
back of the Hall; Barry and Joy, runner beans and brown-skinned
onions from their vegetable plot behind the south pavilion; Judy
will bake bread; there will be pumpkins and prize marrows,
dahlias and chrysanths galore. What should I take? Apples?
Plenty of those already. Honey? Quinces? I ponder the choice.
But I already know what I would take if I could: I would take the
smell of the garden after rain, the spiders' webs lacing the tapestry
hedge in autumn, the reflection of the pear tree in the Canal at
blossom time.

The ladies of the parish have been busy in the village hall, laying
the long centre table with two dozen different salads, piles of
sausage rolls and slices of quiche, pork pies and hardboiled eggs,
mounds of sliced roast beef and boiled ham, baskets of bread, jugs
of celery, cheeses, apple pies – the white tablecloth wreathed with
ivy leaves. The band plays so loudly that the pints of beer vibrate
on the table. Old men and tiny children dance hand in hand,
mothers dance with small sons, sisters with each other. The
teenagers hobnob outside, swapping gossip; light spills from
the windows on to the clustering cars.

By the end of the eighteenth century the grand formal gardens of
previous centuries had been almost entirely swept away, obliterated by the vogue for landscape gardening. But the tradition of
flower gardening survived, albeit in smaller, less formal, more

intimate settings. For Arthur Blayney, Arthur Weaver III's cousin who inherited Morville in 1762 upon the death of their mutual uncle Edward Weaver, I decided to make just such a garden, a personal retreat from the world.

Arthur Blayney was from the Montgomery side of the family. He never married, but at Gregynog, his house near Newtown, he entertained a large circle of family, friends, tenants and stray travellers from 'the titled tourist to the poor, benighted, wayworn exciseman who knew not where else to turn in either for refreshment or lodging'. His table was 'every day plentifully covered with the best things the country and season afforded, for he never indulged in far-sought delicacies, preferring the ducks and chickens of his poor neighbours, which he bought in all numbers, whether he wanted them or not'. It seems to have been he who added the top storey of Morville Hall, the better perhaps to accommodate his many visitors. Perhaps it was also he who enlarged the already spacious drawing room to provide a more commodious setting for the many sociable gatherings over which he presided.

As a model for Arthur Blayney's garden I took the garden made at Nuneham Courtenay by Lord Nuneham, the 1st Earl Harcourt's republican son. Lord Nuneham's garden was based on that made by the heroine of Rousseau's novel *La Nouvelle Héloise*, published in 1761. In Rousseau's tale, Julie retires from the court to live a life of rural simplicity. A former lover seeks her out and finds her in her *Elysée*, a secluded flower garden, enclosed on all sides, where animals and birds live in harmony, wild flowers and garden flowers grow together, and honeysuckles and other climbers trail from the trees and shrubs 'negligently, as they do in the forest'. Rousseau was drawing on the classical notion of Elysium, the heaven of the Greek poets, and also on ideas of the virtues of the simple life as propounded by Virgil, Horace and others, to mount a savage attack on the life and *mores* of the court and the ruling class of his own time. Lord Nuneham was captivated. He begged an acre from his father and in his absence laid out a garden with the help of William Mason, Professor of Poetry at the nearby University of Oxford. The garden featured groups of flowing, asymmetrical flower-beds, winding walks and an axial view leading to a Temple of Flora, the Roman goddess of flowers, all planted with 'a poet's feeling and a painter's eye'. Upon his return from France that autumn, the Earl was said to have been 'disgusted' by the garden's faded state, comparing it unfavourably with the year-round elegance of formal gardens (as live an issue today as it was then, with proponents still on both sides).

Paul Sandby, Lord Nuneham's drawing master, painted a number of views of the garden in 1777, widely circulated at the time in the form of engravings. One of the views shows several slim dark conifers dotted among the flower-beds to lead the eye towards the temple. Mason must have had in mind the pencil-slim cypresses of the Mediterranean (*Cupressus sempervirens*, familiar from Italian gardens) but, knowing that they were not hardy in England, found a substitute. Perhaps he used the narrowly fastigiate Swedish juniper (*Juniperus communis* var. *suecica*), introduced into cultivation in 1768. (The even narrower Irish juniper, *J. vulgaris* var. *hibernica*, was not introduced until 1838.) The Swedish juniper is flame-shaped, silvery-green with softly drooping shoot tips. It took me years to track them down, four of them, knee-high – tall as the Temple now, dark columns thrown into relief against the butter-yellow September foliage of the old mulberry, the bonfire of red and orange that is the cockspur thorn, the vivid scarlet of the maples behind.

Autumn colours come soonest to this part of the garden. I

planted the flower-beds with eighteenth-century roses – *pimpinellifolias* and old damasks, the Portland rose and the first Chinas; with spring- and summer-flowering shrubs such as daphnes, lilacs and mock oranges; with the foxglove spires of *Digitalis grandiflora* and *D. ferruginea* (the 'rusty' foxglove); thickets of sweet white rocket and tangles of climbing roses; drifts of *Phlox* and wild Michaelmas daisies. But in autumn it is the trees here which catch the eye: robinias and acers (red maple and sugar maple), *Nyssa sylvatica* and the cockspur thorn (*Crataegus crus galli*), all trees introduced into English gardens during the seventeenth and eighteenth centuries from the new colonies of North America. These are woodland trees, with leaves high in anthocyanin – a defence mechanism against harsh light – and it is the anthocyanin which gives them their vivid autumn colours. Masked by the green pigment of chorophyll all summer, it is only in autumn as the production of chlorophyll slows and then ceases, and again in early spring when the young leaves emerge, that the anthocyanin shows its true colours: scarlet and wine, crimson and plum, purple and flame. The horse chestnut (*Aesculus hippocastanum*) is another foreigner, introduced from Greece in 1616. By the beginning of September the old tree in the churchyard is already showing its autumn colouring of bright orange and scarlet and gold. Our own native trees are slower to colour, and less vivid. They have a higher proportion of carotenes in their leaves, producing the bright mustard of the native field maple (*Acer campestris*), the pale gold of the birches on either side of the Plat, the deep yellow of the hazels down in the nuttery – the whole garden awash now with gold, punctuated here and there by the reds and purples of viburnum and wild service, the crimson of rowan, the wine-red of medlar, all wrapped around with the green of the hedges.

*

The Temple at Morville is dedicated not to Flora, as Lord Nuneham's was, but to the Hours:

ENTHA TEMENOS HORŌN

– three beautiful words of Greek composed by a friend from Oxford as we sat one day with the tea cooling, the plans spread out before us on the kitchen table: 'This is the Temple of the Hours.' Temple, she said, in its original sense of sacred space: not the building that encloses, but the holy ground which is enclosed; hence originally a garden or sacred grove. And Hours not just in the sense of weeks, months, years – like Vaughan's 'vast shadow', or even as in the Horae, those goddesses of the seasons whose coming blessed marriages and gave fruitfulness to mortals and fields alike (though all of that is implicit, she said) – but Hours as in history, chronicle: stories.

After my mother died, my brother and I made the Temple together. We keep in touch now. I went to his daughter's wedding. She is researching the family history, and we sometimes swap information. And when I sit in the Temple now I sometimes think of that other girl, the laughing girl in the photograph, with one heel raised, about to embark upon her life.

Perhaps my Temple is dedicated to Flora after all.

Throughout their long history gardens have always reflected the *mores* of the times; only rarely have they challenged them in the way that the flower garden at Nuneham did, or Little Sparta, the garden made in the second half of the twentieth century by the poet and sculptor Ian Hamilton Finlay. Rousseau and his heroine Julie have an honoured place in Hamilton Finlay's garden, too. Little Sparta is a garden of inscriptions in the manner of the Leasowes, the celebrated garden made at Halesowen (in what was part of Shropshire at that time) by William Shenstone – the recipient of Thomas Percy's disobliging comments on the Weavers' garden at Morville. In all three gardens, inscriptions are placed so as to invite the passer-by to contemplate the scene while reflecting upon the meaning of the text. Lord Nuneham's texts cited Rousseau. Shenstone's often memorialised his friends. Hamilton Finlay's typically comment on, or playfully undercut, their surroundings, as in

THESIS
fence
ANTITHESIS
gate

inscribed upon a stile.

 But the most striking inscriptions at Little Sparta invoke the shades of philosophers, poets and thinkers from Horace and Virgil to Rousseau and Saint-Just to call for a neoclassical rearmament – the garden abounds in images of war and conflict – against a society which Hamilton Finlay considered to be morally and aesthetically bankrupt (hence the name Little Sparta, in deliberate contrast to Edinburgh, 'the Athens of the North', just over the hills from the garden).

Shenstone set down his ideas on the theory of garden-making in his 'Unconnected Thoughts on Gardening', published in his *Works in Verse and Prose* in 1764. In imitation of Shenstone Hamilton Finlay wrote his own series of garden aphorisms, 'Detached Sentences on Gardening'. They include: 'Certain gardens are described as retreats when they are really attacks.'

Perhaps we gardeners underestimate ourselves: for what else are our twenty-first-century gardens – with their passion for wildlife, their refusal to denude foreign ecosystems by stripping them of rare plants, their rejection of fossil peat as a growing medium, their turning away from chemicals as a means of controlling pests, their emphasis on water-recycling, solar power, composting – if not a critique of modern consumer society, the very society that has brought our planet to the brink of catastrophe?

The mornings are cooler now, with night-time temperatures hovering a degree or two above zero. When I open the door in the morning the smell of quinces wafts across the garden – sweet and musky on the chilled air. The cold breath of condensation lies on the red berries of the honeysuckle. I cross the lawn, my footsteps trailing behind me in the cold dew. Spangled spiders' webs lace the tapestry hedge. The quinces are furred like cats, weighing down the little trees like great golden pears. One or two lie in the silvered grass. They will hang on the trees until late October or even November, perfuming the air around the house. But once picked they will not keep. Cooked, their plump goldenness is transformed into the dark red of cornelian. Raw, they light up the garden like lanterns.

*

Sacred to Aphrodite, quinces have been emblems of happiness, love and fruitfulness ever since classical times. The Greek lawgiver Solon decreed that quinces should be served to every newly married couple on their wedding night. Chaucer wove them into his tales of courtly love. Slices of quince were even on the menu at the wedding breakfast of the Owl and the Pussycat. But beware. The tree of golden apples given to Hera and so zealously guarded by the Hesperides in their garden at the rim of the world may well have been a quince. It was fruit from this tree that was thrown under Atalanta's feet (with the connivance of Aphrodite), causing her to lose the race against her suitor Hippomenes and submit to marriage. Not in itself an unhappy ending, you might have thought, had not Aphrodite, piqued by Hippomenes's failure to thank her properly, inflamed him with lust and then engineered it that the couple were turned into lions on their wedding night. And as everyone knows, lions only mate with leopards . . .

It may well have been a quince too that caused the Trojan War – the golden apple awarded by Paris to Aphrodite after she had bribed him with the promise of Helen, slighting the other goddesses and setting in train a sequence of events that culminated in the fall of Troy. And were it not for the quince, we might all still be in Paradise, for scholars now believe that the Tree of Knowledge was not an apple but a quince, and that it was a quince which was offered by Satan to Eve and by Eve to Adam, thus causing the Fall and the expulsion of mankind from the Garden of Eden.

(If it was, it would have to have been a different variety from mine: rock hard when raw, gritty in texture and with a taste as astringent as lemons, European quinces have to be cooked to release their flavour. Middle Eastern varieties are reputed to be softer and sweeter.) But you get the point. A single quince will perfume an entire room or transform a lowly apple pie into a gastronomic delight. Whole culinary traditions have been built upon quince from Morocco to Iran, Portugal to Serbia: *tagines* and *marmelo, cotignac* and *membrillo*; quince marmalade and quince paste, quince sweetmeats and quince jelly; preserved in honey, spiced with cardamoms, simmered with quails. Quinces are food for the gods.

The mornings may be cold but the days are still hot, full of the shimmer of bees' wings. The ivy in the yard is being mobbed by clouds of honeybees and hoverflies. I can hear the din over the wall as I walk past. In the knots the bumblebees are feeding on the last of the lavender, their long tongues probing the deep throats of the flowers – too deep for the tongues of the honeybees – their note lower, more resonant, like the buzz of their name: *Bombus*. A pair of plump young mated queens (red-tailed bumblebees, *Bombus lapidarius*), move at a stately pace from flower to flower, their fur as black as sables upon their expensive backs; a flotilla of tiny female carder bees (*Bombus pascuorum*), vivid as fox fur and moving at twice the speed of their bigger cousins, dart among the swaying stems; a scrum of big black-and-gold-striped male *Bombus terrestris* and *Bombus hortorum* bomb about with nothing much to do, their wings flashing topaz, amber and crystal in the sun.

As the shadows lengthen and the temperature falls, the lavender is gradually abandoned by all except the male bumblebees, moving ever more slowly, their big bodies clambering awkwardly among the stalks, until the moment when the sun finally disappears behind the house and they stop in mid-motion, one leg half-lifted, like furry solar-powered engines running out of charge. Tomorrow morning as the sun's rays begin to creep across the knot again, they will start to wake one by one, slowly raising and lowering each sleep-cramped leg, until the warmth returns to their bodies. They will continue to fly until the last of the autumn nectar is gone – ragwort, soapwort, toadflax, hawkbit; aster, golden rod, sedum, ivy – but eventually the day will come when the sun no longer reaches the knot and they will slumber on in a sleep from which they will not wake. Only the plump young mated queens will survive, tucked up in hibernation with the seed of the next generation safe inside them.

The occupations for October in the Books of Hours are Plough-ing and Sowing, and Thrashing for Acorns. A busy month. In the Earl of Shrewsbury's prayer book and the Shepherds' Calendar, the fields are full of activity – ploughmen with ox teams and teams of horses urge the animals on as they turn the sod and harrow the soil; sacks of grain stand about ready to be sown; crows look on expectantly; everywhere men are broadcasting seed from bulging slings tied slantwise across their bodies. They walk with measured tread, throwing the seed first to this side, then to that, as if walking between a parting crowd, doffing their hats first to this side then to the other, a courtly, stately gesture. In the background, pigs forage, fattening up for Christmas. At Morville the fields around the garden have already been ploughed and drilled with winter wheat and early oilseed, assuming their winter garb. But the oak trees down in Corve Dale are still green; ancient old trees, branches gnarled and zigzag, but still covered with the new Lammas growth put on in July and August, a wash of springtime green above the autumnal fields.

This is oak country, where sessile meets pedunculate – the pedunculate oak (*Quercus robur*) being truly native only in the lowlands of the British Isles (though widely planted everywhere), and the sessile (*Quercus petraea*) characteristic of uplands in the west and north. There are small differences in their leaves and general outline, but it is the acorns that distinguish them – the acorns of the pedunculate having long stems, those of the sessile having short or no stems. It was the acorns that made the oak so important to country-dwellers. Not for them the oak's hard wood, destined for the timbers of great ships or the roofs of lofty halls. Nor the bark used in the stinking vats of the leather tanner. Nor yet the oak galls, used for making ink. Pigs were what mattered to the peasants, and acorns were what mattered to pigs. The medieval English peasant was considerably better fed than his northern French counterpart, and in this the pig played an important part: times might occasionally be lean, but with chickens, a cow or a few sheep, a vegetable patch and a pig or two, starvation was rarely the spectre that it often was across the Channel. Chaucer's 'poor widow' in the 'Nun's Priest's Tale' was only a lowly servant, but she owned three large sows, three 'kine' (cattle) and a sheep, in addition to the cock Chanticleer and his seven hens who form the characters in the story. Extolling the widow's temperate diet, Chaucer says:

> Hir bord was served moost with whit and blak, –
> Milk and broun breed, in which she foond no lak,
> Seynd [broiled] bacoun, and somtyme an ey [egg] or tweye
> > *The Canterbury Tales*, lines 2843–5

Even today, bacon and eggs is still the great British standby.

Pigs by ancient Saxon right of pannage were free to roam the woods in autumn to fatten up on 'mast' (OE *maest*: primarily acorns, but also beech nuts, chestnuts or any other woodland fodder forraged by swine). After the Conquest, rights to pannage were curtailed by emparkment of land by Norman overlords for hunting forests, and further eroded by the enclosures of later centuries, but in the High Middle Ages from which the Books of Hours date the pig was still the winter staple of the peasantry, providing ham and bacon to feed the family through the lean times until spring. The trotters would provide gelatine, the intestines sausage skins, the bladder a means of mending water pipes or a container for lard. Lard was used for baking and would be spread on bread (for there would be no more milk for butter now until the grass started to grow again in spring). Pig meat was in effect virtually free, and everything was used but the squeak.

My neighbour Arthur, Ian's father, was fifty years a pigman. At the age of fifteen he went to work for Mr Pool, the farmer who owned the land opposite the cottage where Arthur and his family lived. Arthur's father Mr Rowe was head gardener to Lord Acton, and the family lived in the gate lodge at the bottom of the drive to Aldenham Park, the big house on the outskirts of the village. Although Arthur's main responsibility was the pigs, in his time he learned to turn his hand to anything on the farm. And so it was Arthur who taught me how to broadcast seed with a fiddle; how to loft the cows' manure, hot from the byre, on a long-pronged pitchfork; how to burn off the stubble field without setting fire to the house; how to load a wheelbarrow (keep the weight of the load over the wheel at the front; turn the barrow to face the direction you are going before you start to load it); how to look after my tools. Arthur's tools and toolshed are a model of order, the implements gleaming darkly in the shed's cedar-smelling interior, the blades sharp and slicked with oil, the handles rubbed smooth by years of use. Some of the tools belonged to Arthur's father. I found a photograph of him at Arthur and Pat's wedding in September 1954 – and yes, he was as small as me – dapper in his dark suit and trilby hat, with a flower in his buttonhole. (He died soon after, from falling out of a damson tree.)

In the wedding photographs Arthur is resplendent, twenty-eight to Pat's twenty, the pair of them ranged before the church door with bridesmaids and matron of honour, best man and bride's father, Pat with a bouquet of carnations and roses, her dress of Leeds lace and her floor-length veil billowing in the wind. You can almost hear the bells ringing: Arthur Dykes from next door on treble, Bert Richards from Shirlett on the second, Cecil Jones on the third, Percy Ingram from Aston Eyre on the fourth, one of the Elkes on fifth, Arthur's place on tenor taken by someone from Chetton. Everyone in Morville was there: Joan and Edna, clutching their hats, and Guy from the farm, and Mr Pool, and Miss Bythell (who attended the ceremony but missed the reception to go and milk the cows), Mrs Bishop (who never missed a wedding), and Joyce and Dennis from the toll house, and Michael and his mother (his sister was a bridesmaid) – and afterwards at the Crown in Bridgnorth, the long tables lined with faces and babies and cigars and good-natured laughter. Pat was Miss Bythell's herdswoman. She had come to live at Morville the year before and met Arthur at a dance in the village hall. Now their son Ian looks after the village-hall bookings and winds the church clock.

Time passes. The sun slides down behind the hill.

The clock strikes again. Six o'clock: Vespers, the most magnificent of all the Hours, originally sung at sunset – the most important of the Day Offices, celebrated with great solemnity. The canticle is the *Magnificat*: 'My soul doth magnify the Lord: And my spirit hath rejoiced in God, my Saviour.' Sunset and dawn, midsummer sunrise and midwinter sunset, the twin poles of our little lives, whether the makers of the round barrows on the hill or the modern users of the M42, pulling down the sunshades to shield our eyes against the blaze in the western sky. We pray towards the East, but we go West to make a fortune, to discover the New World, to find the New-found-land. We look west to tell tomorrow's weather. Westward lies Tir Nan Og, the Land of the Young; Hesiod's Isles of the Blessed; the Garden of the Hesperides, the daughters of Evening; Ynys yr Afallon and King Arthur's Avalon; Atlantis itself.

The sky is the clear blue-green of a song thrush's egg, with clouds of pale peach and rose and silver, luminous as a Tiepolo fresco newly laid over wet plaster. The whole garden on its raised platform above the house is laid open before the grandeur of the western sky. Across the valley, the trees on the high horizon acquire a tactile quality – not flat silhouettes but rich and dense and black like clustered iron filings or the thick lamp-black of the calligrapher's pen. The vault of the sky deepens to violet and indigo, green-blue beneath, a paring of red on the horizon. And then the green flash as the sun finally sinks, when the red light is hidden, the blue scattered in the atmosphere. Paradoxically, with this quenching of the light there seems suddenly more light in the garden, as if before one were blinded by the bonfire in the sky.

Twilight: that time between the setting of the sun and the coming of darkness when one is alone with one's garden. No one else ever sees it like this – not the garden visitors who come at 2 p.m. on a summer's day; nor the sensitive garden photographers who rise at dawn to catch the elusive light; not even my sympathetic husband, cooking dinner down in the house. Sounds are magnified: blackbirds calling from tree to tree; a neighbour shovelling coal. Smoke rises into the sky. White roses gleam. I can't bear to go in. Half an hour? Three-quarters? Lights come on in the houses below. Still loathe to leave, I find last-minute jobs to do, my eyes now accustomed to the dark; make mental lists of what to do tomorrow; think, 'Can I just . . .? Have I time to . . .?' It is only when – with tools safely stowed and barrow emptied, forgotten washing retrieved from the line and muddy vegetables tipped into the sink, firewood brought in and boots left at the door – I come in at last and turn on the electric light that I realise how dark it has become. The evening star which hung upon the south-western horizon after sunset is already gone. Safely come to harbour once more, I remember the ancient hymn always sung at Vespers – *Ave, maris stella*, 'Hail, star of the sea' – and the old familiar hymn we sang at Benediction: 'Mother of Christ, star of the sea / Pray for the wanderer, pray for me.'

After dinner I feel restless. I feel the tug of the tides in my blood. If I were a fox, I'd be abroad now. The moon is as huge and round and close as if it intended to come bowling down the valley towards us. For a whole week in September and again in October the full moon rises as the sun sets, sets as the sun rises – Harvest Moon and Hunter's Moon. There is enough light all night for the farmers to work in the fields. At this time of year the moon is at its perigee: closer now than it will ever be again until the high tides of February. The cats understand.

I put on my coat and go back into the garden. I can smell the frost falling. I bring armfuls of white horticultural fleece from the fruit store and wrap each orange tree, making it snug for the night. I fasten the loose ends with wooden clothes pegs. No need for a torch: the moon is light enough. I drag tubs of myrtle into the porch, close the lids of the cold frames, carry tender lavenders into the shelter of the kitchen, blue *Streptocarpus* up into the bathroom. All summer they have stood outside. Now the tide of the year washes them back inside again: inside out, outside in, the wash of the years.

Compline

The morning dawns misty and chill. In the stillness you can hear the sound of leaves falling after the frost: the slow patter of dry horse-chestnut leaves drifting into a pile against the wall of the bonfire yard; the whisper of big soft mulberry leaves, blanketing the ground in front of the Temple. The cockspur thorn, all fizzing sparks of orange and flame and vermilion, has collapsed into a plummy heap, leaving the glowing embers of its red berries suspended in mid-air. Across the garden, the last of the Michaelmas daisies gleam, blue as the smoke of November bonfires. In their native America their country names are 'frostweed' and 'farewell summer'.

It feels like the end of something, but there is also the sense of a beginning, the opening of a new phase in the life of the garden, when the frost gets to work to purge it of disease and decay; when the mixture of compost and manure dug into the empty vegetable beds begins its long process of rotting down and enriching the soil. All year the box clippings and the vegetable haulm, the dead heads of spring bulbs and summer flowers, last autumn's leaves and this year's grass, have been layering down into a rich dark crumbly cake from which next year's plants will emerge nourished and stronger.

In our end is our beginning. Senses grow keener again in the cooling air. There is a return to the transparency of spring. Without the distractions of leaves and flowers, you see the garden as it really is.

This time of year the memories come thick and fast as falling leaves. All Saints' Day and All Souls' Day, Remembrance Day and Remembrance Sunday, the first few days of November have always been a time when the boundaries between now and then, between this world and the next, blur like hedges disappearing into mist. Hallowe'en, the eve of All Hallows, gets its name from the Christian festival of All Saints, but its unsettling reputation from the pagan festival of Samhain, celebrated at the beginning of November. Samhain marked the opening of winter, when houses and byres and barns were being occupied again after the long summer absence. Samhain Eve, 31 October, was regarded as particularly dangerous, a time when witches and evil spirits were abroad and had to be placated or outwitted if the coming winter was to be successfully negotiated. The adoption by the early Christian Church of 1 November as All Saints' Day, and later of 2 November (All Souls' Day) as a time to say prayers and masses for the dead, seems unconnected with the earlier Celtic festival, though an echo of the propitiatory fires of Samhain may well survive in our enthusiasm for bonfires and fireworks four days later on Guy Fawkes' Day. In medieval times All Saints' Day was celebrated with enormous ceremony. In this country the twin festival of All Saints and All Souls is now an altogether more muted affair. Our modern festival of remembering comes slightly later in the month on the 11th: Remembrance Day and the adjacent Sunday (Remembrance Sunday), when we remember those who died in the two world wars and in other conflicts since. The heroes and martyrs of war have now taken the place of the saints and martyrs of old.

*

The first words my father learned to read were those of his own name on the war memorial. John Unsworth, 1st/5th Loyal North Lancashire Regiment. Every year on Remembrance Day his mother would take him to see the poppy wreaths being laid on the memorial in Bolton. And every day he would see the same letters on the bronze memorial plaque over the mantlepiece at home, where a mourning Britannia held a wreath of bay leaves above his father's name. 'He died for Freedom and Honour.'

Flowers have been rejoicing with us, mourning with us, celebrating with us, for thousands of years. Thomas Browne, the seventeenth-century author of *Religio medici* and *The Garden of Cyrus*, doctor, botanist and all-round polymath, traced the practice of making wreaths or 'coronary garlands' back beyond the Greeks and Romans to the ancient Egyptians, and geographically as far east as ancient India. Wreaths were awarded to victorious generals and conquering athletes, presented to honoured guests and dead heroes, dedicated to the gods or used to lure beneficent spirits. There were wreaths 'gestatory', worn about the head and neck; wreaths 'portatory', carried at solemn festivals; wreaths 'pensile or suspensory', hung at the doorpost in honour of the gods; wreaths 'depository', laid upon the graves and monuments of the dead – of which we now regularly maintain only two, the depository wreaths of funerals and Remembrance Day, and the suspensory wreaths of holly which we hang on the door at Christmas. Browne loved the orotund sound and shape of Latinate words. His prose is studded with obscure vocabulary and abstruse allusions, sonorous as an organ blast. His coinages were legion – three new words for the manufacture of wreaths alone: they could be 'compactile' (put together), 'sutile' (stitched or sewn together) or 'plectile' (woven or plaited together); their functions convivial, festival, sacrificial, nuptial, honorary or funebrial; the times of their use vernal, aestival, autumnal or hyemnal (when artificial flowers of brass or horn were used, or – using a technique learned by the Romans from the ancient Egyptians – roses forced into bloom out of season). But whatever the details of construction or the manner of use, the wreath was essentially connective, an intertwining of elements which linked nature and man, man and the gods, binding all together into a common story. And, like a collection of stories, each wreath had meaning, composed of elements both practical and symbolic. Thus convivial garlands included ivy because ivy had encircled the mast of the ship that first brought Dionysos, the god of wine, to Greece; also because, just as the grapevine had sprung from the tip of the mast, its growth controlled by the ivy, so the ivy, it was believed, would prevent drunkenness. Nuptial garlands included myrtle, because sacred to Aphrodite, goddess of love. Funebrial garlands included rosemary, because it was believed to stimulate the brain, thus aiding memory and recollection – a connotation it retained until Shakespeare's day and beyond. 'There's rosemary, that's for remembrance,' says poor mad Ophelia; 'pray, love, remember.'

In Bridgnorth a row of scarlet poppy wreaths is propped against the piers of the black-and-white Town Hall, a knot of people standing in front. The clock strikes eleven. Cars and buses come to a halt and switch off their engines. Shoppers along the High Street come out of the shops and stand in silence. People in the side streets, unaware, walk up towards the main street, then fall silent as they reach the corner. A waitress in her black-and-white work clothes, unseen by those on the High Street, walks up Cartway and stands looking on, her tray dangling from her hand; the butchers stand outside their shop in their long striped aprons;

the man from the wine shop, wearing a purple shirt, comes out of
his shop and crosses the road to stand with the group near the
Town Hall, the only moving figure in the tableau. A dog barks in
the silence. Then a gust of wind disturbs the fallen leaves, making
the British Legion flags flap briefly, and the trumpeter sounds the
last post.

The wearing of scarlet poppies and the laying of poppy wreaths
on Remembrance Day dates from 1921, though the sheets of
poppies which covered the battlefields of France and Flanders had
been remarked upon as early as the summer of 1915, the first
summer after the war began. An anonymous poem appeared in
the pages of *Punch* for that year which was to be reprinted around
the world:

> In Flanders fields the poppies grow
> Between the crosses, row on row . . .

The old Somerset name for them was 'soldiers'. At the outbreak of
World War I Britain was still largely an agricultural nation, and
poppies in all their silky frailty, their scattered petals like drops of
blood among the harvested corn, must always have been sugges-
tive of spilt blood and sacrifice, the necessity of death for the
continuity of life, the duty to remember. For these are not the
poppies of oblivion (*Papaver somniferum*, the source of opium,
morphine and heroin), but *Papaver rhoeas*, the field poppy, which
springs up wherever soil is cultivated or disturbed, each plant
producing perhaps a dozen flowers, each flower producing a seed
head, each seed head containing thousands of seeds, each seed
viable for eighty or a hundred years – waiting for the right
conditions to germinate. Like the websites now which enable

one to search for the fallen of the two world wars, each site filled with innumerable small facts, each fact inconsiderable in itself, one hardly distinguishable from the next, each biding its time until it is found by the person who seeks it, waiting for the time when it will germinate in the mind, like a poppy seed.

I know that:

It was snowing when he died.

The date was 30 November 1917.

The place: Cambrai.

He was a baker, twenty-one when he marched away to war. He had only just got married. Her name was Alice. I remember her soft white downy cheeks, her breath on my face; an impression of rounded arms and a small, soft, rounded body; a tiny, whistling, breathy little voice like a laugh. They were together for only three weeks. He sent two embroidered cards home from the front, one inscribed in pencil 'With Best Love to My Darling Wife', the other 'Love from Daddy XXXXXXXXXX'. They called the child John, after his father.

Such was the scale of the casualties that the decision was taken not to repatriate the bodies. During the war, the dead were buried by their own or other units, or sometimes by the enemy, close to the front line. Afterwards, the bodies were gathered together by the Imperial War Graves Commission and re-interred in a series of large new purpose-built cemeteries designed by the architect Edwin Lutyens. The decision not to repatriate the dead meant that there was no body for grieving relatives to bury, no grave in the churchyard beside which to mourn. It was as if they had all simply vanished. And with that realisation came the fear that, unnamed, unacknowledged in their own country, the dead might in time be forgotten. In what was an unprecedented outpouring of public sentiment thousands of plaques, pillars, statues, obelisks and memorial crosses were erected by subscription in streets, schools, factories, banks, universities, churchyards and on village greens everywhere, listing the names of the dead like school registers of stone from which everyone was absent – workmates, colleagues, schoolfriends, those big lads at the back of the class longing to be outside and getting on with their lives – gone for good now. And around the monuments, in place of the bodies, people planted flower-beds, memorial gardens, gardens of remembrance.

Back at Morville I watch Michael walking across the Church Meadow to tend the grave of his sister. She died more than fifty years ago, at the age of four. He comes every week, carrying his shears, to clip the grass. Then Helen comes to put fresh flowers on the grave of her father, and Joyce arrives to change the flowers on Ernie's grave and to tell him all the news – still married after all this time – this act of tenderness, this act of tending the flowers, clipping the grass, a metaphor of remembrance, of keeping the memory green.

Some of the earliest private gardens of the ancient world were funerary gardens. In Ancient Greece, cemeteries were divided into family plots, walled precincts planted with trees and shrubs and flowers, with wells for watering. Often there was a pavilion for dining, too. I like that: dining with the dead. We British tend to be shy of our dead, yet one of the most natural and powerful functions of gardens, both public and private, is to act as the repository of our memories. As early as 1916 the Graves Registration Commission (the precursor of the Imperial War Graves Commission, now the Commonwealth War Graves Commission) sought advice from the Royal Botanic Gardens, Kew, about plants for the new cemeteries. Later Edwin Lutyens' colleague, the gardener Gertrude Jekyll, was commissioned to design the planting. At Lutyens' suggestion, each gravestone was to be of white Portland stone, uniform in design, and one of the aims of Jekyll's planting was to prevent soil being splashed up on to the white gravestones in wet weather. A gentle gesture in such a brutal setting. She chose a mixture of simple English cottage garden plants such as columbines, pansies and white thrift, to give a feeling of 'home', taking care that the planting in front of each gravestone should not obscure the inscription. The thrift was a particular favourite of hers. She raised it in her own garden in Surrey for transport to France and Flanders. According to the poet Geoffrey Grigson, the name means 'that which thrives, is evergreen'. But in the Victorian language of flowers, as Jekyll would have been well aware, thrift also means 'sympathy'.

Yet many of the dead had no grave at all: the bodies of 34,710 of the estimated 150,000 British casualties at the Battle of Arras were never found; of the 419,654 casualties of the Somme, the bodies of 73,357 were never recovered. Some had simply been blown to bits; others, buried in temporary burial grounds, had been pulverised as the front line swirled back over them. And in the panic and chaos that followed the German counter-attack at Cambrai, men simply lay where they fell and were trampled into the mud.

I look at my hands, the nails still black with soil from the garden. They are my father's hands, wide and strong, gardener's hands, piano-player's hands. They even have a cropped finger, like his – my father's lopped by mill machinery, mine the result of a car accident. Are they his hands too, I wonder, my grandfather's? I never found the war memorial in Bolton with his name on it (many smaller memorials, as perhaps his was, have been lost along with the buildings that once contained them), and for a moment my grandfather seems as elusive as ever, as absent from my life as he was from my father's. But then I think again of his hands, young hands, white with flour, kneading the bread. How soft they must have been. And now my father's hands in old age, smoking a cigarette, the bent finger trembling a little; and my hands, tending a garden, keeping the memories green.

In 1997 my parents came back to Shropshire, nearly sixty years after they first came here, running away from dead-end jobs in dying towns. In the interim they had wandered from Lancashire to Somerset, Somerset to Lincolnshire, Lincolnshire to Leicestershire, Leicestershire to Gloucestershire, Gloucestershire to Oxfordshire. Now the village they were living in had lost its shop and its regular bus service, and my father, forbidden to drive after a series of small strokes, was walking four miles each way to do their weekly shopping. He was also doing all the cleaning and washing, my mother having fallen prey once more to depression and entrenched psychosomatic illnesses. Just before Christmas the local hospital telephoned, expressing growing concern. The strokes had affected my father's memory; they weren't sure how much longer he could cope. He had, they said, expressed a wish to return to Shropshire. 'What do you feel about that?' they said.

We had kept in touch, just about, over the previous thirty years, by Christmas cards and telephone calls and the occasional visit. And we had even, briefly, lived in neighbouring villages, when they moved to Oxford just before I left for Dublin. But this would be uncharted territory for all of us.

The new bungalow was on a corner site, with a large new raw triangular garden bounded by two long brick walls and a stream along one edge. I bought great quantities of rambling roses from my friend Lindsay Bousfield, collecting them late one night and arriving at the bungalow long after dark. I was determined to get the roses planted, by the light of the street lamps if necessary. 'Go home!' Pa said. 'You're doing too much.' 'I have to get them *in*,' I said. 'Go home!' he said. How we fought! Eventually, exasperated beyond endurance, I said, 'Do it yourself then' – and instantly regretted it, knowing he could not. 'It's an act of love,' I said. 'An act of pride,' he said. We were both right.

It was the year of the Hale-Bopp comet. Every evening as I put my tools away I could see it in the western sky – the rounded, glowing head with its streaming curve of a tail, swinging in from outer space. It passed closest to the Earth on 22 March, heading for its appointment with the Sun on the first day of April. For eight weeks it was brighter than magnitude 0, brighter for longer than any other comet seen in the past thousand years, at its brightest brighter than any star in the sky except Sirius. Then it plunged back into deep space, receding until it was no more than a pinprick in the night sky. Over those few weeks we planted the white philadelphus that had perfumed the summers of my child-hood, the white double lilac we both remembered outside the bedroom window in Somerset, the lavender brought back to him from my garden as cuttings of cuttings of cuttings taken so long ago from his own garden, Housman's wild cherry tree, and the

Michaelmas daisies where the Peacock butterflies had basked in that sandy Lincolnshire garden.

We both know that this is Pa's last garden. But it is *his* garden. Almost every time he returned from shopping he would bring a plant or a new rose, subverting my carefully colour-themed borders with brilliant pink and red hybrid teas. Privately, I fumed. But he was right: his brilliant jolts of colour spiced up my too-tasteful arrangements; his yellow climbing hybrid tea flowered on and on, long after my understated ramblers had shot their bolt. And my mother loved them. He bought a garden bench, and she took to sitting outside in the sun while he fiddled about, weeding the beds with his old fire axe or using the flat side of it to whack in a stake. Then one day he inexplicably set the tea table as if for a dozen visitors, with sliced apples, peeled oranges, buttered bread – plates, tea cups – mounds of cake – chairs ranged around the room. Who was he expecting? Whose company did he crave? Was he remembering his grandmother, the aunts of his childhood, Edith and Belle and his favourite aunt Jenny, the old Belmont days? For there was no one else – years of moves and fallings-out had seen to that. In the end only me and the kindness of strangers: the carers and social workers whose patience seemed inexhaustible; the new neighbours who sent Christmas cards with 'Best wishes from Mabel at No. 6', and 'All the best from Jack at No. 7'.

He began to confuse my mother with his mother, me with his adored half-sister Doris; lost track of the date; offered you tea six times in an hour forgetting that he had made a pot ten minutes ago; would throw the carers out of the house or refuse to let them in.

But then I would find him sitting on the edge of my mother's bed reading to her from Eliot's *Four Quartets*, the bit from 'The Dry Salvages' that ends 'Not fare well, But fare forward, voyagers,' his battered paperback copy of the text spidered over with his annotations from the *Bhagavad Gita*, from Heraclitus, from the Catholic liturgy, from Plato.

> Fare forward, travellers! not escaping from the past
> Into different lives, or into any future;
> You are not the same people who left that station
> Or who will arrive at any terminus,
> While the narrowing rails slide together behind you;
> And on the deck of the drumming liner
> Watching the furrow that widens behind you,
> You shall not think 'the past is finished'
> Or 'the future is before us' . . .
> Here between the hither and the farther shore
> While time is withdrawn, consider the future
> And the past with an equal mind.
>
> T. S. Eliot, 'The Dry Salvages', 1941

Sometimes the old photographs would temporarily re-establish the link between past and present. The memories would come up to the surface, weedy and dripping, like iron boxes attached to an anchor chain which together we pulled from the depths of his life. How he had been raised in a household of women, in a town of women, where every one of them had lost a son, a brother, a husband, a father. Pa loved women: it was men he had trouble with. How Alice fell pregnant again by a married man who lived in the big detached house opposite the row of cottages where they lived. How the child, a girl, was initially given up to its father's wife, to be raised as their own, but after a time Alice had reclaimed the child and fled into the backstreets of Bolton. How they lived in one upstairs room with a sheet slung under the ceiling to catch the cockroaches that fell on your face as you slept. How the children had one pair of boots between them, otherwise went barefoot. How she scrubbed the floors of public houses to make a living. When a Christmas present was a penny orange, a breakfast treat the top of an adult's boiled egg. Her married lover pursued them. When Pa was old enough he threw him out of the house, tumbling downstairs in a flail of arms and legs.

Sometimes the boxes would open. At other times they stayed obstinately shut, the locks rusted into immobility, the keys lost. I would prompt him with memories of my own, memories of his memories, memories of his retellings of the old stories told to us as children long ago when we would still listen, and now told back to him in old age, our two memories entwined like a ship's cable. I hardly know now what is his memory and what mine. Did he as a small child see the body of the young girl who drowned herself in the big pool, her white nightdress wet against the black stones like the wings of a drowned swan? Or was it a dead swan he saw which reminded him of the story of the young girl? Or did I, listening, see the drowned girl at the water's edge, beautiful and white in the dark water like a dead swan? Except that the fragments of Pa's memories which exist in my memory are just that: fragments. Unlike my own memories, which are blurred around the edges and in which I can, if I try, deepen the focus or shift the viewpoint so that other things come into view around the central image, my memories of his memories are small and bright and hard-edged, like pieces of china dug up in the garden. Try as I might, I cannot see any further round them. That's all that there is.

One morning I found neat squares of paper all over the house with his name and address written on them, as if he were afraid of losing himself between one room and the next. 'Oh, he's full of disappearing today,' said my mother. For years he had played the part of the eccentric professor, feigning deafness, deliberately mishearing what you said in order to repeat it back to you with great comic effect. Now, as language slid away from him, he played the part in earnest, his linguistic constructions sometimes hilarious, often beautiful, a surreal kind of poetry. Struggling for words as we watched the lunar eclipse together in September 1997, he coined his own description of the shadow of the Earth moving across the disc of the Moon: 'the moon-bite – the moon-beams – oh you know! The dustbin in the moonbight'.

Are we less human without our memories? Less ourselves? Or more so, like people on a beach, divested of their clothes?

Comet Hale-Bopp last came our way about 4,200 years ago, travelling on a vastly elongated orbit from the frigid realms of deep space to within a few million miles of the Sun. Long-period comets like this are thought to have their origin in the Oort Cloud, a grouping of small objects ejected from the inner solar system and enclosing it like a shell more than a thousand times further out than Pluto. Halley's Comet seems almost neighbourly by comparison: its source is the Kuiper Belt, just beyond Neptune. It reappears every seventy-five years or so. Short-period comets like Halley's are thought to be among the most ancient objects in the solar system, formed at the edge of the proto-planetary disc when it first began to cool. The head of a comet is composed of ice (frozen water, frozen carbon dioxide and other frozen organic substances such as methane), with specks of carbon dust, rock and metal together making up a 'dirty snowball' which starts to melt as it approaches the sun. As it melts, traces of dust are left behind, specks no larger than grains of sand; ordinarily invisible in the blackness of space, they flare up and vaporise when the Earth's orbit next encounters them. We know them as shooting stars. The comet itself may not return for hundreds or even thousands of years, but the shooting stars remain, like a memory, visible traces of our brief encounter with this being from another world.

Cascades of shooting stars (or meteors, to give them their proper name) recur on the same dates each year. Halley's Comet is the souce of the Eta Aquarids of May and the Orionid meteors of October. Comet Swift-Tuttle is the source of the spectacular Perseid meteor shower each August. The source of the Geminid meteors of December is Phaethon, a 'dead' comet named after Phoebus Apollo's headstrong son who tried to drive the chariot of the sun and was sent plunging to earth by Jove's well-aimed thunderbolt.

Mankind has been recording the passage of comets for hundreds, even thousands, of years. The Chinese may have recorded the passage of Halley's Comet as early as 2467 BC. By 240 BC it was being regularly recorded by Chinese, Japanese, Babylonian and Persian astronomers. In 1066 its appearance in the skies over England was recorded in the Anglo-Saxon Chronicle; it was woven into the Bayeux Tapestry as a dramatic foreshadowing of the death of King Harold. Halley himself observed the comet in 1682. Applying his friend Isaac Newton's new planetary theory of closed gravitationally bound orbits, Halley postulated a single comet with an elliptical orbit and a period of seventy-six years which would account for recorded cometary sightings in 1607, 1531 and 1456. If he was right, the same comet would reappear in the winter of 1758–9. Halley himself did not live to see it, but the comet reappeared on Christmas Night 1758, just as he predicted.

Accurate prediction of anything – whether the return of a comet or the date of Easter – depends upon accurate records being kept of the past. But while the sun, moon and stars provide a ready means of calculating the forward passage of time in terms of

lunar months or solar years, the means of calculating backwards
year on year is less obvious. Some agreed starting point has to be
found. The Romans reckoned the past in years *ab urbe condita* –
from the founding of the city of Rome. The ancient Greeks dated
past events by genealogies – in the third year of the reign of such-
and-such a king, or in the year when so-and-so was high priest;
later by Olympiads, held every four years. Christians date years
from the birth of Christ, Muslims from the Year of the Prophet's
Migration. Parliament and lawyers still work by regnal years.

I reckon dates from the year I began the garden. Like a comet
swinging in from outer space, in the ninth year after I began the
garden, in the forty-sixth year of the reign of Elizabeth II, in the
year that Tony Blair came to power, six months before the death
of Princess Diana, in the year that Comet Hale-Bopp amazed the
world, my father came back into my life.

When Arthur Blayney died in 1795 he left Morville to Henry, 8th
and last Viscount Tracy – the widowed husband of Arthur
Blayney's and Arthur Weaver's other cousin, Susannah Weaver
– and through him to Susannah's daughter Henrietta. Henrietta
succeeded her father in 1797, and the following year married her
cousin Charles Hanbury, who took the additional surname of
Tracy in recognition of his wife's superior fortune. Although
Morville held out the promise of a springboard into Liberal
politics for both Charles and his younger son Henry, it is unlikely
that the Hanbury Tracys spent much time in residence here –
Bridgnorth politics had in any case always been dominated by the
Tory faction, led by six generations of the Whitmores of Apley
(there is a local saying which dates from this time, 'All on one side,

like a Bridgnorth election') – and Henrietta's fortune was soon being laid out in the creation of a vast new neo-Gothic mansion at the Tracy seat of Toddington Hall in Gloucestershire.

In 1814 they sold Morville to their neighbour Sir Ferdinand Richard Acton of Aldenham, and for the next sixty years the house was let piecemeal to family and employees of the Actons: to Henry Acton in the 1820s; to the Actons' land agents in the 1840s and 1850s; to the Rev. Nicholas Darnell, who ran it 'as a place for the education of the sons of Catholic gentry' in the 1860s.

Then in 1873 the tenancy was taken by Joseph Loxdale Warren, lawyer by profession and District Registrar of his native Market Drayton; in retirement, a Justice of the Peace and member of the Board of Guardians; a very Victorian patriarch. His wife Mary Ann had borne him seven sons and seven daughters. The boys went out into the world. Joseph became a barrister, Albert went into the Church, George Gordon into the army. Charles was 'shot through the heart, whilst advancing to the relief of his countrymen beseiged in the Residency of Lucknow on September 25th 1857'. The seven girls remained at home. They never married. When their parents died, they stayed on at Morville, growing old together. They outlived the nineteenth century and the Empress-Queen herself, the first motor cars and the horrors of World War I, Picasso's *Demoiselles d'Avignon* and Eliot's 'Love Song of J. Alfred Prufrock', the Jazz Age and 'The Waste Land', dying one by one: first Josephine Martha, then Wilhelmina Christian, Lucy Ann and Mary Lisette, Henrietta Matilda and Georgiana Mary, until finally only Juliana was left.

It must have been in 1925 or early 1926 that Lady L came to visit the last two Misses Warren, Juliana and Georgiana. (Georgiana, known in the family as Mary, died the following spring.) Perhaps they came for Georgiana's birthday, in early September.

Lady L and her grandmother drove over from Dudmaston in the pony and trap. Juliana would have been eighty-two, Georgiana eighty-one. Lady L remembered them as Edwardian ladies, with upswept hair and long skirts. I imagine them ranged outside the front door as if posed for a photograph, the faces a little bleached out by the sun, one of the sisters with her hand raised to shield her eyes, Lady L's grandmother sitting in the trap holding the reins, Lady L, a leggy girl in a white frock, standing to one side. They frown in concentration, with gaze oblique, averted from the glare. The edges of everything are a little blurred by the light, and I imagine spiders' webs everywhere, those webs you only get in autumn, gold filaments strung from tree to tree, from tree to grass, falling through the air like willow down in spring.

They are all here in the churchyard, seven stone crosses with an eighth for Fitz, the youngest son, and an obelisk to commemorate the other boys, presided over, in death as in life, by the monumental presence of Joseph Loxdale Warren, several sizes larger than all the others.

The Victorians were the first post-modern gardeners. They pillaged the past for styles: for Elizabethan knots, Italianate urns, Gothic ruins, Moorish arches. Their gardens were gaudy, gorgeous and hideously expensive to maintain; cutting-edge and nostalgic, sentimental and technologically advanced, all at the same time. They relied on vast quantities of half-hardy plants culled from all over the Empire, raised indoors, bedded out and then thrown away at the end of the season; on tons of coal and acres of glass; on platoons of gardeners to stoke the furnaces and hand-pollinate the peaches; on squadrons of nurserymen producing flowers that were ever bigger and ever brighter.

All this was anathema to William Robinson, a contemporary of

Gertrude Jekyll. Like her he was an early advocate for the use of hardy plants in gardens. But unlike Jekyll with her usually placid demeanour, Robinson was famously hot-tempered. At the age of twenty-one, already in charge of the greenhouses in his first employer's garden at Ballykilcannon in his native Ireland, he is said, after a quarrel with his superiors, to have quenched the greenhouse fires and thrown open the windows to a freezing January night. Robinson believed in plants that could take care of themselves, especially bulbs, herbaceous plants, shrubs and trees, all of which had been neglected in the Victorian craze for bedding. In 1870 he published an extraordinary book – revolutionary even today – called *The Wild Garden*. At first more a manifesto than a manual, it underwent a series of revisions and new editions as he continued to experiment with natural groupings of hardy plants, intended to be left to naturalise in semi-wild settings. While the early editions stressed the use of native British flowers, later ones included more and more hardy exotics such as peonies, lilies and North American plants like Michaelmas daisies, golden rods and compass plants (*Silphiums*), which he had seen in the wild on a visit to America in the year of the book's first publication. He also shared with Gertrude Jekyll a new enthusiasm for wild roses, shunning the over-large over-brilliant products of the breeder's art in favour of the native roses of Europe and the new species roses which were beginning to arrive in England from Asia.

For Joseph Loxdale Warren I decided to make a formal Rose Border, stuffed to the brim with nineteenth-century bourbons, portlands, moss roses and hybrid perpetuals, searching out roses that could be trained up wires and along ropes, on tripods and posts, pegged down, bedded out, grafted as standards and clipped into pyramids. In Victorian gardens, plants as well as gardeners were expected to know their place.

In contrast, William Robinson's Wild Garden was the sort of garden Miss Juliana might have liked, a place where rambling roses were allowed to trail out of trees, or were left to heap themselves up like briars or sucker into thickets, where 'pruning, or any other sort of attention after planting, should not of course be thought of.' I think of her left alone, the garden gently sinking into decay around her: the brilliantly coloured carpet beds grassed over to save the work of the garden boy, the unpruned espaliers growing monstrous and humorously hump-backed, the pony who pulled the lawnmower put out to grass, his leather boots hung up for good. So for her I planted wild roses from all over the world, and beneath them masses of scented white *Narcissus poeticus* from Greece; drifts of blue *Camassia lechtlinii* from the woods of North America; clumps of sky-blue *Iris sibirica*, tall *Campanula lactiflora* and gawky primrose-yellow *Cephalaria gigantea* from the Caucasus and Siberia; inulas galore. I let the grass grow long and watched as it was colonised by native blue cranesbills, speedwell and yellow rattle. I mowed curving paths through it, overhung with lady's lace and wild roses. And I thought of her long skirts brushing the dew in April, her shoulders dappled with rose petals in June, her sleeve yellow with hazel pollen in spring. Perhaps she might even have kept bees.

In November now the rose-hips are spangled with frost, gleaming wet on the sides facing the sun. *R. moyesii*, like scarlet flagons; *R. villosa*, like deep-red cherry tomatoes; *R. roxburghii*, spiny as conkers.

A change in the weather: wind from the north-west, engulfing the house like a tidal wave, crashing down the chimneys and putting out the fires, sinking us fathoms deep. The house recoils from the impact, doors and window frames rattle, curtains sway in the draught. I have never known the house so cold. I put the shutters up early.

Next morning I go up the garden to survey the damage. I fear for the old pear tree. Buffeted by centuries of gales, it already leans away from the wind, its crown shattered. I find silver birch twigs littering the Plat, a wire snapped in the tunnel, one of the pots of box blown over and the pot shattered. But the pear tree is still standing. It's a misconception that trees fall in the direction in which they lean. Things are strongest where tested most.

Manual labour had a pivotal role in St Benedict's monasteries. The day was divided into study, work and prayer, the times and proportions varying according to the season. Between Easter and 1 October the monks spent their mornings after Prime until the fourth hour at whatever work needed to be done; from the fourth hour until Sext they devoted themselves to reading; from Sext until None they were allowed to rest on their beds in silence; then between None and Vespers they were to return to their work. From 1 October to the beginning of Lent the monks read until Terce, after which they worked at their assigned tasks; then after None they were to return to their reading. 'When they live by the labour of their hands,' said Benedict, 'as our fathers and the apostles did, then they are really monks.'

That's what I like best about gardening: not the thinking about it or the designing of it, the talking about it or the admiring of it, but doing it. Doing everything and anything in the garden, from the hardest task to the most menial or the most boring, doing the work as a daily routine, not just when you want or what you want, not just in spring and summer when the weather is good, not just when it's pleasant, but now, in the cold and the wet.

Did you think it would be easy?

> You are not surprised at the force of the storm –
> you have seen it growing.
> The trees flee. Their flight
> sets the boulevards streaming. And you know:
> he whom they flee is the one
> you move toward . . .
>
> Summer was like your house: you knew
> where each thing stood.
> Now you must go out into your heart
> as onto a vast plain. Now
> the immense loneliness begins.
> The days go numb, the wind
> sucks the world from your senses like withered leaves.
>
> Through the empty branches the sky remains.
> It is what you have . . .
>> Rainer Maria Rilke, 'Dich wundert nicht des
>> Sturmes Wucht', from The Book of Pilgrimage,
>> Part II of *The Book of Hours*, 1903, translated
>> by Anita Barrows and Joanna Macy

Now you see it: the garden and the tasks stripped bare, the hard labour. This is what it is all about: soil and manure, spade and pruning knife.

*

The hours of daylight are short now. I dress in thermal vest, dungarees, flannel shirt, sweater, two pairs of socks, boots, knee pads, gloves, hat, body-warmer, wax jacket. People say there is no such thing as bad weather, only bad clothes. But it all depends on what you're doing. As the old assistant gardener at Dudmaston said, dressed in the same tweed jacket he always wore, 'No wonder you be cold, you got too many layers on. You want to keep moving instead.'

In the Books of Hours the activities for November and December are Slaughtering Beasts, Roasting Meat, and Baking Pies. The villagers slaughtered their beasts in autumn because there was not enough green stuff to feed the animals through the winter. With the introduction of turnips in the mid-seventeenth century as a late-summer field crop sown on the stubble, many more beasts could be overwintered; but in the medieval period, once winter set in, the beasts' diet would grow steadily more meagre, and their flesh make poor eating. Killed in autumn, they would be plump from grazing the 'aftermath' (the new growth made in late summer by grass cut for haymaking), and for a short while there would be fresh meat for everyone. I think of Reg, our local butcher, my husband's best friend. A huge, laughing man with a chest like a barrel and a temperament to match, Reg came into our lives almost the first night we arrived at Morville. Presiding over the pool table in the pub across the road, he challenged Ken, the incomer, to a game of pool. On this occasion it was Ken who won, but honour demanded a return match, a match that has gone on being played in pubs and bars on both sides of the Channel now for twenty years. Slaughtering an ox, roasting a pig, baking pies –

this would have been daily fare for a medieval Reg, who feeds half of Shropshire with his pies. Pork pies are his staple, but he makes black puddings, faggots, brawn and chawl; spiced beef and pickled tongue; game pies in fluted oval moulds, made from venison, pheasant, rabbit, hare, pigeon, wild boar; gleaming strings of sausages made to half a dozen different recipes; dry-salted home-cured hams and flitches; and a raised pie of potatoes and cream and tarragon that would make a grown man weep.

It is Advent Sunday. Four weeks to Christmas. Staff and patients from Park Attwood Clinic near Kidderminster arrive to walk the Turf Maze. The patients have a variety of life-threatening, life-impairing illnesses. They bring candles, and at dusk each walks the maze, alone or with a carer, carrying a lighted candle. By the time darkness falls, the centre of the maze is a blaze of light.

People have been coming to visit the garden almost from the beginning: the people who come back year after year just to see how it is all progressing; the children from the village school who come each year and run round the maze in a shrieking, laughing file ('Where's the tramp, miss?' they tease, remembering the night two neighbours stole up the garden and turned the water-filtration unit into the figure of a tramp with an old hat and boots); the local people who pop in to catch the tulips or the roses or the hellebores; the people who were children here, and remember scrumping

apples from the orchard or camping out in the Brownie House
before the garden was even begun; the groups of blind people and
the groups from the inner cities having a day out; the families on
holiday; the WI ladies on their summer outings; the retired people
studying local history or archaeology or the history of gardens; the
visitors from the Netherlands, Switzerland, America, Japan; the
old people rediscovering the scents of their childhood; the young
people finding a secret corner for a kiss and a cuddle; the
horticultural societies, the garden clubs, the flower-arranging
ladies. It has always felt like a communal effort, a shared project.

There is a moment in the service of Compline, the last of the
Hours, when each of those present silently examines his or her
conscience. Gardening has its own share of vices as well as virtues,
and Advent is a good time to take stock, not only of garden (all
those scribbled notes of things to remember for next year) but of
gardener too. Advent, like Lent, used to be kept with fasting and
abstinence, a time of reflection in preparation for the coming birth
at Christmas. The vicar wears purple in recognition of the sombre
mood. And so I ask myself, Why after all did I do it?

Pride, defined as the inordinate sense of one's own superiority,
was traditionally placed first of the Seven Deadly Sins, because it
was regarded as being the sin of Satan and the fallen angels, and
thus historically as the first sin of all. Pride is the gardener's sin par
excellence. Who has not felt a surge of pride when they say for the
first time, 'Oh, we are in the Yellow Book' or 'We are opening for
the church this year' – better still to be able to boast, 'We had 357
visitors and the grass was squashed quite flat!' Pa was right. I
wanted to make a beautiful garden for him because I loved him,
but also because I could.

Covetousness too is the gardener's sin, the inordinate longing for a material possession – for the blackest of black hellebores, the rarest of snowdrops, the latest plant introduction – and Envy, that uncomfortable feeling of displeasure and ill will towards someone whose garden is grander/larger/more beautiful/more expensively maintained than ours. Neither Covetousness nor Envy is any respecter of age or gender. Lust, on the other hand, is principally the female gardener's sin, for there are many more of us than them. How we lust after strapping young gardeners who come with their own tools and smile on us kindly when we bring them a cup of tea.

Then there's Gluttony – oh yes! – this one's mine too: I'm the sort of gardener who plants half a dozen varieties of leeks, the same of potatoes, unfeasible quantities of soft fruit, a dozen different sorts of peas and beans, when a modest one or two would do. And Anger, I hold up my hand to this one as well: poor Ivor! coming up the garden with tinsel in his hair on the last day of work before Christmas, to find me in a fury because a frost was coming and the pots of tender lavenders were still out in the garden in their summer places.

That first hard frost always catches me out. Sloth, the last of the Seven Deadly Sins, is my special sin. I'm a laissez-faire sort of gardener, preferring to let the garden take its own course. In July and August I am capable of abandoning it altogether, and in September and October I drift around as if summer would never end. Under its old name of accidie (from the Greek, meaning 'negligence'), it was characterised in the writings of the mystics as spiritual torpor or depression, later as a state of restless inability either to work or to pray. Sloth is more than mere procrastination. The concept of time being sanctified by use is fundamental to the Hours: to waste it is to waste our most precious asset, time upon this earth. This does not mean we should everlastingly be working in our gardens. Simply sitting and enjoying the garden is not doing nothing: it is the attentiveness of which the Hours speak. To watch time passing, noting the changes month by month, day by day, hour by hour – to live, as Thoreau said, deliberately – is a sort of sanctification in itself. It is Indifference which is the real sin.

One year I had still not planted the hyacinths and tulips and narcissus in the Canal Garden by mid-December. I had delayed and delayed while I planned the planting scheme on paper, then spent days laying the bulbs out on the grass – two thousand of them in an intricately composed pattern of mingled colours and heights and times of flowering, six rows to each *plate-bande*, no two flowers of the same colour or type next to each other, each row stepped in height, the two tallest rows in the middle, the two shortest on the outside, exactly as directed in the eighteenth-century gardening books (except that, in 1710, there would have been a dozen gardeners to do it) – then broken off planting in order to go to a lunchtime pre-Christmas drinks party at the Hall. I emerged mid-afternoon to a weather forecast of –6°C for that night. Pride (too grandiose a scheme), Greed (too many bulbs), Sloth – they are all here. Hyacinths frosted at the root fail to thrive. And these were rare hyacinths, wonderful hyacinths, old intricate recurved doubles and tall slender singles, brought all the way from Alan Shipp's National Collection at Waterbeach near Cambridge, where I had chosen them the previous March, walking the field and annotating Alan's stock list with size and form, colour of stem and scape, shape of petal and tube. And now they were going to freeze solid. The trenches were already dug, six inches deep and six inches wide, one either side of each *plate-bande*. It was half past three and the light was already failing. With three torches (one in the trench, one on the grass, one in my hand) I set to work, shuffling along on my hands and knees. I could feel the temperature dropping as I worked. At –1° the grass started to crunch under the heel of my hand; by –3° the bulbs were glued in place by the frost, the grass growing crisp and white by the light of the torch; by –5° the cold was pinching the sides of my nostrils as I breathed. I was still working at nine o'clock. But I did it. I finished. And then, as I leaned back on my heels to stretch my aching back, a shooting star sprang across the sky from Gemini all the way to Orion, a single flashing arc. If I hadn't been there, at that moment, hadn't lifted my eyes at that precise instant, I would never have seen it.

The next morning the tide of frost has lapped right up to the house. By midday it has melted in the sun, and the garden is green again. But white frost-shadows linger behind the hedges of the Plat, and on the steep north-facing side of the hill the ridge and furrow shows whitely all day – a reminder of the glacier that once ground its way down this valley. I look back, back up the valley, to where the ice came from. We know that the ice has been here before and that it will come again, sooner or later. It is buried in our collective unconscious, expressed in myth and folk memory – not only those frost fairs on the Thames, those Christmas-card images of mail coaches axle-deep in snow, but imaginary lands where it is always winter and never Christmas, the lands of the Wicked Witch of the North and the Ice Queen, the last home of Frankenstein's monster and the stronghold of the warrior-bears of Svalbard.

The cold has returned more than once already: during the Little Ice Age (reckoned to have lasted from about 1500 to the 1920s), glaciers in the Alps and Scandinavia engulfed pastures, fields and even farmhouses. Hundreds of thousands of people from Norway and Sweden were displaced: between 1860 and 1890 alone a quarter of the Swedish population emigrated to the USA. Conditions further south were characterised by bitterly cold winters, cold wet summers and crop failure; broadleaf trees began to die. And yet the Little Ice Age was just a blip in longer, deeper, colder oscillations. We are in an interglacial period at the moment. Notwithstanding global warming, the ice will return, and sooner rather than later if the North Atlantic conveyor switches off.

I watch the frost-flowers grow, silently unfolding their icy fronds across the windowpanes of the hall, blooming unseen behind the shutters in the sitting-room. The water of the Canal freezes hard. Pa is in hospital. Every night on my return from visiting him I walk up the garden to break the ice to stop it cracking the stonework. The first night I can do it with my heel. A couple of nights later I need the sharp edge of a spade. Eventually only a sledgehammer will do, hefted right up over my head. When I finish, my good tweed coat is stiff with frozen water splashed up from the Canal, icicles hanging in my eyes from my frozen hair.

Each morning I fetch a new box of apples from the fruit store for the birds. They devour them greedily, feeding on the soft pulp, hollowing it out and leaving the skin with the central core attached, like so many lost hearts scattered about the lawn.

Pa died in the little Community Hospital at Ludlow. There is a special ward there, devoted to the care of people with degenerative brain conditions. Outside the windows of the ward, Sister Joyce has made a whimsical little seaside garden, looking down to the tower of Ludlow parish church, where Housman's heart is buried. There are three candy-striped chalets, and wooden cut-out seagulls, and a treasure chest spilling out glass jewels and old coins and handfuls of seashells on to the wet soil of this land-locked county. It's a good metaphor for memory, of those almost-forgotten seaside holidays, those old photographs we all hoard, the journey many of the old people on the ward had already embarked upon, sailing away from the moorings of their lives. Two weeks before Pa died, he wrote one last letter, meticulously dating it and giving the hospital as the return address. Sister Joyce gave it to me after his death, unsure as to whom it was addressed. The letter is written in red ink on two small pages torn from a notepad. It describes a journey across a dark landscape which seems to have echoes of the moors he knew as a boy. It begins, 'Dearest Mum . . .

. . . the country is strange + difficult in a large way. Doris has been with me most of the time which has been very pleasant. We had quite a little difficulty getting through one gate or another but managed quite well . . . Just at the moment the day is very closely clouded over – lots of clouds. We are hoping to go further soon. The day is getting darker + darker than ever. We hope you are better and better and we hope the day will get better. Sorry to the dangerous sustained to everybody. All love and believe our love to you all. God bless you both. DAD

Looking out at the garden on the last day before he drifted into a haze of morphine, he suddenly said, 'It's going to be a lovely day tomorrow.' 'Oh, have you been listening to the weather forecast, Pa?' I said, amused. 'No, that's my prediction,' he said.

*

In an interview given to the *New York Times* in 1998 Sir Martin Rees, Astronomer Royal, formulated the now famous proposition that we are all composed of the dust of long-dead stars. When the Milky Way was formed, about ten billion years ago, it contained only the simplest of atoms, hydrogen and helium. Then the first stars formed, and the building blocks of life – carbon, oxygen and the rest of the periodic table – were created from hydrogen and helium through the nuclear fusion that kept the stars shining. In time these stars ran out of fuel, exploded into supernovae, and threw all the atoms back into space. New stars gradually con densed out of the debris. One of them was our sun with our group of planets orbiting it. All the atoms there are – you, me, the garden, Pa – were once inside a star, and will be again.

After he died I found a tape of Sonata No. 2 in G minor by Georg Muffat (1653–1704), still in place in his cassette player. He had recorded it from the radio, but had forgotten to switch off the machine at the end of the concert. The tape ran on after the music had finished and the radio had been switched off. I listened to the silence on the end of the tape – thinking of him sitting there silently, reading or lost in thought – hoping to catch the sound of his breathing, the creak of his chair. But there was nothing.

It has been a long day. I get up and open the door to have one last sniff of the garden before going to bed. The clock strikes the three-quarters as I stand looking into the dark garden and I think of the Warrens, all tucked up in their single beds in their pin-tucked nightdresses listening to the same two notes: the clock, installed by them in memory of their parents in 1890; chiming the bells that rang for Pat and Arthur's wedding, the same bells that tolled for poor Arthur Weaver; in the tower that the monks of Morville built, the same tower that was surrendered by Robert, the last Prior of Morville, in 1540. Everything coheres. The house reverberates slightly as I push the heavy door to in the curved door frame, the sound echoing into its furthest reaches. My footsteps sound on the boards as I cross the hall and sit down again by the fire, which is still flickering in the dark. I'll just sit until the fire is finished. It's too good to leave. Gradually the small sounds of the fire die down. There's the soft collapse of a log, then darkness all around. I sit and listen to the silence.

That's the other thing I really like about gardening: the silence. Not that silence out of doors is ever really silence. But absence of words, space for the thoughts to come. A silence that allows you to listen.

The maze at the centre of the garden is a unicursal maze. Puzzle mazes – the sort of maze with a choice of paths and in which one can therefore get lost – are a Renaissance concept. The unicursal maze in contrast has a single path that leads inevitably to the centre, and because the outcome is never in doubt, there is no need to conceal it by high hedges. Throughout history and prehistory the pattern has always been the same. Found in prehistoric India, classical Rome, the Egypt of Cleopatra, pre-Columbian America, medieval Scandinavia, the Celtic lands of western Europe, at many times and in many lands around the globe, seemingly spontaneously arising in cultures with no cultural connection with one another, carved on stone walls, laid out on the ground in rocks and boulders, inlaid in marble pavements, woven into basketwork, cast on coins, cut out of turf. In medieval Europe it came to be associated with the Christian's path to salvation.

The unicursal maze unites the most ancient of land-shaping impulses and the most modern, leapfrogging the centuries from the Bronze Age to the Space Age. It completes the cycle from life to death, from denial to acceptance, from ignorance to knowledge. Seven rings, seven circles, the path twisting and turning, repeatedly doubling back on itself. Sometimes it feels as if you are going in the wrong direction, but always in fact tending in the right direction. Bringing me here, to Morville; through Pa's gardens, to the making of a garden here and now; to a place where at last I could become rooted, gaining a purpose that my life never had before, gaining a sense of self that I never had by paradoxically first surrendering it, hand and eye, brain and heart, body and soul, merged with the heat and smell and sounds of the garden.

She did not cry for him. Perhaps after a lifetime of tears there were none left to shed. At his funeral she read Coleridge's translation of Mignon's song from Goethe's *Wilhelm Meisters Lehrjahre*, turning slightly towards the coffin, reading from his copy of Coleridge's *Collected Works*:

> Know'st thou the land where the pale citrons grow,
> The golden fruits in darker foliage glow?
> Soft blows the wind that breathes from that blue sky!
> Still stands the myrtle and the laurel high!
> Know'st thou it well, that land, beloved Friend?
> Thither with thee, O, thither would I wend!

She survived him by two years.

When she died, we scattered their ashes together into the wind over Wenlock Edge. Not farewell, but fare forward, voyager. Skyrockets and stardust, Pa; onwards and upwards.

It is St Lucy's Day now, 13 December, and the days are imperceptibly beginning to draw out again. The children from the school are rehearsing their Nativity play in the church. Though the solstice is not until the 21st, from now on the sun will set a minute or two later each day. There is no net gain in daylight hours for another week, as the sun will go on rising later until 30 December. But it feels like a turning point, a first small turning towards the light.

It is no coincidence that St Lucy's feast day is placed at the darkest time of the year. Before the reform of the calendar it coincided with the solstice:

> 'Tis the yeares midnight, and it is the dayes,
> Lucies, who scarce seaven houres herself unmaskes . . .
> John Donne, 'A Nocturnall upon S. Lucies Day'

Her name means 'light', from the Latin verb *lucere*, 'to shine', which also gives us the word 'lucid' (clear, understandable), and 'pellucid', that which allows light to pass through it. In Scandinavian countries her day is still kept with candlelit processions led by the eldest daughter of each household, wearing a wreath of lighted candles upon her head. In her last days, my mother used to say, 'I am grateful, dear, for all you do for me.' And I am grateful too, Mum. For being alive. It's been wonderful. Thank you.

*

Just before Christmas that year I went to listen to Handel's *Messiah* in Hereford Cathedral and, driving back over the Clee Hill in the dark, long after midnight, the car window wound down to prevent me falling asleep at the wheel, I became aware that the ice had melted, that a softness was flooding the land. And when I got back to Morville, and switched off the engine and stepped out of the car, there was a bird singing in the silence, pouring its heart out into the darkness of the garden. I stood and listened, breathing in the warm dark. I didn't know what a nightingale sounded like, but the bird's song was so piercingly sweet that I felt sure that it must be a nightingale. A nightingale in December! Even when I looked it up next morning and discovered that it could not have been a nightingale, that in winter nightingales migrate to warmer climates than ours; even when I read that a number of other birds do sing at night in winter, including robins, wrens and even song thrushes, for me it will always be a nightingale. Nightingales in December.

The word 'Compline' comes from the Old French *complie* (from the Latin *completa*, said with a long 'e') in the sense of 'it is accomplished, complete'. It is the last of the Day Offices, said before retiring for the night. The mood of Compline is of facing the dark, of acknowledging the fear of the unknown, but now with love and confidence. In the form used by tertiaries, Compline includes the serene *Nunc dimittis*, the Canticle of Simeon: 'Now lettest thou thy servant depart in peace.' Our lease runs out in August 2008. We'll go and make a garden by the sea, we said. But Ken went sooner than that. My husband didn't garden. He cooked instead. But he saw the *point* of the garden. He understood – and continues to understand – *why* I can't bear to come in until long after dark, why I spend all my money and then borrow more, why I am always exhausted, always late for everything, never want to go on holiday. Once we did go away, to Paris in winter. We climbed up to the Sacré Coeur. I wanted to light a candle, and we walked round the dim interior of the church, looking at the plaster saints, each with their votive offerings. Then my husband saw one with very few candles in front of it. 'That one,' he said. It was St Joseph, patron saint of understanding husbands.

'Go and make a new garden somewhere else,' said Mirabel. 'Don't cling to the past.' But will I be able to go quietly, to leave it all behind? The white roses and the autumn-tinted trees, the winter nights and the summer dawns? Moonrise and starshine, pear blossom in spring? All the hopes and the joys and the memories?

What happens if I stay? Will there come a time when I can no longer 'cope' with the garden – with its labour intensive *plates-bandes* and hundreds of pots of tulips, its thickets of roses to prune and miles of edges to cut? The word implies a dichotomy between me and the garden which I do not feel. There's more than one way to make a garden. As I grow older, the wild roses press against the outside of the yew hedges; the long grass whispers to me. A garden is a process, not a product. It's not a still life; it changes all the time. Perhaps I will gradually retreat from the garden, as I imagine Miss Juliana doing, giving it more and more say in the decisions about what goes where, playing a game of grandmother's footsteps with it as I peer over my shoulder to see what it's up to now. I made a garden out of a field, gradually expanding into it over the space of twenty years. Perhaps when the time comes I will hand it back to the field, a bit at a time, welcoming the wildness in, returning it to nature. That's the beauty of a garden made of compartments. I'll start with the Cloister Garden, letting the little patches of embroidered turf and beds of herbs morph into the wildflower meadow they always wanted to be. I'll let the New Flower Garden become a wood, where self-sown wildings rub shoulders with their imported transatlantic cousins. I'll mow paths through the garden, so I can see what's happening, but they'll be narrower paths, without edges, like the paths made by the badgers and the voles, tunnels merging into the surrounding greenery. I'll cut the hedges once a year to save my neighbours' blushes, and I'll prune the cordon apples in summer, but I'll give up pruning the roses. I'll let them grow into beautiful tangles like the wood in *Sleeping Beauty*, their thorns protecting the garden from outsiders and prying eyes until at last someone new comes along, like Sleeping Beauty's Prince, to wake them once more from their long sleep.

Or not. No garden is for ever.

Last year the window in the big bedroom was taken apart for repairs. It had only ever opened an inch or two at the top, and last summer the room was stiflingly hot. When we dismantled the frame, the lower sash was found to have been nailed shut. We pulled out the nails and threw up the sash, letting in the breeze and the fresh air. The window stood open all that long hot summer, while the sash was being repaired. By the time the window was reassembled the nights were already growing cooler, and a mist of cold condensation would appear on the inside of the panes in the morning. But the presence that had looked out through the nailed window, who had stood there, warming the windowpane with the soft pulse of their breath, was gone, evaporated into the morning air, vanished out into the garden at last.

It's going to be a green Christmas. The garden is all green and gold, lush grass and low winter sun, full of the wingbeats of birds. A young thrush bathes in the Round Pond, fluttering its wings and dashing the water into the air with its beak. Down in Bridgnorth, the blackbirds feast on the rowan trees of the supermarket car park, eyeing the crowds of shoppers who at half past eight are already making their way to the Christmas Eve market. The stalls in the High Street are piled high with gargantuan leeks and carrots, potatoes as big as yams, knobbly green walking-sticks of Brussels sprouts. The shops overflow with whole cheeses, enormous turkeys dangling by their legs, vast pink-and-white smoked hams suspended from the ceiling. There are mounds of holly and mistletoe, gleaming jars of pickled red cabbage, home-made Christmas pudding and slabs of moist dark Christmas cake. I have lost a family but gained another. Here's Pat and Ian and Arthur, already returning from the market as I make my way up. And Reg, doing a roaring trade on his stall, selling pork pies with apple, pork pies with cherry tomatoes and spring onions on top, reaching over the tops of people's heads with carrier bags and change. There's a fellow beekeeper in the queue outside the baker's. John's wife Brenda waves in passing, her arms full of shopping. One of the flower-arranging ladies from the church pauses to exclaim about the weather: 'The daffodils are up already!'

In the Books of Hours the book itself is often portrayed, open on its owner's prie-dieu, or perhaps held by the Virgin, surprised by Gabriel at the Annunciation. But of all the figures portrayed in the landscape of the Books of Hours – from sheep-shearer and cow-man to vintner and serving woman, butcher and farm labourer to woodman and swineherd – there is one figure missing: the hand that writes or illuminates the text – the copyist, the patient chronicler, writing it all down, passing it on, down the centuries. The literal meaning of the 'transmission of texts' is a handing over, a handing on, like stories, like my mother's Book of Hours, like the plants in a garden, passed hand to hand, planted in new soil where they will grow and thrive, like Miss Jekyll's thrift. When I worked in the Old Library at Trinity College, with its barrel vault and tiers of books twenty-six shelves high, I once had a vision of the library as thousands upon thousands of people, ranged on the shelves, feet outwards, like one of those Continental cemeteries where the coffins are slotted horizontally into walls; and everyone was talking, thousands of different voices, male and female, old and young, telling their own stories. As I have tried to tell the stories of the people here, of the land and how it came to be as it is; of the garden and how it came to be made; of me, and how I came to Morville, and why I am as I am.

When I get back from town Les and Nick have already brought the tree, all sixteen feet of it, a rustling fragrant giant, its freshly cut stem still sticky and oozing with resin. I manoeuvre it into position in the hall, then go out to fetch greenery from the garden: long graceful trails of big-leaved Irish ivy to make the Christmas garland for the mantlepiece, and shorter, stiffer trails of ordinary *Hedera helix* from the garden wall; armfuls of tree ivy with their black angular poppy-seed heads, and branches of holly, covered with brilliant scarlet berries; pungent fans of blue-green juniper, snippings of silver variegated holly from the standards in the *plates-bandes*, fronds of yew trimmed from the big trees by the garden gate. Gradually the house fills with wet green resinous scents. And last of all, as dusk falls, a great globe of mistletoe, cut gleaming gold from the wet black branches of one of the old apple trees in the Orchard, ceremoniously brought indoors and hung up in the hall.

A last-minute dash then to deliver Christmas cards – to Ivor across the road, and Wilf down at The Lye; to Bridget at Acton Round, John and Brenda at Aston Eyre, to Dan down in Bridgnorth – with a drink or a chat or a mince pie with everyone, and then back home to decorate the tree, winding trails of ivy round the trunk, and wedging branches of juniper and red-berried holly to fill in the broad gappy branches at the bottom; sprays of tree ivy to fill the gaps between the smaller branches further up; little white candles at each tip. Then the ivy garland, bound round and round with golden chain and studded with sprigs of holly and black ivy berries, lifted into position above the fireplace. And finally the holly wreath, completed on the stroke of midnight, and hung up on the door to welcome Christmas in.

I light the candles in the windows: two fat golden candles made of the beeswax from the hive, one for each window, to burn every night from now until Epiphany. Then I put my coat on and walk up into the garden. Across the Church Meadow light is streaming from the church out on to the gravestones. The Evangelists are counting heads. Soon they will be balancing their books for the year: the Bell Fund and the Building Fund, the receipts from the May Fair and the Harvest Supper, totting up the births, marriages and deaths; who lived, who died, who came, who went, who got married, who ran away with the milkman; writing their final reports. I wonder what they will have made of *me*, those parish-pump chroniclers of Morville? What have they made of my macaronic cobbling together of Latin and English, elegy and farce, science and fancy? This jumble of fragments tossed together like the made-up ground of the garden, this blackbird's nest of cobwebs and sheep's wool, this day in a life, this life in a day? Reading their version, will it be found that I have romanticised, like the makers of the Books of Hours, with their romantic pastoral version of a fading feudal world, a world that even then scarcely existed any more? Would they even agree among themselves?

The constellations wheel overhead. Here is Orion, the Hunter, striding across the sky with Sirius the Dog Star at his heels, in nightly pursuit of the Seven Sisters, the Pleiades. Here is Ursa Major – the nymph Callisto, beloved of Jupiter, transformed into a bear through Juno's jealous rage and caught up into the heavens by Jupiter to save her from the hunter's spear. Over there Cepheus and seated Cassiopeia, side by side, unlucky parents, condemned nightly to reiterate those boastful words that brought down upon them Poseidon's anger; and their daughter Andromeda stretched upon the rock, forever menaced by Cetus the Sea-monster, nightly rescued by forever-young Perseus, striding the sky with the Gorgon's head swinging from his belt. And there on the western horizon, where the hill touches the sky, is Pegasus the winged horse, born from the blood that spurted from the Gorgon's severed head, unfurling his huge wings across the great steppe of the winter sky; as he leaps upwards his hoof strikes a rock, and out gushes a spring, the spring of the Muses, the perpetual wellspring of story.

Listen.

In the tower the voices of the bell-ringers call to one another once more. The ring has been restored and there's a new team now: Anthony and Harriet, Sharon and Sophie, Ian and Alison.

'Look to.'

'Treble's going.'

'She's gone.'

The bells peal out across the dark land, over the village and the Hall, over the stream and the meadow, pealing down the years.

Grandsire Doubles for Miss Juliana, Cambridge Surprise for Arthur Blayney, Kent Treble Bob Minor for the Arthur Weavers and their wives – pealing down the years, ringing out the old, ringing in the new – Reverse St Bartholomew for George Smith, Stedman Doubles for Frances Cressett, Plain Hunting for Prior Richard.

Disturbed by the clangour of the bells, a barn owl flies low over the village. It's so dark now that only he can see the grassy platform of the abandoned road behind the church, the copperplate of the eighteenth-century gravestones, the gaping mouth of the lych gate; the bell pits at Aldenham, the old stone quarries on the hillside, the line of the old mill race; Miss Bythell's road, the line of the eighteenth-century turnpike, the faint swell of the Roman road. On white moth-wings he swoops low over the garden, banking over the swirl of the maze, the pale squares of the knots, the arches of the cloister. His reflection is caught briefly in the Canal, among the branches of the old pear tree, which towers up into the night sky and down into the dark water beneath, like the axle-tree of the universe, joining past and present, present and future.

'That's all . . .'

'Stand.'

They are ringing down now, faster and faster, round and round, the reverberations from the bells setting up reverberations in the stonework of the tower, until the whole bell chamber is singing with stone and metal. Then one last chime from each of the six bells: Treble, Second, Third, Fourth, Fifth, Tenor – 'Peace & Good Neighbourhood', 'Prosperity to this Parish' – the harmonics dying away in the tower, the multicoloured sallies looped up again on the pegs on the wall.

After the clatter of departing boots on the tower stairs the silence surges back. In the darkened church the goose-feather quills scratch on, writing someone else's story now.

Acknowledgements

The Morville Hours, like the garden, has always felt like a shared enterprise. I owe a great debt of gratitude first of all to Ken Swift, who found Morville, and for his love and support in the making of the garden and the writing of the book; also to Paul and Ruth Heslop and Tony Bradley for helping the dream become a reality. Thanks too to all my Shropshire friends and neighbours for sharing their stories with me: Pat, Arthur and Ian Rowe; John and Brenda Lane; Joyce Needham; Sir George and Lady Labouchere; Rachel and John Norbury; Ivor Bishop; Les, Dennis and Joyce Cooper; Nick Watkins; Derek and Harold Pugh; Dan Rudge; Wilf, Roger and Toni Cantrill; David Meredith; Reg May; Karl Liebscher; Alan George; John James; Tom Smith and Liz Beazley; Natalie Hodgson; Ioan Davies; Mirabel Osler; and John and Pauline Napper. I am grateful also to Prof. Vincent Gillespie for his early encouragement and advice about liturgical matters; Dr Margaret Howatson for patiently fielding queries about classical mythology and much else besides; Emma-Kate Lanyon, Curator of Archaeology and Social History, Shropshire County Museum Service, for access to and information about the Romano-Celtic figurine in Much Wenlock Museum; Daniel Lockett, Curator of Geology at Ludlow Museum, for identifying the pebbles from the garden; the staff of the Shropshire Records and Research Centre, Shrewsbury, for help in deciphering the obliterated first page of the Morville Parish Register; the Rev. Hugh Patterson for information about the patron saints of Morville; Simon Cowan for help with tracing the lost roads of Morville; Ann Scard for answering my questions about tufa; Patricia Scott for sharing information about the Warren and Weaver families and for help with genealogies. Thanks also to Brian Goodwin, who first taught me about bees, and the bellringers of Arley and Alveley for teaching me how to ring church bells. In addition I would like to thank Dr Paul Stamper of English Heritage and Dr Jeremy Milln of the National Trust and the team at ArchaeoPhysica for trying to anchor my wilder flights of fancy in solid archaeological fact; any remaining pieces of folly are, needless to say, of my own devising. Thanks too to Julia Williamson and Peter Cooper for lending me the cottage at Shelve where the closing chapters were written, and to Denville, Angela and Barbara Wyke for making me so welcome there. I would also like to thank my agent Felicity Bryan for her patience and her enthusiasm; Bill Swainson, Emily Sweet and all at Bloomsbury for taking such care with the text and the design of the book; Dawn Burford for the wonderful illustrations; and finally Sandy Saunders, without whom this book might well have been written sooner, but life would have been much less fun.

Notes

Many books over many years have gone into the making of this book. Sometimes something as small as a word or a phrase has caught my imagination; at other times whole books have been filleted for facts in areas which lay far beyond my own compass. In the process, much scholarly information has been hijacked in an imaginative retelling that few of the authors would recognise, still less wish to own up to. But my debts are immense, and I would like to acknowledge them here. If I have inadvertently omitted any fellow traveller on what was, inevitably, a long and winding road, I offer my apologies.

Roger S. Wieck's *Time Sanctified: The Book of Hours in Medieval Art and Life* (George Braziller, 1988) was the source of much information both liturgical and iconographical. I am indebted to Prof. Eamon Duffy's *Marking the Hours: English People and their Prayers 1240–1570* (Yale University Press, 2006) for placing the Hours in their personal and historical context, and to Dom David Steindl-Rast's *The Music of Silence: Entering the Sacred Space of Monastic Experience* (HarperSanFrancisco, 1995) for adding to my perception of their spiritual dimension. Ronald Hutton's *The Stations of the Sun: A History of the Ritual Year in Britain* (Oxford University Press, 1996) and Geoffrey Grigson's *The Englishman's Flora* (Phoenix House, 1958) were never far from my side. The work of Richard Mabey, and in particular his monumental *Flora Britannica* (Sinclair-Stevenson, 1996), has always been, and continues to be, an inspiration.

Information about herbs, their histories and their uses, was in the main taken from Mrs M. Grieve's *A Modern Herbal* (Jonathan Cape, 1931), and information about the stars and constellations from the various editions of Ian Ridpath and Will Trion's *The Monthly Sky Guide* (Cambridge University Press). Quotations from the liturgy of the Hours are from my mother's copy of the *Dominican Prayer Book* (4th revised edition, 1962); quotations from the Rule of St Benedict are from Timothy Fry (ed.), *The*

Rule of St Benedict in English (Liturgical Press, 1982). Other references to saints, figures of classical mythology and various matters relating to the calendar are from the *Oxford Classical Dictionary* (2nd edition, 1970) and the *Oxford Dictionary of the Christian Church* (2nd edition, 1974).

I come to Morville

For the early history of Morville I am indebted to W. Watkins-Pitchford, 'The History of Morville' (reprinted from the *Bridgnorth Journal*, 23 and 30 June, 1934); D. S. Cranage, *An Architectural Account of the Churches of Shropshire*, parts1–10 (1894–1912); Francis Leach, *County Seats of Shropshire* (1891); and R. W. Eyton, *Antiquities of Shropshire*, 12 vols (1854–60), all to various degrees revised and augmented by the various volumes of the *Victoria County History of Shropshire*. Where I have followed a new line of enquiry of my own, I have given references to original manuscript sources and archive collections at the appropriate places below. I am grateful to the Bodleian Library, Oxford, for access to microfilm of and printed images from MS Auct.D.inf.2.11 (the Hours of the Fastolf Master) and MS Gough Liturg.7 (the Earl of Shrewsbury's prayer book). The Shepherds Great Calendar was last printed for the year 1931 as *The Kalendar and Compost of Shepherds*, ed. G. C. Heseltine (Peter Davies, 1930).

Vigils

For information on local place names I am indebted to Dr Margaret Gelling's *Place-Names of Shropshire* (English Place-Name Society, vol. LXII/LXIII, Part One, 1990), and for their wider interpretation to her *Place-Names in the Landscape* (Dent, 1984). For the geology of Morville and the surrounding district I have drawn principally upon vols 166 and 167 of the Geological Survey of Great Britain (*Geology of the Country around Church Stretton, Craven Arms, Wenlock Edge and Brown Clee* (HMSO, 1968) and *Dudley and Bridgnorth* (HMSO, 1947), respectively). Information about soils came from vol. 166 of the Soil Survey of Great Britain: *The Soils of the Church Stretton District of Shropshire* (Agricultural Research Council, 1966). Brian S. John's *The Ice Age, Past and Present* (Collins, 1977) was a revelation about the workings of ice. I met the Shropshire mammoth in person: in 1999 an exhibition was mounted at Condover by the Shropshire Museum Service to welcome back the conserved bodies of the group of four mammoths discovered in 1986; their remains are now housed in Ludlow Museum. My account of prehistoric man in Shropshire draws principally upon S. C. Stanford's *The Archaeology of the Welsh Marches* (2nd revised edition, 1991), with additional information about local sites from the Shropshire Sites and Monuments Record (available on http://ads.ahds.ac.uk), though their interpretation in connection with the settlement of the village is my own. Margaret Gelling's *The West Midlands in the Early Middle Ages* (Leicester University Press, 1992) and Brendan Lehane's *Early Celtic Christianity* (Constable, 1994) both provided valuable insights on the Anglo-Saxon period.

Lauds

The idea of patterning the book around an exploration of the five senses arose from the first words of Benedict's Rule, 'Listen . . . with the ear of your heart.' (For anyone who's counting, the extra senses are Anticipation (in 'Lauds') and Memory (in 'Compline'); absence or dullness of sensual experience (as in depression) is a topic explored in 'None'.) I am grateful to my friend Harriet Strachan for introducing me to Gaston Bachelard's *The Poetics of Space* (Beacon Press, 1969), and to Sue Whalley of Park Attwood Clinic for drawing my attention to the anthroposophical view of the senses as described by Albert Saesman in *Our Twelve Senses: Wellsprings of the Soul* (Hawthorn Press, 1990). The reference to the Aislabie family's 'respectable pause for anticipation' is from the chapter on Studley Royal in Mavis Batey and David Lambert's *The English Garden Tour: A View of the Past* (John Murray, 1990). I am indebted to Christopher Taylor's *Roads and Tracks of Britain* (Dent, 1979) for a more secure historical underpinning to my longstanding fascination with roads. The paraphrases of Tacitus are from the *Agricola*, translated H. Mattingley, in *Tacitus on Britain and Germany* (Penguin, 1948). The account of Roman Shropshire draws heavily upon Roger White and Philip Barker's excellent *Wroxeter: Life and Death of a Roman City* (Tempus, 1998, reprinted 1999). A fuller explanation of Hooper's Rule for dating hedges will be found in Dr Oliver Rackham's *The History of the Countryside* (Weidenfeld & Nicolson, 1995, reprinted 1996), from which I have borrowed the quotation from Caesar's *De bello Gallico*, and to which I am also indebted for information about other matters such as coppicing. Information about the history of vine cultivation (and other fruits, *passim*) is from F. A. Roach, *Cultivated Fruits of Britain: Their Origin and History* (Blackwell, 1985).

Prime

Much of the information about water mills comes from Dr Barrie Trinder's *The Industrial Archaeology of Shropshire* (Phillimore, 1996). The quotation from Wassily Kandinsky is taken from *Bright Earth: The Invention of Colour* by Philip Ball (Penguin, 2002). I am indebted to Laura Mason and Catherine Brown's *Traditional Foods of Britain: An Inventory* (compiled for the GEIE/Euroterroirs project, 1999) for information about simnel cake and its local variations, and to Victoria Finlay's *Colour: Travels through the Paintbox* (Hodder & Stoughton, 2002) for information about saffron. The account of Robert de Bellême is based upon that contained in the *Ecclesiastical History* of Orderic Vitalis, Robert's contemporary and fellow Salopian, edited and translated Marjorie Chibnall (Oxford University Press, 1969–78), vols II, III and VI. Information about marling came principally from Nigel Harvey's *The Industrial Archaeology of Farming in England and Wales* (Batsford, 1980). The quotation from Virgil's *Georgics*, Book IV, is from the verse translation by C. Day Lewis (Jonathan Cape, 1940; also available as a World's Classics paperback, 1983). Inspiration for 'Do moles dream of the wind?' was provided by Kenneth Mellanby's monograph *The Mole* (New Naturalist series, Collins, 1971).

Terce

Material about the interpretation and sources of Botticelli's *Primavera* came from many sources, of which the most useful was Roberto Marini's 'Analisi di Capolavoro: Botticelli's La Primavera' (http://www.thais.it, retrieved 8/ 12/05). The story of John Leland's madness comes from *The Itinerary of John Leland in or about the years 1535–1543*, 5 vols, ed. Lucy Toulmin Smith (1907; facsimile reprint, Southern Illinois University Press, 1964). I am indebted to William Fiennes' *The Snow Geese* (Picador, 2003) for alerting me to the extraordinary aerial life of swifts, and to, among others, J. Zahradnik's *Bees, Wasps and Ants* (Hamlyn, 1991), Karl von Frisch's *Animal Architecture* (Hutchinson, 1975), Miroslav Bouchner's *Animal Tracks and Traces* (Octopus, 1982), and Michael Chinery's *The Natural History of the Garden* (Collins, 1977) for illumination on the lives of the other residents I encountered while making the garden at Morville – bumble bees, ants, dragonflies, harvestmen, birds of every sort, foxes and badgers.

Sext

Quite the best book I know about learning to appreciate roses (as distinct from growing them) is Edward A. Bunyard's *Old Garden Roses* (Country Life, 1936), and it is to him that I am indebted for the rosebud riddle. The poems of Thomas Traherne are quoted from Alan Bradford's Penguin edition (1991). 'The Celestial Stranger' was printed for the first time in *Thomas Traherne: Poetry and Prose* (SPCK, 2002), ed. Denise Inge, and I am grateful to both Denise Inge and Alan Bradford for details of the still-unfolding discovery of Traherne's manuscripts. Information about prehistoric dragonflies and horsetails comes from W. S. McKerrow's *The Ecology of Fossils* (Duckworth, 1978). For the method of 'setting' a scythe and the explanation of the use of the 'strickle' (as for much else besides) I am indebted to Dorothy Hartley's *Lost Country Life* (Pantheon Books, 1979). The account of the eglantine as a symbol of Queen Elizabeth I is based upon Roy Strong's in *The Renaissance Garden in England* (Thames and Hudson, 1979).

My account of the purchases of church property made by Roger Smyth in the 1540s and 1550s follows that in the *Victoria County History*; background information came from Dom David Knowles' *Bare Ruined Choirs: The Dissolution of the English Monasteries* (Cambridge University Press, 1976). Manuscript pedigrees of the Smyth, Cressett, Hopton, Horde and Clench families are in the Shropshire Records and Research Centre, Shrewsbury. The 1562 will of Roger Smyth and 1584 ruling on its validity are in the National Archives at Kew (PROB/11/46/64 and PROB/11/67/184, respectively). Details of the burial of Roger Smyth on 26 June 1562, the birth of his and Frances's daughter Maria on 2 July, and the subsequent marriage of Frances Smyth to John Hopton on 13 January 1562/3, are from Morville Parish Register (f.1 recto, examined under ultra-violet light).

The contemporary gardening manuals on which the account of the design and planting of Elizabethan and Jacobean knots is based include, in addition to Thomas Hill's *The Profitable Art of Gardening* and *The Gardeners Labyrinth*, Gervase Markham, *The English Husbandman* (1613); *Maison Rustique, Or, The Country Farme*, translated into English by Richard Surfleet (1616), and John Parkinson, *Paradisi in Sole Paradisus Terrestris* (1629). The ruminations on pastoral were prompted by Helen Cooper's scholarly investigation *Pastoral: Medieval into Renaissance* (Brewer, 1977).

None

The Latin text of the *Chronicon ex chronicis* is printed as *Florentii Wigorniensis Monachi Chronicon ex chronicis*, ed. B. Thorpe (2 vols, 1848), and was translated into English by Joseph Stevenson as *The Chronicle of Florence of Worcester*, Church Historians of England II (1853; facsimile reprint, Llanerch Publishers, 1996). Modern historians now customarily attribute authorship, at least in part, to John of Worcester. The accounts of reaping and threshing are based on Hartley, *Lost Country Life*, and Harvey, *Industrial Archaeology of Farming* (from whom the details of subsequent mechanisation are also drawn). The tithe maps of Shropshire, transcribed by H.D.G. Foxall, are available at the Shropshire Records and Research Centre, Shrewsbury. I am also indebted to Mr Foxall's *Shropshire Field Names* (Shropshire Archaeological Society, 1980) for their interpretation. Iain Sinclair's *The Edge of the Orison* (Hamish Hamilton, 2005) provided details of John Clare's journey from London to Northampton.

George Smyth was buried at Morville on 9 January 1600/01; his will (proved 24 January 1600/01) is in the National Archives, Kew (PROB/11/

97/390). His son John was buried in St. Leonard's, Bridgnorth, on 28 January 1635/6 and his will (proved 27 August 1636, Bridgnorth Peculiar Court) is in Staffordshire County Record Office, Lichfield. The account of the Civil War period in Bridgnorth is based on Clive Simpson's 'Bridgnorth and the Civil War' (typescript, Bridgnorth Library); for the Battle of Edghill see Philip Warner, *British Battlefields* (Cassell, 2002). It has been suggested (*Transactions of the Shropshire Archaeological Society*, Series 4, vol. 5, p. 54) that George Smyth II disappeared and may have died in Ireland; however, there seems no reason to suppose that the burial at Morville of 'George Smith Esq.' on 10 November 1641 (Morville Parish Register) is not his; no will has been traced. For documents suggesting that George Smyth II mortgaged the estate see Worcester County Record Office, Bulk Accession no. 8782, ref. 899: 749, parcel 84 (iii), 7,9 & 11. The will of Arthur Weaver (proved 28 May 1689) is in the National Archives, Kew (PROB/11/394/889).

Sir Thomas Hanmer's *Garden Book*, printed with an introduction by Eleanour Sinclair Rohde (1933), was reissued as a facsimile reprint by Clwyd Library and Information Service in 1991; since Rohde's transcription the manuscript itself seems to have disappeared. I am grateful to the late Ruth Duthie for corrections to Rohde's transcript and for sharing her research on the layout of Sir Thomas's garden (subsequently printed as 'Planting plans of some 17th-century flower gardens', in *Garden History*, vol. 18, no. 2 (1990)), and to Jenny Robinson for her 'New Light on Sir Thomas Hanmer', *Garden History*, vol. 16, no. 1 (1988). For the whole milieu of florists and their flowers see Ruth Duthie's *Florists' Flowers and Societies* (Shire, 1988).

I am indebted to Camilla Stewart for her observation that the medieval window at Morville is composed of fragments from two separate images. I am also grateful to Amanda Harris-Lea and Dr Jeremy Milln for their suggestion that the avenue at Morville is aligned on Aldenham. Sir Whitmore Acton's estate plans (1721–2) are in the Shropshire Records and Research Centre, Shrewsbury. Thomas Percy's letter to William Shenstone is printed in *The Percy Letters: The Correspondence of Thomas Percy & William Shenstone*, ed. Cleanth Brooks (Yale University Press, 1977). Among the many books consulted on the geology of Shropshire I am especially indebted to Peter Toghill and Keith Chell's *Shropshire Geology: Stratigraphic and Tectonic History* (Field Studies Council, 1984), Richard Fortey's *The Hidden Landscape: A Journey into the Geological Past* (Jonathan Cape, 1993) and Ann Scard's *The Building Stones of Shropshire* (Swan Hill Press, 1990).

Vespers

Ruskin first expounded the notion of the 'pathetic fallacy' in *Modern Painters*, vol. III, part 4 (1856). Quotations from the poems of Herbert, Vaughan and Donne are from the selection edited by Helen Gardner as *The*

Metaphysical Poets (Penguin, 1957). I am indebted to John Stubbs' biography, *John Donne: The Reformed Soul* (W. W. Norton, 2007), for the quotation from Donne's letters, and for the reconstruction of Donne's journey from Warwickshire to Montgomery in 1613. Like the mythological figures which are its subject, Ovid's *Metamorphoses* has been translated, reworked and woven into countless other books; in addition to Ted Hughes' selected *Tales from Ovid* (Faber, 1997), I am indebted to Ciaran Carson's *Fishing for Amber* (Granta, 1999) and to David Raeburn's verse translation of the complete *Metamorphoses* (Penguin, 2004), from which I have freely borrowed here.

For a detailed analysis of the architecture of Morville Hall see Arthur Oswald, 'Morville Hall, Shropshire', parts I–II, *Country Life*, August 1952. The garden historian Mavis Batey has been hot on the trail of Lord Nuneham and the Earl of Harcourt for many years, and I am indebted to her chapter on the garden at Nuneham Courtenay in *The English Garden Tour*, and her article 'The Gentle Executioner' in *Oxford Today*, Trinity Term, 2000. The painting of Morville Hall showing the architectural improvements of William Baker (1748–9) is in the Government Art Collection (ref. 10663); a modern copy also hangs at Morville Hall in the collection of Dr and Mrs J. C. Douglas, and I am grateful to them for allowing me access to it. The papers of the Papillon family of Lubenham and Acrise Park, Kent, are divided between the Northamptonshire County Record Office and the Centre for Kentish Studies, Maidstone; for some of the strange stories surrounding Papillon Hall see http://web.ukonline.co.uk/lubenham/folklore. The will of Arthur Weaver III (made 6 January 1747, proved 2 May 1759) is in the National Archives at Kew (PROB/11/846/473).

For the idea of butterflies as 'beautiful airheads' I am indebted to Miriam Rothschild's enchanting *The Butterfly Gardener* (Michael Joseph, 1983). The reference to Arthur Blayney's legendary hospitality is from Philip Yorke's *The Royal Tribes of Wales* (1799), quoted in the guidebook to Gregynog (now part of the University of Wales). For information about quinces I am indebted to Roach, *Cultivated Fruits of Britain*, and to Jane Grigson's marvellous *Fruit Book* (Penguin, 1983). For the suggestion that lions only mate with leopards (with which I end the story of Atalanta) I am indebted to Ciaran Carson's *Fishing for Amber*. Observations on the diet of the English peasant were prompted by J. C. Drummond and Anne Wilbraham's *The Englishman's Food: Five Centuries of English Diet*, new edition by Tom Jaine (Pimlico, 1991).

Compline

Sir Thomas Browne's observations on wreaths and garlands are contained in a letter to the diarist John Evelyn, printed in Browne's posthumously published *Miscellany Tracts* II (1683) and reprinted separately in 1962 as a keepsake by the Gehenna Press, Northampton, Massachusetts. I am indebted to Richard Mabey, *Flora Britannica*, for the origin of 'Poppy Day'. The idea of dining with the dead was prompted by a reference to funerary gardens in the American School of Classical Studies at Athens' *Garden Lore of Ancient Athens* (1963). Information about war graves came principally from the website of the Commonwealth War Graves Commission (http://www.cwgc.org); Gertrude Jekyll's use of thrift in this connection is from Betty Massingham's biography, *Miss Jekyll* (Country Life, 1966). The literature on comets is immense, but the NASA website, especially Donald K. Yeoman's article 'Great Comets in History', was especially helpful (http//ssd/jpl.nasa.gov). The will of Arthur Blayney (proved 30 October 1795) is in the National Archives at Kew (PROB/11/1266/173). For Bridgnorth elections see *Victoria County History of Shropshire*, vol. III. The Members of Parliament for Bridgnorth from 1295 to 1800 are listed with brief biographies in *Transactions of the Shropshire Archaeological Society*, Series 4, vol. 5. Information about Joseph Loxdale Warren and his family is taken from gravestones and memorials at Morville, together with contemporary newspaper reports and other material kindly supplied by Patricia Scott.

Index

A NOTE ON THE AUTHOR

Katherine Swift lives at the Dower House, Morville Hall, in Shropshire. She worked as a rare-book librarian in Oxford and Dublin before becoming a full-time gardener and writer in 1988. She was for four years gardening columnist of *The Times*, and has written widely in the gardening press, including an acclaimed series on the gardens and landscapes of Orkeny for Hortus. She is the author of *Pergolas, Arbours and Arches: Their History and How to Make Them* (with Paul Edwards and Jessica Smith) and *Jim Partridge* (with Alison Britton).

A NOTE ON THE TYPE

The text of this book is set in Linotype Stempel Garamond, a version of Garamond adapted and first used by the Stempel foundry in 1924. It's one of several versions of Garamond based on the designs of Claude Garamond. It is thought that Garamond based his font on Bembo, cut in 1495 by Francesco Griffo in collaboration with the Italian printer Aldus Manutius. Garamond types were first used in books printed in Paris around 1532. Many of the present-day versions of this type are based on the *Typi Academiae* of Jean Jannon cut in Sedan in 1615.

Claude Garamond was born in Paris in 1480. He learned how to cut type from his father and by the age of fifteen he was able to fashion steel punches the size of a pica with great precision. At the age of sixty he was commissioned by King Francis I to design a Greek alphabet, for this he was given the honourable title of royal type founder. He died in 1561.